CHRISTINA KEIM M ED. MFA

Unwanted

The Causes and Effects of America's Horse Population Crisis

TRAFALGAR SQUARE

First published in 2025 by
Trafalgar Square Books
An Imprint of the Stable Book Group
32 Court Street, Suite 2109, Brooklyn, New York 11201

Disclaimer of Liability

Library of Congress Cataloging-in-Publication Data

Names: Keim, Christina, author.
Title: Unwanted : the causes and effects of America's horse population
    crisis / Christina Keim.
Description: North Pomfret, Vermont : Trafalgar Square Books, 2025. |
    Includes bibliographical references.
Identifiers: LCCN 2024051549 (print) | LCCN 2024051550 (ebook) | ISBN
    9781646012367 (paperback) | ISBN 9781646012374 (epub)
Subjects: LCSH: Horses--United States. | Horse adoption--United States. |
    Horse industry--United States. | Animal shelters--United States. |
    Animal welfare--United States.
Classification: LCC HV4749 .K45 2025 (print) | LCC HV4749 (ebook) | DDC
    636.1/08320973--dc23/eng/20250109
LC record available at https://lccn.loc.gov/2024051549
LC ebook record available at https://lccn.loc.gov/2024051550

Interior and cover design by RM Didier

Printed in the United States of America

10 9 8 7 6 5 4 3 2 1

THIS BOOK IS DEDICATED
to anyone who ever witnessed an injustice and thought,
"Someone ought to do something,"
and then realized they were that someone.

Contents

Note:
Both first names and surnames are used in reference to interviewees
in this book. This editorial choice was intentional.

*"A good man will take care of his horses and dogs
not only while they are young,
but also when they are old and past service."*

PLUTARCH
GREEK PHILOSOPHER AND HISTORIAN, 100 AD

Introduction

MORE QUESTIONS THAN ANSWERS

IT IS NEARING FOUR IN THE AFTERNOON on the second Saturday of July 2019 when I turn into the gravel lot of the Lebanon Valley Livestock Auction in rural Lebanon, Pennsylvania. Just six miles off the interstate, the facility comprises several nondescript farm buildings, all covered with the same beige metal sheeting; one contains a country store, outside of which a hand-painted sign offers "fresh baked pies." To one side, a dozen or more horse and stock trailers are parked, attached to dusty towing vehicles. Mostly, these trailers are the hallmarks of professional haulers; some are so long I can't even guess how many animals could potentially be sandwiched into their interiors.

To the left of the main buildings, I can see horses through a large doorway. They are packed closely, and I hear them calling. I have been told that for a first-timer such as myself, the Lebanon Valley sale is a good one to attend. It isn't quite as notorious as the New Holland Auction, located 27 miles to the southeast in the heart of Lancaster County. To equestrians, the name New Holland is synonymous with last chances: according to some sources, at least a quarter of the animals running through its weekly equine sale end up on a truck bound for the United States border, and ultimately a Canadian or Mexican slaughterhouse. Generally, it is said, the horses at Lebanon Valley are in better condition, of higher quality, and sell for decent prices, all of which can help keep them off the meat buyer's truck. Even so, horses from one sale sometimes end up at the other, and many of the significant human figures at each venue are the same.

I am here to see this world for myself, to better understand the players—the dealers, the rescuers and activists, the regular buyers and the random bidders. And, of course, to see the horses, who find themselves traveling along a mobius strip of an uncertain future. I have heard stories of auction horses that have endured horrible neglect and abuse, of animals so emaciated they can barely stand. I have read accounts of horses shipped thousands of miles from auction to auction, compressed into tight quarters on trailers so ill-suited for the species that many disembark with significant injury. I have heard that young, healthy Thoroughbreds still wearing racing plates often show up at auctions on Mondays after failing to deliver at the weekend's meet.

At the auction, lines between good and evil blur.

A long-time equine advocate told me she thought I was very brave to come here alone. Her comment has spooked me enough that I park my car nose facing out for an easy exit, although another individual familiar with the sale had reminded me that it is a place of business, and I have as much reason to be there as anyone else. However, my vehicle is the only non-truck in the lot, and I feel acutely aware of my out-of-state plates. I carry nothing with identifying insignia, no logos of my own farm or other equine groups I am connected to. I have chosen to wear muted colors. My goal is to blend in.

People who only know horses from television and the movies think they vocalize all the time. In reality, contented horses generally don't say much out loud. Theirs is largely a nonverbal language, one of posture and movement. Horses tend to only vocalize when there is something quite important at stake—socialization, food, or fear. As I hear the horses whinnying from the pens at Lebanon Valley, I have no doubt as to which biological imperative they are speaking.

These are the unwanted.

AS ITS NAME IMPLIES, the Lebanon Valley Livestock Auction caters to a particular niche in the regional agricultural market, mostly specializing in the sale of swine and cattle, species aligned with the traditional definition of "livestock." But on the second Saturday each month, its holding pens are filled with a different category of livestock species—equines, including riding horses, working drafts, donkeys, and mules.

Equines have long been classified as "livestock" by legal entities such as the US Department of Agriculture (USDA), alongside those species that produce meat, eggs, milk, or other food products, or wool, fur, or leather. But in the United States, horses are raised for none of these purposes. In fact, in America, for the most part, eating horses is taboo.

In some definitions, "livestock" includes those species that provide "work" for humans. Yet only 8 percent of American horses are still used for "work," primarily in ranching, mounted police units, carriage operations, small-scale sustainable farming and logging, and Amish and Mennonite communities that still rely upon horses for transportation and tilling crops. Is this output enough to justify the horse's continued "livestock" designation? It is a reasonable question, because, in reality, the horse's use in the United States today is largely recreational, and horse ownership is considered by most to be a luxury.

Despite this, as an industry, the equine community has been quite willing to accept benefits of having the horse classified as "livestock." Some of these perks relate to laws establishing minimum standards of care and protection from neglect. But in some regions, benefits also extend to tax breaks and other agricultural exemptions that would be lost if horses were to become classified as companion animals. These benefits are what make horse farm ownership financially possible in some communities. Legally, it is a slippery slope.

It is perhaps the ambiguous status of the horse—not quite livestock, not quite companion animal—that has left the equine industry in such conflict over the question of how to manage unwanted animals. For decades, unneeded, unsound, or older horses often ended their lives in American slaughterhouses, just like members of any other livestock species. But modern sensibilities toward the horse changed, and the idea of equine slaughter became largely unpalatable to the general American public.

The partnership between horse and rider is one of extreme trust and violates natural law: a prey species turning its well-being wholly over to the care and attention of a predator. Together, the pair—

predator and prey—is capable of tackling seemingly impossible tasks. Developing this bond and the empowering experience that comes with it is what drives many people to become equestrians. Horses are named, loved, and embraced. It is an almost sacred relationship; when an owner or rider must say a final goodbye, the pain can be almost like losing a close family member.

This is perhaps why people who sell horses at auctions are often considered "less than" by many equestrians. It is thought by some that rather than "doing right" by their partners after injury or at the end of their careers, these individuals instead seek a quick sale and a few hundred dollars in their pockets. Maybe some of them feel a sense of relief or carry the conviction that someone else will be willing to deal with their horse's problems. Maybe some of them don't know any better or simply don't care.

The reality of what happens to an older, lame, or otherwise compromised horse that goes to auction is beyond what most horse lovers care to fully consider.

HARRISBURG, PENNSYLVANIA'S capital city, is just a 45-minute drive from Lebanon. But beyond city limits, it is striking how quickly the hustle of urbanization fades. Interstate 81 slices through miles of agricultural land; cornfields planted in symmetrical rows are interspersed with pastures where dairy and beef cattle graze. This is farm country, politically and socially conservative; the region is known for its large concentration of Amish and Mennonite families. Lebanon County is home to six Amish church districts and is adjacent to Lancaster County, home to the oldest and largest Amish community in the world. Farming remains a critical element of this culture, and their continued use of equines in traditional roles ties these Anabaptists intimately to the local livestock sales.

It is a Mennonite woman I first see as I search for the entrance to the auction hall. She is hurrying around the corner of the building, her beige skirt swirling around her feet, the color nearly blending with the building behind her. Only her white *kapp* stands out. She seems to have mastered the art of not being seen and has vanished almost before I notice she is there. I follow her steps and discover a simple glass door with a metal handle. Through it I see a short hallway leading to a tiered room lined with plastic chairs. I simultaneously fear and am fascinated by the world a few steps away. I grasp the handle and pull the door open.

A few minutes later, I survey the room from the highest row of chairs at the back. Before me, a narrow chute connects a small, covered riding arena to the holding zone where I'd seen the horses waiting. The auctioneer, a heavy-set man with cropped dark hair, sits above the chute, its white-washed walls scarred with strike marks and manure. A crowd of men stand at the edge of the chute. They are a mix of ages; most wear jeans and cowboy boots. A few wear the straw hats common to Mennonite men.

One of these, who I later learn is named Henry, stands out in his vibrant lime-colored shirt and black pants held up with black suspenders. He is narrow and lithe and moves with quick gestures. He bounds up the steps from the auction floor two by two, holding a paper cup of French fries, stopping to chat with an elderly man seated to my left.

"Not many folks here," says the elderly fellow, his accent thick with country overtones. He seems to be just one of a number of audience members who are in attendance more for Saturday evening entertainment than because they are actually planning on bidding.

Henry nods and wipes a swipe of ketchup from his full yet neatly trimmed beard.

"Bunch of 'em 'll just end up in New Holland on Monday," the elderly man continues.

Henry's pocket vibrates, and he pulls out what is possibly the oldest remaining flip phone on the planet. On the whole, the Mennonite community embraces more modern technology than their Amish cousins, yet the incongruity of using a cell phone while driving a horse-drawn buggy is still jarring.

"I just can't have mares around," says Henry into the phone. He is back down the stairs in a few bounds.

"Oh, I never had a problem with mares," says the elderly man to me. I smile in response and scan the crowd. A Mennonite family—parents, daughter, and two sons, the males wearing matching purple shirts—sits together, holding a bidding ticket. The daughter's blonde hair is tucked up, but she does not yet wear the *kapp* of her mother. The young girl smiles shyly at me.

The elderly man continues talking, describing now a pair of women who'd come to the auction the previous month. They'd purchased a donkey but couldn't convince the animal to load after the sale. A few of the dealers had linked arms together, got behind the small animal, and shoved it on the trailer.

"I hoped they wasn't plannin' to unload it before gettin' home!" He nearly snorts as he starts laughing.

A trio of mini donkeys are moved into the chute; the sale is about to start. The tiny animals mill nervously around the pen, always staying in physical contact with each other. Sale animals are tagged with a hip number when they arrive; collectively, these donkeys are numbers one through three. We will be into the mid-hundreds by the end of the night.

HOW DOES A HORSE BECOME UNWANTED? If we hope to stop it from happening, this is, perhaps, one of the most important questions to answer.

Firstly, young horses can be sensitive and unpredictable, and require experienced handling. When not provided a solid, basic education, a mature domesticated horse can behave much like a feral one—fearful, defensive, and ready to run. Animals with these characteristics have few prospects for homes that can accommodate their needs.

But it is not just the untrained who are unwanted. As a species, horses are long-lived and expensive to maintain due to an increasing loss of open space and the costs of producing feed and providing veterinary and farrier care. So older animals, as well as those with long-term medical conditions, lameness, or other issues that preclude them from use or increase the cost of their maintenance, can become undesirable. Like an older car with high miles, equestrians understand these animals' usefulness is likely limited and the cost of "repairs" high.

And there are more: Foals produced by high-end breeders who do not meet exacting standards. Racehorses who no longer win enough to pay their keep. Mustangs gathered by the federal government and adopted out to owners lacking knowledge and experience, or sent to long-term holding pens. Once-loved animals whose owners can no longer afford to keep them.

Any horse can become unwanted.

The question of what to do with unwanted horses is not new, and it is one that many equestrians have long been unwilling or unable to face. But in the mid to late 2000s, two events occurred that brought the crisis to a head. The first was in 2007, when the last three US-based equine slaughter plants closed in Texas and Illinois, largely due to legal battles between their Belgian owners and local municipalities. Prior to this, as many as 100,000 horses were slaughtered annually in the United States.

A lifelong vegetarian, I have always been troubled by large-scale factory farming and the widespread ill-treatment of any species of animal involved in that system. But as an equestrian and horse owner, I believe equine slaughter to be not just inhumane but immoral, and I applauded when those slaughterhouses closed. However, like many others, I had never stopped to interrogate the most important question: What would happen to the unwanted animals now?

The second event was the major economic downturn of 2008. For American families facing reduced wages and job loss, horses—if they had them—were at the bottom of the financial priority list. Farm owners found horses abandoned on their properties, and national parks reported finding domestic horses that appeared to have been turned loose on federal land. Organizations across the country set up to offer custodial care of equines in need of help, such as equine rescues, were overrun with unwanted animals while simultaneously facing a reduction in charitable giving.

But the horses just kept coming.

In the ensuing years, a civil war of sorts has raged within the equestrian community, between those who believe that surplus American horses should be humanely slaughtered here at home, and those who do not. This is perhaps putting too sharp of a distinction between the two factions, but ultimately, those who do not stand firmly in one camp or the other—in favor of "solving" the problem by slaughtering horses domestically or in opposition to it—seem to instead become caught in an ever-swirling vortex of rhetoric, judgment, and conflict. They are so spun around that they seek to avoid the discussion altogether, rather than take meaningful steps to solve it.

How did the equestrian industry end up here? More importantly, what can we do to fix it?

It is these uncomfortable truths that I seek to better understand.

"DO I HAVE ONE? One here, now one and a quarter, give me half, now one half give me two…."

The auctioneer begins his rolling buzz. He is hard to follow and clearly knows where the main buyers are sitting, even knows what type of animal they like. Henry (who I now realize is a "bid catcher," there to assist the auctioneer in noticing a buyer's interest) and a smooth-faced middle-aged man in a white cowboy hat and mauve shirt are working the crowd, driving up bids.

I study the bidders. It is hard to tell when or how they acknowledge their interest. Most wear a stern poker face, but Henry and the other man (who I later learn is the auction's owner, Brian Moore, also a dealer) seem able to quickly read them. The three men work as a unit, the auctioneer calling out a number (quarter or half to indicate twenty-five or fifty on the hundred dollar), and the bid catchers bellowing and pointing as a bidder throws in. Henry, in particular, comes alive—his eyes widen brightly, his colorful shirt a stark contrast to the manure-splattered, cracked plywood lining the gate behind him. Once Henry finds a bidder, he holds their gaze, unblinking, arm extended and fingers folded to indicate the bid, while somehow still scanning the crowd for competition. Finding a higher offer, he rapidly shifts his stare to the new leader, sometimes pausing only for a second before snapping back to the former.

Representatives from equine rescues often frequent auctions, looking to "pull" horses. Some specialize in animals they deem "rehomeable," and dealers have been known to bid against rescues in such cases with no intention other than driving up the price. It isn't unusual for a rescue to fight to "win" an animal so extremely compromised that it is likely the next step will be humane euthanasia, sometimes without even leaving the auction yard.

A small pony is brought out. The purple-shirted Mennonite family now begins to bid. A small battle ensues, with a dealer on the floor running the total up to $300. The man I presume to be the father hesitates to answer the auctioneer's call for another quarter.

"This is why you came," says the auctioneer, speaking directly to the father. "Seems a shame to sit here the whole time and not get him."

The father whispers to the younger son, who is sitting on his lap. The daughter is holding her cup of fries tightly and the elder son has stopped eating his burger. Almost imperceptibly, the father nods.

"Sale!" yells the auctioneer, as though the family has hit a homerun, and the rest of us are just fans at the ball field on a Saturday night.

FREE TO GOOD HOME.

Ads with this tag line once appeared in the print classifieds of local newspapers, and agricultural and equine publications. Today, they are on social media and Craigslist. There is always a story: *Beloved older animal seeks soft landing. Companion animal only. Sound for light riding. Getting married. Having a baby. Lost my job.*

Free to good home.

When people must part ways with a horse, they usually want desperately to believe that their horse will find a good home—that a fair and kind new owner will take on the fiscal and physical responsibility for the animal they can no longer keep. And sometimes, it all works out.

For the rest, there is the horse auction.

I can see that most of the horses at Lebanon Valley are sound and rideable. A number seem to come from somewhere "out west" and are described as "ranch broke" and "quiet and gentle." The last words are used so frequently in the auctioneer's descriptions I begin to laugh when he says it—as though "quiet and gentle" are static equine qualities like height or coat color, rather than characteristics of genetics combined with good training and kind handling. Despite the frequency of these qualities, the most expensive sale all night is only $4,000—a bargain in today's horse market.

Some of the horses are untrained. Some are clearly terrified of the chute and the loudspeakers and the audience. They whinny their worry to the others in the holding area, looking for support. A teenaged Appaloosa seems quiet as she is ridden through, all business but no flash. "Hasn't been off the farm in five years, never seen so many people. Nice horse," says the auctioneer. I imagine the mare was someone's pet. The dealers are unimpressed, and she sells for $750—a meat price.

Others sell for even less. Usually, these animals are awkward or unappealing in appearance—too plain or disfigured or homely. Some are older and some are thin, although not, by my eye, "emaciated." Mares appear to be undesirable. Smaller horses, unless clearly ponies, also are not popular. Some are a little lame. "Needs shoes," Henry's bid catcher partner offers whenever a horse shuffles through the lane, too uncomfortable to take an even stride.

Horses that are ridden appear in Western tack—a heavy-horned saddle and a shanked curb bit. A few Warmbloods come through, elegant and clearly bred for English sport performance. They are out of place in the Western gear.

The "catch riders" are mostly men—some in cowboy hats, all without helmets. There are two women; one rides with a strong posture and a soft hand, while the other is younger and wilder. The back pockets of her jeans are bedazzled with an embroidered pattern, and as the night wears on her loose blonde hair becomes stringy and stuck to her face, a small braid pulling just a few pieces back. She flirts with the dealers and shows off, removing the bridles from some horses and steering them with just the reins wrapped around their necks. Once or twice, she stands on a horse's back to demonstrate his docility. She slides off the haunches of a black Walking Horse mare, remounts, then somersaults off the horse's side, steps underneath her belly, and finally remounts by vaulting up the hindquarters. The mare doesn't flinch, yet she sells for less than $2,000.

Some horses are "no sales"—that's when the bidding never gets high enough to make the sale worthwhile to the dealer. These horses are sent back to holding, to return to the dealer's home lot and perhaps be sold another day.

THE AIR IN THE AUCTION HALL has become stifling, but I am not sure whether it is due to the actual temperature or the ambient energy in the room. The crowd has thinned to about 40 people, and the auctioneer is clearly becoming frustrated by the number of "no sales." My presence suddenly feels more obvious; I hold no bidding ticket and speak to no one. I'd been instructed by those familiar with livestock auctions to keep a low profile and to be extremely careful with my phone. Auctions like this one have been visited so many times by animal rights and welfare advocates that most now prohibit any form of recording, whether photo or video. Auction staff are known to forcibly evict anyone whom they deem to be a threat or nuisance.

I decide it is time to leave. But before I do, I step through a set of swinging doors that lead to the "warm-up" ring, where the catch riders prepare the horses prior to sale. A pile of extra arena footing is heaped in one corner; children run and chase each other up the pile and slide down, shrieking.

The flirty blonde is on a rough-coated chestnut; the pair is standing next to a black-and-white pinto carrying an overweight man whose size dwarfs his horse's petite frame. Suddenly the chestnut pins her ears and threatens to kick; like lightning, the girl flips the ends of her reins overhand and smacks the horse over the head. She does it again and then violently spurs the horse forward into a swift canter. The horse runs, whites of eyes showing and head held high in fear.

A middle-aged Mennonite woman in a green dress looks at me and asks, "How are you with breeds?"

She nods toward the little pinto. Based on her conformation and style of movement, I guess the mare is a Tennessee Walker, a breed known for its comfortable, smooth, running walk—a special gait not all horses can do. The woman expresses disbelief—the mare is small, barely over pony-size.

"I've seen Tennessee Walkers that size," I reply. My voice feels boggy from humidity and being silent for nearly four hours. "But maybe Spotted Saddle Horse. Or Foxtrotter."

The woman has two daughters with her. All three are excited about this horse, who wears a hip number in the low hundreds. One daughter tells me their neighbors have Rocky Mountain horses, another gaited breed, and she has ridden their stud and one of their mares.

"The mare is sort of common," she says. "But the stallion…he is so fancy!"

Her eyes glitter, and I recognize in them a spark I have seen countless times before. She is horse-crazy.

The attendant swings open the pipe gate to the chute, and the overweight man rides the pinto in. The women run through the swinging door, and I know the family is bidding. I hear the announcer call the horse a Tennessee Walker, but without registration papers, no one really knows.

They do not offer enough money.

No sale.

THE LEBANON VALLEY AUCTION is a place to sell livestock, pure and simple. The equines here are no more than commodities to be bought and sold. I wonder if any of the people running this sale genuinely *like* horses. Or are these animals simply a means to an end, a way to make a profit, regardless of where the animal ends up? Are the dealers and catch riders and auctioneer any different than ribbon-chasing competitors who sell their horses without concern for the horses' futures when they are no longer able to perform?

For someone with my philosophy—I believe horse ownership means committing to ensuring lifelong care of the animal—this auction has been overwhelming. Horse after horse coming through the chute looked pleasant enough. Functional and competent, the kind of animals that anyone could have fun with. But I know the kinds of buyers who need horses like these should not be shopping here, or at any auction, where a dealer's predatory eye would no doubt recognize their heartfelt longing, driving up the price of a cheap horse or encouraging the purchase of an animal with serious problems. Livestock auctions are a business. When demand goes up, so do prices. And when the supply exceeds demand, prices drop, and any horse deemed to be flawed or imperfect doesn't stand a chance.

I feel sick thinking about what is likely to happen to those horses who are too nervous or too untrained to show their potential. To those who are just not attractive enough to catch someone's eye. I think of the sweet-faced Appaloosa, of a shiny black pony mare with a kind eye, of a nondescript, awkwardly assembled bay that seemed like he'd be a wonderful family horse.

Legally, horses are considered livestock, yet many equestrians staunchly object to businesses such as Lebanon Valley that treat them as such. Perhaps what we need is a third category, one somewhere between livestock and companion animal, and out of this gray zone the horse will surely emerge. It would seem that the way to solve the problem of "too many horses and not enough homes" is simple—stop producing so many horses. But reality is never so cut and dry. There is clearly a complexity to this puzzle, and no doubt its solution will be equally multifaceted. By the end of the night, I have more questions about the problem of unwanted horse than answers. If those in the equestrian community truly love horses, and they do not want to see them sent to slaughter, what other solutions can we propose to manage the near-constant stream of surplus animals? But what do you do with a long-lived, expensive herbivore once his "useful" years are behind him? What role does the horse truly hold in modern America, and in the America of the future?

The auction is still going when I drive out of the lot after nearly five hours. I am immediately swallowed by cornfields that lie to the horizon, and the dusky sky is painted with an array of pastels, purple and pink and melon orange. I haven't driven a mile when I come upon a black-topped buggy pulled by a lanky bay, containing the Mennonite family in matching purple I had seen earlier in the stands. I slow to a crawl and pull into the other lane, waving to the children. The girl and her older brother wave back, she with a tiny smile, he wearing a stern mask. Their new pony is nowhere to be seen.

THE ROAD TO SALVATION?
A LOOK AT EQUINE RESCUE

ANYONE WHO HAS SPENT TIME in the horse world will tell you that, as a community, equestrians can be a rather opinionated bunch. No matter the topic—tack, shoeing, blanketing, turnout, even the best age to start training a horse—equestrian "best practices" vary across the industry, sometimes (but not always) along breed, discipline, regional, and socioeconomic lines. It is not uncommon for a "horse person" to believe their way is "right" and "best."

This mindset carries over into the conversation around unwanted equines. Among some industry leaders working to solve the problem, the term "unwanted" is now passé; instead, they prefer to describe these animals as being "in transition" (defined as a horse changing owners, careers, or homes, sometimes due to an owner's change of circumstance) or "at risk" (less desirable animals more likely to suffer from abuse or neglect, or to be shipped abroad to slaughter). But preferred nomenclature is only one way in which conflicting perspectives emerge. Even among equine rescue advocates, there is disagreement about how best to serve and support these unique populations in their time of need, as well as how to prevent them from needing help in the first place.

In Part I, I'll introduce you to several of these advocates, each of whom is living in the day-to-day space of helping and healing displaced, discarded, or otherwise unwanted equines. We will learn how they found themselves working within the field, hear about their triumphs and struggles, and discover how their perspectives on the subject of equine rescue have evolved along the way. Each advocate and organization plays a unique role within the wider web of equine welfare. And although they may not agree on all points, universally, they are resolved to do the best they possibly can for those individual animals ending up within their orbit of influence.

These advocates will show how any horse can become unwanted, how when it comes to working with people in the realm of unwanted horses, it can be hard to tell the "good guys" from the "bad," and how for some horses, ending up in what is known as the "slaughter pipeline" is a fate worse than death.

Chapter 1

RESCUE ME

SOMETIMES, PHYLLIS ELLIOTT THINKS her lifelong passion for horses is simply encoded in her DNA. Her grandfather kept both a store and draft horses in historic Faneuil Hall in Boston, Massachusetts, and her father, Bernard Altieri, seemed to have the "horse gene" too. It was he who bought Phyllis her first pony, and he would later raise Thoroughbred racehorses.

As a young adult, Phyllis also ended up working in the racing industry for a time (her sister Lillian Klesaris still does, training Thoroughbreds alongside her husband Steve in Florida). Phyllis's youth was spent riding and horse showing all around the Northeast. Her horses lived in her backyard, and she had the opportunity to learn from some individuals in the industry she deems "wonderful people," who taught her that when it comes to horses, she should always keep an open mind. She met her husband Bill Elliott, also an equestrian, while caring for his mother's horses. As newlyweds, Phyllis tried to practice financial caution and urged Bill to sell his horses. But as soon as their first child Nicole was born, Bernard bought his new granddaughter a pony named Buddy, and Phyllis and Bill were back in it again.

As Nicole and her younger sister Jessica became more involved in riding and showing, Phyllis did everything she could behind the scenes to support them. In 1995, the family moved to a thirty-acre former cattle farm in Brentwood, New Hampshire, so they could keep their horses at home. (Buddy came with them and is buried on the property.) Phyllis tried her hand at breeding, producing a total of seven animals, three of whom still live with her as they approach their thirtieth birthdays. She served on advisory boards and held leadership roles within equestrian organizations serving youth, like 4-H and the New Hampshire Quarter Horse Association. Throughout her children's junior careers, Phyllis was the quintessential "horse show mom," staying largely behind the scenes and serving as trailer driver, boot polisher, and perhaps most importantly, bill-payer.

One day Phyllis came to the same crossroads many middle-aged women do when they wake up and realize their principal work of raising children is concluded. Phyllis and Bill still owned their farm, and Phyllis's love for horses remained undiminished. She began considering alternative ways horses could remain a focus in her life.

As a child, Phyllis had read a slender book about a horse called "Snowman," which recounted the story of how, in the 1950s, professional trainer Harry deLeyer pulled an unassuming, unregistered carthorse off the slaughter truck and made him into a national show jumping superstar. This was years before a longer recounting of the tale drafted by Elizabeth Letts would become the bestselling book *The 80-Dollar Champion* (2011) and the subject of a documentary called *Harry & Snowman* (2015). Phyllis had gone to horse auctions with her father; in fact, her first pony, Edge Hill Agate, had been purchased at one as a yearling. Even then, it was well-known that most auctions were a conduit to the slaughterhouse, and Phyllis was well-versed in the world that Snowman had come from. His rags-to-riches story stayed with her, always.

After keeping nearly all her children's former show horses for the entirety of their lives, offering them to other local kids to ride and take lessons on, the idea of sending any horse to auction, and quite possibly to slaughter, was repugnant to Phyllis. She began researching how modern-day auctions worked, and started to ponder the idea of pulling a few horses herself.

One spring day in 2014, Phyllis was scrolling Facebook, and she paused on a post made by one of her daughter's childhood friends. This young woman was sponsoring a "GoFundMe" to raise money in support of the rehabilitation of several rescued horses. Phyllis had never heard of "crowdfunding" and looked up how it worked. She thought it seemed pretty straightforward, so one morning, she wrote out a story about how she wanted to go to the New Holland auction in Pennsylvania to save some horses, and made a GoFundMe page of her own. On a Sunday in late

May, with the $2,200 she'd raised online, Phyllis, her younger daughter Jessica, and her friend Sue Jones headed to Pennsylvania with an empty horse trailer and a goal—to save as many horses as possible.

The women ended up successfully bidding on eight animals—four ponies and four Miniature Horses—and had enough money left to purchase fuel for the drive home. One of the ponies had been Phyllis's pick—a walking skeleton with a thick coat they'd dubbed "Hairy." The pony had no expression in his dull eyes. In fact, he had so little affect they'd wondered if he was blind—it appeared he had just given up.

"He had absolutely zero emotion," remembers Phyllis. "None. He didn't blink, he didn't look at you. He had hay, but he didn't eat it. He was the epitome of pitiful."

At the auction, Phyllis was so anxious she would miss Hairy's turn in the ring she wouldn't leave her seat. When the pony finally came into the chute, the bidding started at just $10, but once Phyllis put in a bid, unbeknownst to her, dealers sitting across the aisle began driving up the price, until it reached around $250. That was when the bid catcher got annoyed, looked straight at the auctioneer, and announced "Sold."

Once Phyllis got Hairy home, it took her several days and multiple types of forage to convince him to eat, but in time, he did. His expression brightened, and his weight improved. It was determined he was probably somewhere between 25 and 30 years old. Hairy was adopted by a woman who chose to leave him on Phyllis's farm, where he thrived until old age finally took him, one New Year's Eve.

Phyllis was deeply affected by what she had seen at the auction. Most of the horses had looked good—fat, healthy, and sound—yet they sold for a pittance, often no more than $600. The auctioneer had announced each of these horses "came with a signed paper," and Phyllis had assumed that meant they were registered. It was only later she learned the truth—the seller was guaranteeing the horse had received no medications within the previous 30 days, clearing them for human consumption.

"Talk about being naive," says Phyllis with a grim smile.

After more crowdfunding and trips to the auction, followed by successfully placing the rescued animals in homes, a donor encouraged

Phyllis to establish a formal 501(c)3 nonprofit. At first, Phyllis resisted the idea, but her donor was insistent.

"I'd been on other boards of directors, and I didn't want to do all that," says Phyllis. "I just wanted to save some horses, and I didn't want to be told what I could or couldn't do."

But ultimately, Phyllis caved, and Hidden Pond Farm Equine Rescue became an official registered nonprofit with the state of New Hampshire, complete with a board of directors. She admits now that doing so drew together resources, both human and financial, that might otherwise have remained out of reach.

"It changed the landscape for us, totally, including what we're doing, and how and why we are doing it," says Phyllis. "One thing about our board of directors is everyone is brilliant in their own professions. The people who help run this organization are unbelievable. The volunteers— also unbelievable."

In just under a decade, Hidden Pond has helped to successfully rehabilitate and rehome an average of 27 horses, ponies, donkeys, and mules each year, and has offered lifetime sanctuary on Phyllis's farm to many more. And Phyllis can't count the number of other animals whose fate she has altered—animals in such poor condition they were beyond rehabilitation, for whom her organization arranged humane euthanasia, and some whose owners simply needed help finding resources to better support the equines in their care. In recognition for her efforts, the New Hampshire Horse Council named Phyllis its 2022 New Hampshire Horseperson of the Year.

But Phyllis is quick to credit those around her with Hidden Pond's success.

"You are depending on people to help you in your mission, and raising money is very difficult," says Phyllis. "I try to not turn my back on anything or anyone. Our main focus will always be a horse in need."

FROM THE ROAD, it is hard to see the full extent of the Hidden Pond property, but a multi-tiered stack of round bales piled out front, two large horse trailers parked in the short driveway, and glimpses of horses resting behind a hodgepodge of wood and metal fencing in the distance are enough to indicate that it is likely more than a family with "backyard horses." A well-worn dirt path leads around the Elliotts' home, a gray Cape Codder with an attached garage, and in following this path, visitors are greeted by an array of fowl—a sea of loose roosters, geese, and a duck or two. It is only after you walk behind the home that you view the true expanse of the farm.

There are equines everywhere.

They are housed singly and in small groups, in large paddocks and small dry lots; there are shaggy ponies, leggy Warmbloods, Thoroughbreds retired from the track. There are bays, and palominos, and grays, too. I visit on an unseasonably warm day in late November, and the sun's long, low rays seem to have caused an outbreak of napping among the equine residents. Those still awake are delicately nibbling hay from nets or have shoved the entirety of their heads and necks into hay huts. A group of perhaps half a dozen children in shorts and muck boots are cleaning stalls in the largest barn and helping to tidy several smaller paddocks attached to run-in sheds.

Hidden Pond's horses now come from many sources. Some have been seized by law enforcement and gone through the court system; others are auction pulls. A handful of residents are the remaining members of the Elliott family's original herd; others are horses that have been adopted but are boarded on the property. Occasionally, the farm becomes home to an unexpected "bonus horse"—a foal born to a rescued mare who was not known to be pregnant (it has now become the organization's policy to run a hormone test on all mares with an unknown history). In the year of my visit, Hidden Pond has taken in a larger than usual number of "owner surrenders," an event not uncommon when an individual is no longer physically or financially capable of caring for a horse.

Phyllis points out Noah, a pinto gelding who is in his mid-twenties. He was surrendered by his owners for financial reasons, and despite being a lovely, experienced animal, his age makes him less desirable to adopters. Noah has become good buddies with an aged chestnut gelding named Moose, who spent the summer of 2022 wandering loose around neighborhoods in Sterling, Massachusetts, alongside a female moose (hence the name). Noah helps teach children enrolled in Hidden Pond's Camp Desperado, which Phyllis started so horse-loving youth can learn to ride, even if they don't have the financial means to do so in a traditional riding program. (Many participants are only able to attend camp thanks to scholarships sponsored by generous donors.) She also teaches them basic horsemanship skills, so they learn all that goes into the daily care of these animals. Campers learn everything from how to clean paddocks to grooming, tacking up, basic riding fundamentals, and post-ride care. When the veterinarian or farrier stop by, the campers get front-row seats to watch these professionals at work. Campers even receive a crash-course on what a nonprofit is and fundraising, collaborating with each other to design their own web-based campaigns.

"They work on a specific need and an easy goal," explains Phyllis. "They learn what a nonprofit is."

Long-term Hidden Pond residents like Noah find a new purpose in life through their work with campers, even though other equestrians might consider some of them to be "too old" to be useful.

"Twenty-three years old? No one wants that old horse," says Phyllis about Noah. "But I gotta tell you what—that old horse is the best teacher. He was amazing this summer."

Then there are Athena and Ruby, two bonded mares. Athena, a petite bay, first arrived at Hidden Pond in 2015, and was fostered and adopted twice before returning to the rescue for good in 2019. She is approaching 30 years old and isn't totally sound. Ruby Shoes, a chunky chestnut with a thick white star on her forehead, was pulled from an auction in 2020. She is sounder than Athena, but with scars all over her legs, it is clear she has her own story to tell. Both mares have a permanent sanctuary home at Hidden Pond and also assist in the youth programming.

"They can still teach a child what it's like to love and touch a horse," says Phyllis. "For us, it works out, because they are teachers."

And in so many ways, Phyllis believes that education is the key to making progress toward solving the unwanted horse crisis. Not only does she want to connect horse-loving youth with good horsemanship education, she believes it is crucial to teach prospective owners about both the long-term and hidden costs of horse ownership, *before* they make an expensive investment. Just as important is teaching owners, in all corners and levels of the industry, that not every horse should be bred.

"The whole, 'I can't ride my horse so I'm going to breed her,' and running studs with mares and just culling what you don't want—what do you think is going to happen to that foal?" asks Phyllis. "If you don't have a plan for that baby, or don't know what that baby's going to do…. Hey, I bred horses. I *know* what it's like to bring horses up, and I know what it's like to sell them—and keep them. Overbreeding needs to stop."

At that moment, there is a shriek, followed by raucous laughter, and we both look over to where the children are wrapping up their morning at the farm. Phyllis explains that they are all homeschooled, and they volunteer at the farm each week as part of their curriculum. We watch as the kids take turns hanging their pitchforks beneath an overhang outside the main barn.

"Think about what those kids are learning being here, about a work ethic—about how to contribute to society when they grow up," says Phyllis with obvious pride. "My volunteers, they learn everything. They come, they get schooled by someone who knows the ropes that will show them what to do, then they find what they like the most, and they go off on their own."

Phyllis has never actually counted how many volunteers visit the rescue each month—she thinks there may be as many as 40—and even without a specific volunteer coordinator, somehow it all just works. There is Dwayne, who comes every weekend and "works his butt off" because he enjoys learning everything he can about horses. There is a dedicated group Phyllis calls her "Sunday Morning Wake-Up Crew," who used to just clean up manure but has now learned to fill and stuff hay nets and top off water tubs. Volunteers have told Phyllis that coming to the farm is "the best part" of their week.

Then there is Mary, who during my visit seems to be doing a bit of everything from feeding horses to assisting the homeschoolers to repairing a broken pitchfork head. Mary has adopted five special needs horses from

Hidden Pond, and in the next few months, she will adopt a sixth—Spirit, a dun-colored, drafty-looking gelding. When Spirit arrived at the rescue he was a fearful, highly distrusting, traumatized animal. But Mary has spent countless patient, slow hours with him, mostly just sitting nearby, and eventually inside, his paddock, working to earn his trust. Mary tells me she has recently submitted paperwork with the state to establish a nonprofit equine sanctuary of her own.

"The opportunity to work at Hidden Pond fills a void for us, and it fills a void for the volunteer," says Phyllis.

But by far the biggest void Phyllis, her board, and the rest of her volunteers must tackle is the expense of running the rescue. The need for money is constant, and Phyllis participates in what she calls "fundraising school"—seminars put on by a Tennessee-based organization called Get Fully Funded (helmed by fundraising consultant Sandy Rees) every year.

"There's always something to learn," says Phyllis. "You are asking people to help you, and there are all these different programs and support. Then there are all these rules and regulations, and documents. You don't go to college for this—I learned by the seat of my pants."

At fundraising school, Phyllis learned it was important for nonprofits to host one "audacious event" per year, so Hidden Pond began running an open house each June. The open house has evolved from a one-day event to a four-day extravaganza, complete with educational speakers, farm tours, and a special "intro to horses" session for children. But it also includes several non-equine themed activities, ranging from chainsaw sharpening to wine tasting to a BBQ rib cookoff.

"You try to build your donor base to at least 1,000 people," says Phyllis. "You have your events, which for us have grown. And you apply for 10 grants a year."

The rescue's biggest expense is hay. Thanks to the volunteers, labor costs are kept to a minimum, but the rescue does maintain two paid employees whose salaries must be covered (neither one of whom is Phyllis). She's heard plenty of stories about rescues that have gotten in over their heads—too many equines, too little funds—and she knows that effective fundraising is essential to Hidden Pond's success.

"Don't think I don't get scared—you have to be careful, and you can't waste anything," says Phyllis. "Everyone out there doing rescue is doing it because they love the animals, not to get rich—trust me."

We are sitting beside a small turnout area, adjacent to a shed row of stalls and a farm access road, muddy after recent heavy rain. Further up the road, Mary the volunteer is supervising two horses eating a supplemental lunch feed; they are Phyllis's homebreds, living out their last years on the farm where they were born. One of them finishes his meal and is taken back to his fenced turnout, but the other flops down on the brown grass of late November, rolls, and then stretches out in the sun.

"Re-opening slaughter is not the answer, because it gives everyone an excuse," says Phyllis, who is watching her horse luxuriate in the rays of the late fall sun. "We have become a 'throwaway society,' where we want everything yesterday and if something doesn't work anymore, you get rid of it. Remember, only 20 percent of people who have horses show. Most are recreational riders. Just because your horse can't do the 4' [show jumps] anymore doesn't mean he's not going to be a great horse for somebody else."

A metal sign attached to the barn door reads, "Full Circle of Life Shelter." It represents that Hidden Pond is part of a network of shelters across the country that will accept an equine in need, no matter the stage of life, especially if that animal is not likely to be an "adoptable" animal, or is in need of end-of-life care. Phyllis knows there are still many problems to be solved in equine rescue, but she remains optimistic that the passion she sees among rescuers means they are collectively moving closer to a solution.

"I am encouraged [the unwanted horse crisis] will come to an end—the more we work together," says Phyllis. "That's the hard part, because everyone's a type A, opinionated personality, and it's gotta be 'their way or the highway.' I think we *can* work together, and if we get a handle on the overbreeding, and open up horses again to those who can't afford it, I think it's possible to fix this."

WHILE PHYLLIS WAS LOOKING AT CELEBRATING the tenth anniversary of her first trip to New Holland when I spoke with her—the one during which she purchased Hairy and began her unexpected journey into the world of equine rescue—the Maine State Society for the Protection of Animals (MSSPA) has been serving horses in the Northeast for over 150 years. Originally established in Portland, Maine, to provide retirement care for horses that pulled the city's fire engines and street cars, today the MSSPA remains the only organization within the state wholly dedicated to the care and rehabilitation of abused or neglected equines.

When I visit the MSSPA on a gray winter's day, I am immediately struck by the impression of workmanlike efficiency on the property. Despite the season, everything looks neat, tidy, and organized. The facility is centrally situated among expansive, rolling fields in an agricultural area on the edge of South Windham, Maine, not far from one of the state's correctional facilities. Its white-sided Visitor's Center, built in 2018, faces the road and holds pride of place. On the side of the building, the silhouette of a large cantering horse hangs below the organization's name and website, spelled out in forest green letters. Positioned adjacent to and behind the Visitor's Center, respectively, sit a classic New England-style barn with 26 stalls, also white with forest green sliding doors, and a moderately sized indoor arena. Surrounding these core facilities are white-fenced paddocks with run-in sheds, populated by horses mostly hanging out in pairs or trios.

In 2020, the entire MSSPA property was christened the Lawrence J. Keddy and Marilyn L. Goodreau Equine Rehabilitation Facility. It is an appropriate, and perhaps understated, tribute to the couple who are widely credited as being the MSSPA's "modern-day founders." Keddy and Goodreau, who shared a passion for helping injured and abused animals, met while volunteering for the organization in the late 1960s. By the time Keddy, a philanthropist and self-made millionaire, became president of the MSSPA in 1974, there were no shelters in Maine equipped to handle large farm animals. At the time, the state was seeking to sell or lease a farmhouse, barn, and 124 acres of land on River Road in South Windham—and the couple saw an opportunity for the MSSPA to establish a true farm animal sanctuary. In 1978, Keddy personally leased the property and moved the organization's activities there; in 1989, he purchased it for "fair market value" and donated it to the MSSPA, giving the organization a permanent base and the opportunity to expand its mission. Under the direction of Keddy and Goodreau, over the next several decades, the MSSPA grew to become the largest horse rescue facility in all of New England.

Despite its name, the MSSPA is not state-run or funded (a common misconception), but rather has always been an independent nonprofit organization, with no legal oversight or jurisdiction in cases of abuse or neglect. But after the acquisition of its new facility on River Road, the MSSPA established a "one-of-the-first-of-its-kind" public/private partnership with the state of Maine—the organization agreed to shelter and provide care and rehabilitation for any and all equines seized by state agencies, at no cost to the state.

But Keddy wasn't done expanding the MSSPA's impact on animals in need. Upon reviewing state statues regarding animal welfare and finding them lacking, he successfully lobbied for the extensive revision and strengthening of Maine's animal-welfare related codes and laws. The effects of his efforts are still felt in the state today. In fact, due to the quality and enforcement of Maine's animal protection laws, from 2020 through 2022, the state was ranked first in the nation by the Animal Legal Defense Fund in its Annual Report on the subject (the state slipped to second in 2023, behind Oregon).

When Keddy died in 2000, Goodreau assumed the duties of MSSPA president, a role she held until 2011. That was when attorney Meris Bickford stepped in as the organization's first CEO. Bickford brought her extensive experience in bank management and trust administration to the MSSPA, and was instrumental in establishing a $10 million endowment for the organization, as well as revitalizing its adoption and volunteer programs. Bickford is the one responsible for the construction of the Visitor's Center and indoor arena, which was dedicated in her honor upon her retirement in 2022.

Today, not only is the MSSPA well-known within the state as a resource in assisting neglected or abused equines, or those at risk of becoming so, the organization continues to enjoy a close working relationship with local and state agencies responsible for enforcing Maine's animal welfare regulations. As a result, the majority of equines finding safety under the auspices of the MSSPA still do so as a direct result of seizures made by law enforcement.

In spite of its strong animal protection and welfare statutes, Maine is a fairly large state with many small towns, and the personnel responsible for enforcing the rules are often overextended. The state's Animal Welfare Program (AWP)—which is tasked with developing and implementing policies and programs to address animal cruelty complaints, as well as inspecting and licensing animal shelters, pet stores, kennels, and animal research facilities—has just six District Humane Agents, who serve the entire state. Meanwhile, the AWP may receive as many as 800 complaints a year, each pertaining to concerns about the care and well-being of horses, cats, dogs, other livestock, and even exotics. In order to adequately investigate such a large volume of calls, the AWP partners with other agencies such as the state police, local law enforcement, and Maine's 300-plus municipal animal control officers. When these investigations result in the seizure of an equine, the MSSPA is most often the animal's next stop—and when a horse arrives, the experienced staff knows exactly what to expect.

"They're all underweight," says Jeff Greenleaf, who has been the MSSPA barn manager since 2014. "They're all full of parasites. They all have poor hoof care. They all have poor dentition." He ticks off the problems on his fingers, then repeats them for emphasis. "That's why they're seized by law enforcement or state officials," he continues. "The majority of them have those individual issues. Every horse that comes in."

All new arrivals are promptly evaluated by the MSSPA's core staff, as well as one of three veterinary practices and a team of farriers. And remaining true to Keddy and Goodreau's original vision, the MSSPA will ensure these animals are treated, healed, and rehabilitated, if possible. To be clear—all MSSPA intakes will receive this essential care. But what happens beyond that will depend on whether the animal's owner is willing to immediately sign custody over to the state, or if the individual chooses to fight the charges in court.

"There are many times where the owners end up surrendering the animals to the state of Maine, then the state transfers title to the MSSPA," explains Kathy Woodbrey. She's been with the organization since 2011 and took over as MSSPA CEO and vice president of its board of directors when Bickford retired in 2022, during which time she has seen hundreds of animals come through the facility's tall wooden doors.

When it comes to ensuring the best future for a seized animal, a prompt transfer of title to the MSSPA is perhaps the preferred outcome. This means that Greenleaf and his team—which includes his six-person staff, volunteers, and a network of organizational partners throughout the region—can assess each animal's level of training, identify their needs, and make a plan to help them find a suitable new home.

"We evaluate them physically to see what they need to get back in shape and do the best we can for all of them," says Greenleaf. "Some are limited by the physical and metabolic issues they may have, and those are best suited as pasture pets or companions.... We start at square one, even if we know the horse is a Grand Prix horse. Ground manners, like haltering, leading, stopping, backing up, and yielding the hindquarters. We work up from there to long-lining, light longeing, and basic saddle work."

As staff members become more familiar with each horse, they get a better sense of the type of handler or rider that might be best suited for them. Although some animals arrive nearly feral, and gentling them typically requires the more specialized expertise of outside trainers, new intakes usually have at least basic handling experience. With well over 100 volunteers working at the facility each month, horses are handled by individuals with varying levels of proficiency in their horsemanship skills. Watching how horses respond to a range of handlers gives staff useful information in matching them with a potential adopter.

"You don't know who is going to come and want the horse," says Greenleaf. "They could be an Olympic rider, or they could be someone who just wants a horse to look at while they're drinking coffee at their kitchen table."

The MSSPA places anywhere from 25 to 30 horses into new homes annually. Some adopters are looking for a specific type of horse—a Miniature Horse, a donkey, a 16.2-hand Thoroughbred—and are willing to wait until that type of animal arrives. Others are more open-minded in finding their match and are happy to work with MSSPA staff to find just the right equine for their specific situation. All prospective adopters must pass a rigorous approval process and complete an in-person "meet-and-greet" with the animal they hope to bring home. Once an animal is placed, MSSPA volunteers will do annual post-adoption site visits; in 2023, they visited 99 facilities to check on equine adoptees placed by the organization.

"We have horses all around the country—Massachusetts, Texas, Florida, even Colorado," says Woodbrey, who notes that most of those horses moved out of state with their owners *after* being adopted. "We do get applications from out of state, but a meet-and-greet for somebody who lives in Florida is a little difficult!"

Several horses living on the farm when I visit—like Alibar, a bay Morgan/Arabian gelding, and Romeo, a small liver chestnut with a long star and adorable snip—are horses previously adopted out by the MSSPA and later returned when their families' situations changed.

"Part of our adoption contract agreement is that for any reason, at any time, if they do not want the horse, can't take care of the horse, we get the horse back," says Greenleaf. "No selling, trading, leasing, or anything like that is allowed."

Although the MSSPA has a maximum capacity of 120 equines, in general they try to keep the farm's population much lower than that. At the time of my visit, they had 29 equines under their care, with several scheduled to leave for new homes the following week. While it is the organization's goal to place all adoptable horses into a new home, Greenleaf acknowledges that for some animals, staying at the shelter long-term may be the most realistic outcome.

"The way we look at it, no horse on this property is actually a 'sanctuary horse' [permanent resident of the rescue], because it is possible that any horse on this property could go to a good home," says Greenleaf with a smile. "We do, though, have horses who most likely will remain here for the rest of their lives, because of their age, conditions, medications—that kind of stuff."

But there is another type of horse that may also experience an extended stay at the facility. These are animals seized from individuals unwilling to relinquish ownership without a fight; caught up in a backlogged court system, these equines remain in limbo at the MSSPA until their case is resolved. They are, of course, well looked after and receive all necessary basic care. But beyond that, the staff is unable to further their education, never mind adopt them out.

"We don't publicize or post photos of these animals, but we are open to the public, so people see them and say, 'What a wonderful-looking horse. I would love to know more about him,'" says Greenleaf with a sigh. "We can't say anything except, 'We'll let you know when they come available'— *if* they come available and don't go back to the owner."

It's a frustrating position for all involved. Post-pandemic, some otherwise adoptable animals have remained at the MSSPA for nearly two years, while their owners await their day in court. Often, these animals have ready homes waiting. One time, after a case involving a trio of animals held at the MSSPA for over a year was finally resolved, the organization had them placed in new homes within weeks.

"The court systems are backed up, and we understand that," says Woodbrey. "The district attorneys and everyone else are doing the best they can. But as these horses sit here without conclusion on their case, and we don't have title to them…." She pauses and lets out a large sigh before continuing. "They have a difficult job, and I believe they care about the animals, but sometimes things that are out of their control may hamper their ability."

ALTHOUGH THEY RECEIVE MANY REQUESTS, only a handful of MSSPA intakes each year are direct owner surrenders—and even this is a departure from long-time policy. When they call, owners cite many reasons they are looking for help—health issues, financial challenges, a child who has lost interest—but the reason they come to the MSSPA specifically about taking their horse or pony is almost always due to one main concern.

"Most folks are worried about their horse getting into a bad situation—that's the majority of the calls we get from people who want to surrender animals," explains Greenleaf.

The MSSPA has worked hard to create options *beyond* surrender to support these horses (and owners) in need, thereby saving their own resources for the most vulnerable, challenging, or neglected cases. Each call for help is handled on a case-by-case basis, and after MSSPA staff hears the details of the specific situation, many owners are instead referred to one of the organization's direct owner-support programs designed to keep horses both safe and out of shelters.

The first of these is the Maine Horse Matchmaker, a free online rehoming program begun by the MSSPA in 2015. At that time, the organization did not accept direct owner surrenders under any circumstances, yet they still wanted to find a way to help facilitate the process of finding these animals a new home.

"It was a way to connect someone who is not able to keep their horse any longer with someone who is looking for a horse," says Woodbrey. "It's better for the horse if it can go from one caring owner to the next caring owner, and bypass the shelter."

Maine Horse Matchmaker is hosted on Facebook and facilitated by the MSSPA—the organization processes and posts each animal's profile, and monitors the page's activity and comments to ensure all discussion remains focused on the best interests of each horse. All animals posted on Maine Horse Matchmaker must be offered for free; they cannot be leased, sold, or "rehomed with a fee." Further, all placements are made directly by the original owner, not the MSSPA, leaving the selection of the most appropriate home for the horse up to the person who knows the animal best. The program has been largely successful, with about 65 percent of the animals placed on its social media finding a new home.

Sometimes, though, what owners need is assistance getting through a financial tough patch. To support the owners of horses in this situation, the

MSSPA runs a Feed and Care Bank, which provides temporary, emergency assistance to cover the cost of hay, feed, farrier or dental services, routine vaccinations, and veterinary care. Owners must apply for this assistance, and for those who qualify, the MSSPA will pay service providers and vendors directly. The Feed and Care Bank will also assist with the cost of euthanasia—a process that often also begins with an owner calling to request that the MSSPA take a horse.

"It's a tough conversation to have, but sometimes, for those older horses who have lived in one place for a long time, it would be the kindest gift that animal could receive," says Woodbrey. "It is assessed on a case-by-case basis, and it is all related to the animal's quality of life. Euthanasia is costly, and if that is a barrier to the horse being released from pain and suffering, that is something we are able to help with. We are focused on the animal, and the animal's needs, whether that animal is coming to us from law enforcement or from an owner. We are all horse lovers here, and our MSSPA community knows horse people."

ON THE FRONT EDGE of the MSSPA property, adjacent to the visitor's parking lot and within sight of River Road, is a small green shed labeled "Treasure's Tack Shack." Named for a beloved and recently departed Miniature Horse who was a longtime MSSPA resident, the shed contains gently used horse equipment, ranging from blankets to riding boots to high-end saddles, all donated to the organization. Twice a week, staff and volunteers open its doors to local equestrians, whose purchases help to support the organization's work. It is a natural symbiosis of resource sharing, and much like the Maine Horse Matchmaker and Feed and Care Bank programs, this type of grassroots connection to the state's equestrian community is one of the MSSPA's hallmarks.

In addition to the work the MSSPA does directly for equines, they also prioritize creating opportunities for human education. In the middle of the Visitor's Center is a spacious classroom and meeting space, with a large wooden table and windows looking into the indoor arena. Here, the MSSPA has hosted seminars such as an equine-specific animal control officer training, and "So You Want to Own a Horse," an educational offering for prospective horse owners. The organization has also welcomed youth attending summer camp programs at the Animal Refuge League in Westbrook, Maine, and the Animal Welfare Society in Kennebunk, Maine, as well as students from the Windham School District, offering them basic horsemanship education and the opportunity to learn to groom and lead a horse.

In the main entrance of the Visitor's Center hangs a series of partnered photographs, showing "before" and "after" images of animals the MSSPA has played a role in saving. To see the transformation in the animals is truly inspirational and reminds me how powerful an act it is to extend compassion to creatures who have fallen into unfortunate circumstances. But for even some experienced horsemen, it can be difficult to see the animal in the "after" photo when what stands before them is an equine who looks like the one "before." Woodbrey and Greenleaf have almost a quarter century of combined experience in the field of saving neglected horses; I ask if they think it is possible to reduce or even eliminate the number of unwanted horses, perhaps someday rendering this photo wall irrelevant.

"Whether teaching children from a young age what responsible pet ownership is, or for adults considering getting a horse—it's all important," says Woodbrey. "Education is a big piece of solving this problem. But if you're talking at a national level, I don't think there is one answer." She pauses, then continues, "It's not breed-specific. I think there is some overbreeding, and backyard breeding, and there are issues with the wild horse population, and then you add in the competition horses. But I wouldn't say, 'Oh, the Standardbreds are the problem,' or, 'It's the Thoroughbreds.'"

Greenleaf nods and adds, "It's equines in general, not just the racing industry, the show industry, the reining industry. It's a combination of all that. It would be great if I didn't have a job, but I honestly don't see that happening, based on the horses I see come through this place."

But both agree moving toward eliminating the issue of unwanted horses requires stakeholders from around the industry to come together to work toward a common goal. To that end, the MSSPA has recently partnered with several other Maine-based equine rescue organizations, including Horses with Hope in Hope, Maine, Bagaduce River Equine Rescue in Brooksville, and Futures for Standardbreds in southern Maine, to create the Maine Equine Rescue Network, with the intention of sharing resources and ideas, offering support, and continuing collaborative efforts toward finding solutions.

"The size of this organization here may be larger than others, but we all share a common goal—the care and well-being of the animals," says Greenleaf. "It doesn't matter if it is 5 or 500. We all have the same goal—for the animal to have the best life it can have. It is about collaborating on what we *can* agree on. Put six people in a room and they are going to have six different opinions on a subject, so collaborating on what you *can* agree on may take a while. But it's all in the common interest of the good of the animals."

I have been strolling around the property with Woodbrey and Greenleaf, visiting with many of the equine residents, and we now pause in the main barn's wide aisle. A farrier is nailing corrective shoes onto the hooves of a fuzzy chestnut Quarter Horse named Creek. I'm told the young gelding arrived at the MSSPA last July and is now looking for a companion home. In a stall and waiting his turn with the farrier is Simon, an owner surrender. He peers at us quizzically, tiny and pert ears almost touching, begging for a treat. This aged purebred American Saddlebred gelding just had a few meet-and-greet visits with adopters this morning; Greenleaf is hopeful that one will prove to be just the right fit. Then there is the newly dubbed "Misty," a chestnut pony mare who has been at the MSSPA for over a year. She is finally leaving for her new home next week. Part of a seizure case that was tied up in court, Misty was given her new name in honor of starting a new chapter in her life.

As we move back outside, toward the paddocks, I am struck that these horses could be any horses, in any barn.

"So many adopters have come in and said, 'I had no idea I'd get such a great horse from a rescue or a shelter,'" says Greenleaf. "These animals may come from horrible situations, but now some are Second or Third Level dressage horses."

Woodbrey nods affirmatively and smiles.

"We had a little pony that came in two or three winters ago, laminitic," she says. "But with a medication change and a feed change, now he's a little competitive driving pony in New England and doing amazing. I'd like to debunk the myth that they're just a bunch of old broke-down nags—that's just not true."

Greenleaf reaches out to stroke the forehead of a dark bay Quarter Horse named Violet, who is reaching over the fence toward us. The tips of the ex-barrel racer's long mane are sun-kissed, she wears the most expensive shoes of any horse on the property, and her strong personality necessitates an experienced handler. But when horses arrive on the farm who need a bit of a refresher on proper equine manners and behavior, the staff puts them out with Violet, and she sets them right.

In that moment, Violet abruptly turns away and pivots her body toward her companion, forcing him to move his feet in an act of equine submissiveness. She looks satisfied with his reaction and wanders over toward her hay feeder. Greenleaf watches her a moment, then turns to face me.

"They're not all broken," he says. "They come to us broken, but they don't stay that way."

"We all have the same goal—
for the animal to have the best life it can have. It is about
collaborating on what we can agree on."

JEFF GREENLEAF
MSSPA BARN MANAGER

Chapter 2

FINDING YOUR NICHE

ALI BAKER HAS ALWAYS LOVED ANIMALS. It's hard to say if this quality is the result of nature, or nurture—her parents, David and Karen Chipman, are also animal lovers, and as Ali grew up in their home on the North Shore of Massachusetts, the family cared for everything from stray dogs and cats to ducks, chickens, and rabbits. When Ali was five or six, her parents leased a Shetland pony for her to learn to ride, and when she was eight, Karen bought a horse named Bo to share with her daughter. Later, the family also took in a Miniature Horse named Gigi, who for a time lived behind a privacy fence on their suburban lawn.

Ali was a member of both Pony Club and 4-H, and enjoyed taking lessons and competing at horse shows; when she was a little older, it was no surprise to anyone that she chose to enroll in the animal science program at the local agricultural and technical high school. She went on from there to complete an equine-focused animal science degree at a state university, with an eye toward veterinary school (although she later chose not to apply).

Karen thought it was important for her daughter to understand that not all domestic animals were lucky enough to be afforded the compassionate care and life-long home that their family offered. In addition to regularly participating in the annual Massachusetts Society for the Prevention of Cruelty to Animals (MSPCA) fundraising walk, at least once a year, Karen brought her daughter to a horse auction in western Massachusetts.

"She felt it was really important for me to bear witness to all the horses and donkeys that were essentially given up on, because I came from a different world," explains Ali. "She helped me understand where equines go once they are no longer 'of use' to humans."

With the memory of those trips seared in her mind, Ali says that as an undergraduate, she believed equine slaughter to be an ethical method for managing unwanted horses. But she doesn't feel that way anymore, and for nearly a decade, she has been hard at work trying to make a positive impact on outcomes for some of the smallest of the unwanted—Miniature Horses, donkeys, and mules.

It all started on a 5-acre farm in Raymond, New Hampshire, in 2015. That was the year Ali bought her first home; the land had become a bit overgrown, but it was zoned for livestock and she knew with a bit of time and effort, it could be restored to order. By then, it had been a few years since the passing of her "heart horse," an Appendix Quarter Horse gelding named Todd. Ali had found it necessary to take a break from horses altogether to recover from his loss. But with the new property came an opportunity for new beginnings.

One of the first equine residents on the property was Gigi, the Miniature Horse from Ali's childhood. While in college, Ali had made the difficult decision to rehome Gigi for financial reasons; after she graduated and needed a companion for Todd, Gigi's adopters had offered her back to Ali. Giving up Gigi had taught Ali that anyone could end up in the position of needing to responsibly rehome a well-loved horse—and how important it was to be able to do so without judgment.

It wasn't long before a small herd of goats joined Gigi on the property. Ali affectionately refers to them as "freeloaders" who did not help with clearing the property as she'd hoped they would. Dogs, cats, and chickens increased in number. Somehow, word got out about this kindhearted, dark-haired, tattooed, animal-savvy young woman, and soon, people began calling and asking her for help with various animals in need. Ali found it hard to say no.

"Before I knew it, I started to take in animals," she remembers. "I started to have people asking how they could donate. I was like, 'I'm a person, not an organization.'"

But Ali finally succumbed to the suggestion made by several close friends and supporters that she officially found a nonprofit, and in 2018, she filed the necessary paperwork to establish Home At Last Farm (HALF).

Initially, their stated mission was "to rescue, rehabilitate, and re-home farm animals, as well as provide permanent residency for the extra special animals who are not adoptable."

"Our focus was not just horses," says Ali. "We wanted to think about farm animals in general."

But when people began dropping off roosters in the middle of the night, much to her neighbors' chagrin, and she started to run out of space, Ali quickly realized her new organization needed to become more specialized. By then, she was working from home, trying to balance the needs of her fledgling rescue with the demanding, non-animal-related corporate career she relied on to help support it. In her limited spare time, she became aware of what seemed to be an uptick of posts on social media sharing information about auction horses living in deplorable conditions, along with requests to donate "bail" to rescue them.

Soon, Ali was reviewing online debates around "kill buyers" and "kill pens"—terms commonly used to describe the middlemen who either directly purchase equines to ship to slaughter, or who purchase them to sell to feedlots or others who are under contract to fill a slaughterhouse's quota, as well as the "holding spaces" animals with this likely fate are kept in.

However, Ali noticed that most "keyboard warriors" didn't distinguish between a dealer with a contracted quota to fill for a foreign slaughterhouse (a true "kill buyer"), and those dealers who *called themselves* "kill buyers," but in reality lacked such contracts. She noticed the naysayers claimed that none of the horses appearing in the heartbreaking posts she kept seeing online would ever ship to slaughter; Ali suspected there was some truth to this. But when those same people would argue that purchasing a horse from that circumstance wasn't "rescue," she had to disagree.

"You hear the word 'kill pen,' and some people will have a totally visceral reaction," says Ali, shaking her head. "They'll say, 'Kill pens aren't real! Those horses will never ship to Mexico or Canada, because they don't have a contract.' Fair. But there are a certain number of *actual* kill pens in the United States that *do* have contracts, and you'll see those kill buyers go around the auctions. They'll pull horses that are, in fact, going to ship.

"If we look at the situation in the most simple terms, you have an unwanted horse population," she continues. "You don't have homes for them. You do not have rescues for them to go to. No matter what, they are going to have to funnel 'down' to somewhere, and that funnel usually ends at the lowest of the low places. That's going to be someone who doesn't give a shit about them and wants to flip them to make money."

The question of whether the purchase of animals from these middlemen is helping or hindering the plight of equines in the auction pipeline is perhaps one of the most divisive among those who seek change. Ali prefers the term "bad dealers" to "kill buyers," and she acknowledges that purchasing an animal from one of them—or someone pretending to be one—means these individuals will make a profit, and will likely then purchase more horses, so the cycle continues. But when it comes to alleviating the suffering of an animal, that is a compromise she is willing to make.

"These are the most disgusting, deplorable places you could even imagine," Ali says. "The things that go on there—the sicknesses animals have—I can tell you, any donkey that's going to end up at a bad dealer is going to have pneumonia. Most of those donkeys die, or get shot on the back of the lot, if people don't come in and pull them." Her voice breaks as she continues, "I have had people pull animals from kill pens, and ask me to take them on, and they have all broken my heart." She pauses and takes a deep breath. "At the end of the day, they're always going to need to land somewhere. And they are suffering there. I can tell you, those animals need rescue."

Ali began pondering the question of whether HALF could possibly make a positive impact on outcomes for horses stuck in the slaughter pipeline. At first, she explored the possibility of bidding on young, unhandled horses at auctions, and partnering with a trainer who could give them a good foundation. Her rescue would cover most of the animals' expenses, and when they were ready, facilitate their adoption. She hoped that in so doing, HALF's work would not only set at-risk horses on a safer path, it could help to change the belief many people hold that quality riding horses don't come from low-end auctions. But despite the efforts of Ali and her organization's board, they struggled to find trainers interested in being involved.

"It was a little bit heartbreaking, to be honest," says Ali.

But she had barely filed away the disappointment when she noticed a new trend emerging in the online dialogue she followed. Perhaps thanks to Gigi, Ali has always had a soft spot for Miniature Horses, small equines purpose-bred to display the physical characteristics of full-size horses but measuring only 34 inches at the withers or less. Most Miniature Horses are kept as pets; too small to ride, some "Mini" enthusiasts enjoy driving them, or taking them in hand through obstacle courses and over fences. Thanks to their small size, Minis are also increasingly popular in certain types of equine-assisted therapy work. Despite this, in the eyes of many involved in the online debates around kill pens, Ali noticed that Minis seemed to be considered to be something like second-class citizens.

"I started to realize there was a big buzz around Miniature Horses," says Ali. "People would say, 'Miniature Horses don't go to slaughter,' or, 'If you're pulling Miniature Horses, you're not saving them, because they don't really ship.'"

So Ali started to watch auction livestreams, and realized just how often Minis did, in fact, end up on the sales manifest—sometimes, loose herds of them, one or two studs mixed in with a group of pregnant mares, most barely handled. She watched who bought them, and for how much. Even now, she doesn't know if, or how many, Miniature Horses ship to slaughter. But what she does know is the luckiest Minis at auction were those purchased by a rescue, while the others went from dealer to dealer to dealer, and auction to auction, looking worse and worse as time went on.

"All these unhandled Miniature Horses, going to auction—where do they go?" says Ali. "If they don't get pulled by someone with a good home offer, where do they go? It's a big question I still have. Where… do…they...go?"

Ali found that only a handful of other rescue groups were asking these same questions, and she came back to her board with a proposal to focus their work on Miniature Horses, for several reasons. First, there was a clear and demonstrated need. Secondly, Ali had the skills to work with unhandled Minis and prepare them for adoption, so there would be less need to recruit outside trainers. And finally, Miniature Horses typically use fewer consumable resources (hay, grain, bedding) than full-sized horses, reducing the cost of these essential expenses. Her board was "on board," so to speak, and HALF expanded its name to become Home At Last Farm Mini Horse and Donkey Rescue—because Ali recognized that donkeys (often smaller in size and kept as pets or companions) faced many of the same challenges as Minis. (Since the transition in focus, Ali's rescue has also extended its services to a handful of mules and ponies as well.)

In 2020, Ali and her husband Chris purchased a larger facility in Wales, Maine. Not only would there be capacity to shelter more rescues (alongside a growing herd of Ali's own horses and other assorted livestock), but the property had an indoor arena—a tremendous advantage when it comes to keeping horses in work year-round in the snowy Northeast. In Wales, the couple found a welcoming community and many local residents eager to volunteer in support of the rescue's work. But after two years of trying to balance her job with providing the animals high-quality care through the rugged Maine winter, in 2022, Ali, Chris, their animals, and HALF's physical facilities relocated to Statesville, North Carolina.

HALF LEADERSHIP KNEW they needed to be strategic in deciding how to fulfill their new mission to "do big things for little horses." From the beginning, Ali has used her personal funds to cover any shortfalls in HALF's treasury (most notably, the cost of decent quality hay, which at the time of writing she says is averaging around $16 a bale in North Carolina), and she also has funded everything related to the physical infrastructure where the animals live. It is a model many small rescues follow, but one which is not, in the long run, sustainable.

"There is this misconception, if you are a 501(c)3, that you get government grants, government assistance, or that the ASPCA is just sending you a check every month," says Ali. "The reality is, none of that happens."

Ali has frequent conversations with her board members—and others working in the world of equine rescue—on the subject of ways to make HALF a more financially sustainable organization. Most recently, she has created a subscriber-based account on Patreon, the online creator-space for running digital shops or paid memberships in order to establish community support for an idea, business, or organization. In exchange for a monthly donation of as little as $5, subscribers are granted "insider access" to educational and outreach content related to the rescue. HALF also recruits monthly sponsors to support their small sanctuary herd (two of whom are former lesson horses from Ali's high school), and runs regular social media fundraising campaigns, including giving donors the opportunity to suggest names for new intakes. Despite these efforts, there are days where the question of how to fund the rescue keeps Ali up at night.

"Our donors do a really good job of covering our vet bills, covering our grain, covering our medications, our farrier," says Ali. "We never really have to worry about those challenges. But we do not have the money coming in to cover the hay and infrastructure expenses, today." She pauses, then admits bluntly, "I feel like HALF is at an okay place right now because I'm in a position where I can fund it. But it's not sustainable, and it's honestly not a very smart personal decision for me either. I do recognize that, and I haven't quite been able to solve that challenge."

When HALF was brand new, Ali was excited to network with other organizations; she believed that with different groups addressing different aspects of equine rescue, there was an opportunity to increase positive outcomes for all through collaboration. Looking back, she admits she was perhaps a little naive to the reality that some groups would perceive a new organization as just one more competitor for limited funds. Despite the frosty reception on some fronts—a reception Ali admits felt personal at times—HALF was ultimately successful in establishing partnerships with several East Coast-based organizations whose values and approaches were similar to her own.

"There is no one organization that is going to operate the same as another," says Ali. "But if you keep looking, there are many organizations that can put differences aside, and find ways to work with one another to really focus on what's important. To me, that is, 'How can we help the equine?'"

To this end, because they are able to offer specialized training and support for Minis, HALF has taken them in from other rescues, and because HALF only has limited space in its own sanctuary, it has sent larger animals to other organizations. But perhaps just as importantly, HALF has worked to establish a network of foster homes to help further extend its impact and reach.

"In general, fostering has allowed us to help more horses, because space is finite, time is finite, and resources are finite," Ali explains. "For fosters, we cover the cost of medical care, and generally, but not always, the fosters will cover the cost of farrier, feed, and bedding." She pauses and gives me a knowing smile. "We've had dozens of fosters, and every foster tells me, 'There's no way I'm going to 'fail'—I've fostered full-sized horses for other rescues,'" she continues, almost laughing now, referring to the frequency with which the foster homes turn into permanent ones. "I've only had two people *not* 'fail.' It's wonderful, because we've placed these horses into great adoptive homes, but it also means we are always looking for new fosters."

Sometimes, owners need assistance with rehoming their Mini or donkey, but their circumstances don't require HALF take physical custody of the animal. HALF offers these owners a "courtesy share" about their animal to the organization's network, usually leaving the screening of potential matches up to the owners; at other times, they assist with this process as well. In this way, HALF has helped to facilitate the rehoming of "dozens upon dozens" of animals.

HALF's goal is to create the best outcome for all animals coming under its care, even if doing so means they will stay with the organization for a longer timeframe.

"It is about taking as much time as they need to come around, feel secure, and get the proper training for a successful adoption," says Ali. "Then, it's about finding the right adopters, who are adopting for the right reasons. I would rather take a year to adopt a horse than have the horse come back to us multiple times, or get lost in the pipeline."

The use of humane euthanasia in equine welfare work is another somewhat contentious subject. By the time some animals arrive under the care of an organization like HALF, they may be facing an array of challenging and life-limiting health conditions. Sometimes, even if it might be medically possible to resolve some of these animals' issues, they will not enjoy a good quality of life, and the kindest and most humane choice may be to let them go. But equine welfare groups sometimes come under fire when they choose to euthanize animals rather than rehabilitate them.

"We are not afraid to euthanize if we need to," says Ali. "That's a sticky point as well, making those decisions without worrying about the optics around it."

Each of the deliberate choices Ali makes may come at a financial cost—donating to an organization with a lower number of annual placements, or one that sometimes makes the humane choice to euthanize a rescued animal, may not be the right fit for every donor. Transparency in communication between HALF and its supporters is required, and Ali and her board must nurture a network of individuals who share a similar ethos.

Ali admits she's met people who believe other organizations are more worthy of funding because they make a broader impact. Given how hard it appears she is working to make a change for a designated segment of the equine population, I ask how she handles this kind of feedback.

In response, Ali purses her lips, and I can see her sit a little straighter as she says, "I'm less concerned with the number of adoptions, and I'm very much more concerned around providing every equine that comes into our care with lifelong protection, or a peaceful passing—whatever they may need."

In speaking with Ali, it doesn't take long to recognize both her passion and commitment to equine rescue work—or to understand that investing so much of her time, energy, and personal financial resources into it can take a toll, particularly when it seems as if there is always another animal in need. I ask her if she thinks we can solve the problem of unwanted equines.

"It's such a complex issue—and where I am is very much downstream," she replies. "I feel like a floppy little band aid, barely hanging on, trying to cover this massive, infected wound. It's like taking a teaspoon to empty out the ocean. But there is still a need for operations like ours, very much."

But to truly solve the problem, says Ali, we must stop the flow of horses upstream, at the source. She ticks off contributing factors on her fingers:

legislative challenges, excess and poorly regulated breeding practices, breed and discipline organizations that do not promote an ethos of accountability to the equine across his life cycle, the rising costs of horsekeeping—and, of course, lack of education.

"There's a view within the equine community—and maybe it's coming from an uneducated place—that once a horse is done being 'serviceable,' you can 'get rid of them' or look for somebody else who wants to retire them," says Ali. "I don't think people fully understand where those horses end up. Those are the ones I feel the worst for, that end up in the auction pipeline." She pauses before continuing, "They are bewildered. They went from a loving home to something they should never experience."

Despite the low moments, it is perhaps knowing she has the ability to intervene, where others may not, that continues to fuel Ali in her work. And she hopes someday, HALF will be on such solid footing she can hand the reins over to someone else, and move her efforts upstream, where she could make even more of a difference for even more animals.

"A lot of us are so entrenched in the day-to-day, that to be able to pick our head up and think 'big picture' is hard," says Ali. "Some days it feels like we are only making a small dent, because we are downstream trying to catch this mess."

WITH SO MANY DIFFERENT FACETS of this complex problem to consider, the benefits of specialization—as in the case of HALF—seem clear, particularly for a new organization. Focusing on one piece of the puzzle could, perhaps, lead to greater success and better outcomes, and be less overwhelming.

Horses With Hope is a privately funded organization based at the 350-acre Broadview Farm in Hope, Maine, that, like HALF, has created its own niche—offering training (or re-training) from the ground up to horses taken in by other rescues. Its founder (and funder) Tannetta "Tet" Fentener van Vlissingen comes from a Dutch family known for its philanthropic work, particularly in the field of conservation (her late father Paul Fentener van Vlissingen contributed to the creation of game reserves in Scotland, South Africa, Malawi, Zambia, and Ethiopia). But Tet's deep, lifelong love for cats, dogs, and horses eventually led her to expand her philanthropic reach to include work focusing on efforts to help domestic species.

Tet grew up in Europe and spent time in both the United Kingdom and South Africa before returning to the United States in 2009, not long after the last US-based slaughterhouses closed their doors. Intuitively, she felt this wasn't a victory for horses, because it didn't address the causative problem—and with their closure, there was now nowhere for the still-flowing stream of animals to go.

"We were still left with many people not wanting their horses, for whatever reason," says Tet. "The only difference now was we were shipping them, horribly, to Mexico or Canada. But the numbers, in terms of how many unwanted horses there were—particularly in those years—didn't change."

For years, Tet had wanted to do something to help improve outcomes for horses that were slaughter-bound, or otherwise unwanted or discarded. In the aftermath of the US slaughterhouse closure, she heard a call to action, not just for her personally, but for the entire industry.

"I really wanted, and hoped, that anybody who was involved with a horse, or cared for a horse, would feel that we could get to a more community feeling of responsibility to those animals," says Tet. "To say, 'Well, we'll just close the slaughterhouses, and therefore, we can close our eyes to it—it's not happening anymore,' to me, felt like not addressing the issue. And we were not educating the public about what really happens."

Like many others, initially, Tet started in rescue work by pulling a few horses from auctions, bringing them home, and then doing whatever it took to help them heal physically and mentally from the experience. Although she later developed conflicted feelings around the role well-intentioned rescuers play in perpetuating the auction cycle, her early experiences there proved eye-opening. She recognized there were a few different categories of horse that frequently ended up unwanted and in the auction system—and often, the reason they were there had more to do with the animal's former owner than the horse himself.

"You've got horses that are there because someone's financial status changed, and they can't take care of it anymore—that's one whole category," says Tet. "Then, you have those who have done something wrong in the eyes of the human—they have behavior issues, something the human can't handle, and the only way the owner knows how to get rid of [the horse] is to go to an auction. Then, you've got those with physical issues, sometimes so crippled that the kindest thing for us to do is to euthanize them."

It was around assisting the latter two categories of animal in particular that the work of Horses With Hope fully began to take shape. Neither of these types of animal is overly appealing to the average horse owner, and therefore they are more at risk of being purchased by "bad dealers" for slaughter.

"At Horses With Hope, what I really wanted to provide was help for a combination of those two, and also to show people that with time and consistent training and understanding, some of the horses that were deemed 'too far gone,' you can actually turn around," says Tet. "Through consistency, and a lot of work, they can become solid citizens again." She pauses, seeming to choose her next words carefully. "In my opinion, if you give a horse good ground manners, and good behavior and good training, that almost guarantees that horse a lifetime home. Everybody wants that horse—who is safe, and not spooky, right from the beginning."

But Tet recognized many existing rescues lacked the resources—human, financial, and physical—to offer consistent training for horses that were unpredictable, difficult or dangerous to handle, or otherwise had significant holes in their training. She decided rather than owning or taking in horses themselves, Horses With Hope would partner with other established equine rescue organizations operating within the northeastern region. Horses With Hope would agree to take on the care and training of sound, otherwise adoptable horses with behavioral or training issues at their expense, and once the animal was ready, work alongside the original intake organization to place him in the most appropriate new home.

"This was one of those areas where we can do more good together than separately," says Tet. "Sometimes, it takes a village to figure out what is wrong with a horse, whether physically or emotionally."

Horses entering the program at Horses With Hope must be sound—not "mostly" sound—meaning they are healthy and physically comfortable enough to handle the demands of ridden work, without the use of medications or other intensive therapies. This is one area in which there has been occasional friction between the organization and its rescue partners. But in an effort to be fully transparent with potential new owners, Tet feels it is imperative to ensure each animal is comfortable enough to fill his future role as a riding or driving partner for the long-term.

"Some people will feel even if [a horse] has a slight limp, it should still be able to work for people, and that becomes an ethical question," Tet explains. "To what extent are you willing to put a horse that's sort of 'off' into work? We feel quite strongly that's a hard ask of a horse. If you adopt a horse, and get home and ride it and it's lame, what are people going to do with it?"

Today, Horses With Hope employs two full-time rider/trainers, as well as four crew members who assist with the animals' daily care. But Tet emphasizes all Horses With Hope employees help with the animals' training, simply by being consistent, kind, and clear in every interaction. Sometimes, says Tet, that consistency, over a long period of time, is the piece which seems to make the largest difference—and it is one of the reasons Horses With Hope keeps the number of horses in training low, usually no more than nine animals at a time.

"Right from the beginning, I wanted to focus not on doing 50 horses a year, but doing a smaller group, and doing them well," says Tet. "I was never a believer in 'take them in, a week later, adopt them out' when we haven't even really figured out why they ended up where they did in the first place."

A few years ago, Tet was approached by a large, national-level rescue organization that wanted to partner with Horses With Hope. But the group's priorities seemed to be, first, getting horses in and out of the rescue within just two months, and second, increasing the total number of animals onsite at any given time. After several meetings, and despite the fact that she is "very supportive of the overall work they do for all animals," Tet decided she simply could not align with them in terms of equine rescue.

"We find that, on average, when we take a horse in, they spend at least six months with us," says Tet. "It gives us the time to really provide them with a 're-set'—everything from leading nicely, standing for the farrier or grooming, to being ridden. We have found that all the basics need to be reinforced and be really solid, because a horse that is unruly while being led can quickly overwhelm and scare a new owner—and then they tend to end up back in bad places."

As an example, Tet recounts the story of one mare whose first response to most any request was to rear, then flee. The mare was wary and extremely distrustful of humans in general, but even routine farm activities could set her off. To help desensitize her and build her confidence, one of the trainers spent three months simply taking the mare with her, wherever she was working on the farm.

"The horse just became an attachment to her," remembers Tet with a chuckle. "The goal was to expose her to as much as she possibly could and get that reactiveness out of her, and to get her to trust humans—so she could learn opening and closing a gate was not a death threat.

"That's want I love about my trainers—the dedication," she continues. "That's how basic it can be, for the first couple months, when [horses are] that reactive. It's not all about, 'We're going in the round pen, because I have to sit on you by next week.'"

Eventually, the mare did settle down, and later was successfully adopted out. But had she been in a program committed to a quicker turn-around, Tet isn't sure the mare's future would have been so positive. Taking time to understand each animal's unique needs and personality, she believes, is critical, because that is what it takes to ultimately achieve a successful placement.

"Transparency in this labor of love is so important," says Tet. "We are really open about what an adopter is getting into—there's no point hiding. If we hide things, [the horses] just end up back where they came from."

FROM THE BEGINNING, Horses With Hope has been a privately funded organization. In many ways, this is a luxury, relieving the organization from the ever-present pressures of fundraising faced by traditional non-profits. It also means Horses With Hope is immune to the burden of any restrictions on organizational practice or philosophy sometimes imposed by grant-making bodies as a condition of funding.

"I do this out of my love of horses, and my gift back to the horse world is to help these unwanted horses," says Tet. "But every single person in the United States that's involved with horses needs to figure out what part they take responsibility for."

She points out that the horse is perceived and used differently across the country, and even among disciplines and breeds, leading to varied beliefs around best practices for their care and management. But regardless of how and why they keep horses, she feels all equestrians need to examine how their actions impact the unwanted horse cycle.

"If we really want to fix it, we all have to look within ourselves," says Tet. "Something has to change at the root level. We can all blame New Holland [auction], and the slaughterhouses in Mexico and Canada, but we all have a role to play in the responsibility for this."

She speaks specifically about breeding—about the common belief that a mare who can't be ridden should instead be bred (regardless of the reason why she is unrideable, and whether these traits might be passed to her foal), as well as a general lack of accountability for the resulting foal's long-term well-being.

"A lot of people forget, in the excitement of breeding, that it's a long-term project," says Tet. "You've got at least three to four years of putting money in and caring for the animal, and technically, you shouldn't be riding them yet. Everybody loves a foal, but unless you know you have a home for the next 30 years for that animal—don't breed. It goes back again to the education aspect—there are just too many horses. So, can we get it back down from the 'kill pen level' to a 'personal ownership level,' where we don't breed so many? It's a difficult topic, but unless we talk about the difficult things, we're not going to fix it."

Which leads back to the other group of vulnerable horses Tet set out to do something about through the work of Horses With Hope—those animals who, whether due to age, illness, injury, or some combination thereof, are perhaps best served if humanely euthanized. Discussing euthanasia as a viable alternative for animals that others might not reasonably want to take on is often an unpopular subject, but when the alternative is an uncertain and likely difficult future in the auction pipeline, she believes the option must be considered.

As an example, Tet tells me about one draft mare she picked up from auction during her early days working in equine rescue. The mare was ataxic, showing poor coordination and balance, and her hind end was extremely weak. She clearly needed help. After coming under Tet's care, she was diagnosed with a severe case of equine protozoal myelitis (a neurological disease that often causes permanent physical impairment), and with a poor prognosis for recovery, she was euthanized.

"Whoever brought her [to the auction] had an option to just put her down at home," says Tet. "So often, people immediately presume that under no circumstances should that happen. But people should be made to feel that, when appropriate, euthanasia is a kind thing to do. Sending a crippled horse to an auction is really *not* kind. Yes, there is a financial aspect to euthanasia. Can we make it affordable, so we don't end up with those types of horses going into that situation? But there is this, also: it is easier to 'dump them,' for some people. I hate to think that, but there are people who can dump [a horse] at New Holland [auction] and walk away, and go buy another one tomorrow."

Even though Horses With Hope does not offer sanctuary services, they are regularly asked by horse owners to take on aged or permanently lame animals. Tet and her team find that often, these owners are emotionally and financially exhausted, and Horses With Hope tries to not only direct them toward financial resources, but to offer them emotional support.

"We try to encourage those people to see the kindest thing to do is let your horse be with you, and peacefully die at your place," says Tet. "We always offer if we can help in any way, even to go be with them.

"It's not an easy subject to discuss, but it is a necessary subject," she emphasizes. "To prolong the suffering of an animal because it makes us feel uncomfortable doesn't feel right to me. We take them into our lives, and part of what is our responsibility is to provide the best care we can, up until the very end."

Horses With Hope has plans to further enhance its owner education programs around the subject of humane euthanasia, and has recently partnered with the Maine State Society for the Protection of Animals (MSSPA) in Windham to secure additional financial assistance for owners in need to make this option more accessible. She is equally supportive of collaborative efforts to educate prospective horse owners about the overall cost of care—not just of regular upkeep, but of the need for additional funds to handle emergencies.

"We are still working toward a more educational aspect of Horses With Hope, to encompass all these points," explains Tet. "How can we make it a better world for the horses, and more sustainable, so we don't end up with this surplus that is still going through New Holland?"

And although she personally has moved away from purchasing animals who end up there, she understands why some rescues still do.

"We are the problem and the solution as rescues, in a way," says Tet. "We're in it because our hearts break for these animals, and we want to do good. I know that sometimes, unintentionally, we add to the problem. It isn't black and white." She pauses, then continues, "As rescues, we can all learn from each other, or help each other, or figure out a way we can help more horses."

Chapter 3

THE BUSINESS OF EQUINE RESCUE

IT ISN'T REALLY SO DIFFICULT to understand why kill pen pages on social media platforms gain such large followings, despite the horrific images and near-constant pleas for financial assistance shared on them, which under other circumstances might feel oppressive, even desperate. Intuitively, I believe there are many horse lovers who feel somewhat powerless to effect change when faced with the knowledge that some horses do, in fact, still ship to slaughter, and that most equines in the auction pipeline face deplorable conditions. For these horse lovers, perhaps the act of sending a small donation toward "bail"—a colloquial term used to describe the purchase price of a kill pen animal, set by the dealer—feels like a minimal positive step; perhaps they feel if they cannot change things for *all* horses in the pipeline, they might be able to make a change for *this one*.

It is always harder to say "no" when a face and a name are put on a problem.

For those seeking to obtain a horse from either an auction or a dealer's lot, it is very much a case of *caveat emptor*. Horses there are sold "as is," and it is almost never possible to "vet" the animal prior to purchase. There are plenty of stories about horses sold while medicated—sedatives, painkillers, antibiotics—all to mask an underlying condition. Once the animal gets home, even experienced equestrians can be surprised to learn what they are actually dealing with in terms of both health care management and behavioral issues. The cost of bail, whether inflated or not, is often the least of the expenses to follow. And for those equines purchased by the underinformed or inexperienced, without the right support, their well-intentioned new owners may end up in need of rescuing themselves.

The whole process reminds me of going shopping on the lot of a less-than-scrupulous used car dealer. Most of them won't lie to you outright, but if you don't ask exactly the right questions, or lack the necessary expertise to verify details for yourself, it is easy to be deceived. Navigating these potential pitfalls successfully will always require a bit of luck, a good eye, and if possible, the assistance of someone intimately familiar with the process.

That is the role Penny Parker has played over the past decade for hundreds, if not thousands, of buyers seeking to purchase animals heading through auctions in the Mid-Atlantic region of the United States. Through a combination of pre-sale and live video streams, and an ever-expanding network of online followers, Penny says her mission is to keep horses out of the pipeline, out of the auctions, and ultimately, out of the kill pens themselves. Not only do she and her partner Dave Manning attend the sales, where they network animals and offer proxy bidding to followers at home, they provide quarantine services and hauling to points all over the East Coast.

Penny is an interesting figure in the world of rescue, and by her own admission, sometimes the subject of controversy. Her personal motto, "Save a horse, no matter where they are," speaks to both her own ethos about equine rescue and the criticisms of her detractors. Penny has cultivated close working relationships with several dealers, and as a result, has been accused of being in league with them; further, because she now makes her living primarily through offering quarantine board and hauling services, some critics have called her a "mass bailer"—someone just looking to turn a profit with no regard to who buys the horse or where they end up.

"There's a lot of controversy about what I do, because I do so much of everything," says Penny. "People didn't care for me, and maybe some still don't, because they believe I'm in bed with Marlon, then Brian, and in their pockets."

Penny is referring to Marlon Garcia, the owner of a now-defunct weekly equine auction at Cranbury Sales Stable in Cranbury, New Jersey, and Brian Moore, who along with wife Jen, owns and operates the Lebanon Valley Livestock Auction in Lebanon, Pennsylvania—the one I visited in 2019. Penny first provided weekly livestream video services at Garcia's auction, but about six years ago, they parted ways, and now she videos almost exclusively for the Moores. She doesn't like the fact that Brian

Moore has sold horses to slaughterhouses and feed lots, but she believes he does a better job caring for his horses than most, and appreciates that the Moore family has been willing to let her into their barns and to document their animals.

"I'm a people pleaser, and I obsess about it, and I want everyone to love me—who doesn't?" says Penny. "But I've learned, and I've become hardened over the years. These horses need us, and it's not their fault who gets the horse. I hate that Brian [Moore] buys animals and he ships them, but now these animals have me, and we've saved thousands.

"They don't pay me," Penny continues, speaking about her relationship with the Moores. "I don't make any money going there for hours on end, and seeing sick animals and dead and dying animals, the worst of the worst. I go there because it's my mission to help these animals, and they need us."

A former optician, Penny already owned two horses and was involved in the world of Pit Bull and Great Dane rescue before making her first trip to New Holland's equine auction over a decade ago. She admits now she was equal parts intrigued and terrified to attend and see the kill buyers in action; that day, she ended up purchasing an Arabian mare she named Miranda Lambert. From there, her involvement in equine rescue work "snowballed."

At first, Penny mostly volunteered, taking photos and videos of dealer-owned animals for equine rescue groups working at the auctions to share on social media, hoping to raise awareness in the equine community and beyond. As she started to become better known among those who regularly attended the auctions, people began sending her money and asking her to use it to save horses. In 2020, she filed paperwork to establish Horse Angels Rescue as a 501(c)3 nonprofit, to better be able to manage donations toward the purchase, rehabilitation, and care of animals coming either directly from auctions and dealers, or occasionally, those "intercepted" from private owners before they officially made it onto the manifest at a sale.

These days, Penny has as many as 180 animals under her care at any given time, spread across four facilities in two states (her Heartland 1 and two quarantine locations straddle the Pennsylvania-Maryland border). These equines represent a combination of Penny's own animals, long-term boarders, horses currently in quarantine or laying over, and nearly fifty equines living in permanent sanctuary. When she is not on the road or at an auction, Penny spends the majority of her time attending to the care of these animals, which often entails addressing significant veterinary and farrier needs, and sometimes almost herculean efforts to support exhausted, sick, and emaciated rescues. Recently, she and Dave moved into a cottage located at the idyllic Thornbury Farm in West Chester, Pennsylvania, owned by the Spackman family and home to their CSA, an event facility, and Penny's equine sanctuary.

In a way, the sanctuary herd is a microcosm of the scope and breadth of the equine species. Penny has almost every kind of horse imaginable living there, from former stallions (now gelded), to aged Amish draft horses, regular and draft-sized mules, Standardbreds, donkeys, a herd of ex bronc horses, a trio of bonded Thoroughbreds, a group of Appaloosas from a major seizure in Maryland, and a few Miniature Horses. Some are young, some are old; some are sound, some are not. Some have been trained to ride or drive; some were barely handled before arriving at Thornbury. But with Penny, they are all living an idyllic life, grouped in compatible herds and grazing on luxurious grass fields.

"They are the unwanted—the misfits," says Penny simply. "They were throwaways, and now they are horses who are going to stay and live their life."

She admits it can be overwhelming at times managing the logistics of caring for so many horses; due to the importance of adhering to strict protocols at her three quarantine facilities, Penny doesn't feel she can rely on volunteers, and instead employs a handful of trusted staff members to handle the day-to-day care of the animals staying there. However, she is hoping to develop a volunteer program to assist with the care of animals in sanctuary at Thornbury in the future.

WHEN PENNY FIRST PLUNGED into the world of equine auctions, dealers, and kill pens, she thought briefly about putting her efforts "upstream" instead, working to reduce the flow of animals into the pipeline.

"I gave up really fast," she admits. "I think I'd still be fighting and not getting anywhere. In the end, I decided to just start rescuing horses, and doing what I could as a rescue."

In 2017, Penny set up a private Facebook group, also called Horse Angels, and began sharing her livestreams there, along with photos and other information gathered from her visits to dealers' lots. Many posts there are positive and encouraging; Penny documents the recovery of particularly hard-luck cases she has rescued, and shares information about rehabilitated horses still needing to find their adoptive homes. Group members share photos about animals they have adopted from Horse Angels Rescue, or those they have asked Penny to pull for them at an auction, now looking healthy and well-fed and living their best lives in new homes.

But not every story in rescue has a happy ending, and Penny is prepared to share this reality with the Facebook group's members (32,000 and climbing). She has had animals collapse in her trailer on the way home from a sale or go down later in her barn—in fact, it's happened so many times they now have a sling, and a process, for helping these horses get back up and stay that way, if the animal still seems willing to fight. But when they are not, she is prepared to let them go. Based on the comments, it is hard to tell who feels these losses most acutely—Penny, or her followers.

Sometimes, a supporter will offer to sponsor an auction horse of Penny's choosing; when this happens, she says she "will pull the worst of the worst." She shares these stories, too—horses dropped at auction with untreated illnesses or old improperly healed injuries (or new ones); horses with obvious disfigurements or tumors; horses that look worn out and dejected. To try to save these animals, Penny works with some of the best veterinarians in the greater Philadelphia area, including Unionville Equine Associates and Penn Vet's New Bolton Center. But sometimes, it is simply not possible to overcome a combination of neglect and bad luck.

"I'm an empath, so I can walk [into an auction], and feel who's down, and who's sick, and who's dying, and who's giving up, and I go right to them," Penny says. "I can't say no, and I bring them home, and they stay—because of the way they looked, and the loss of hope in their eyes. It's devastating."

Typically, Penny visits the Moores' facility about a week before their monthly sale, walks through the pens, and shares information about some of the animals there with members of Horse Angels.

"When I go in there, I walk around and I look for eye contact, or who comes up to me—or who is standing in the corner with their head down low," says Penny. "It's an energy thing for me. I just want to see who needs me the most."

After seeing her posts, people will sometimes ask Penny to evaluate certain horses on their behalf; other times, they will give her a general idea of the type of horse they are looking for, and she will see if any of the animals available match the description. Once the sale starts, she or Dave will stand right down front taking video, and as horses come through the chute, Penny will proxy bid for those who ask her to do so. Ideally, the bidder is watching the livestream before Penny bids, in case the horse ends up being lame (she won't bid on an unsound horse unless specifically asked).

Despite what some have alleged, Penny says she makes no money in this process—no cutbacks or commissions from either buyer or seller. In fact, when Penny wins a proxy bid, the buyer must call the sales office and pay the dealer directly. From there, buyers can either pick up the horse themselves, or ask Penny or any other quarantine provider to do so on their behalf.

Quarantining a recent auction purchase is a necessity. Given the stressful, crowded conditions the horses experience in such an environment, it is nearly impossible for them to avoid exposure to communicable equine diseases, particularly respiratory disorders, among which strangles is by far the most rampant. This highly contagious disease is often described as the equine equivalent of strep throat. It is caused by an equine-specific bacterium, *Streptococcus equi*, with symptoms appearing anywhere from two to four weeks after initial exposure. Once strangles shows up on a property, it can be hard to manage, spreading easily from horse to horse. And although most previously healthy horses eventually recover, it is a disease that can prove devastating to an already debilitated animal.

For these reasons, animals quarantining with Penny usually stay a minimum of 30 days; for horses that end up developing strangles, a typical stay is closer to 60 days. Before they leave quarantine, horses must test negative for strangles through a polymerase chain reaction (PCR) test, a fairly sensitive assay which screens for bacterial DNA.

Penny charges just $625 per month for quarantine board, which covers daily care and feed, and handling for the veterinarian and farrier (these professionals bill their services separately).

RECENTLY, BRIAN MOORE acquired a load of 26 Standardbreds; according to Penny, ex-racehorses like these are among the most common type of animal he ships to feedlots, so when he offered her the opportunity to head into his pen and network them specifically, she jumped at it. Thanks to her efforts and online presence, within days, she managed to rehome every single one. A few weeks later, she repeated the process, this time for 38 "Standies," as she calls them.

"People claim I am a 'mass bailer,'" she says with a hint of scorn. "So, where do these horses go? Well, if they freaking watch me, these horses get into homes. They don't go into my field."

But yet, the flow of horses continues, and auction pens refill, and I can't help but think eventually, Penny will run out of people to network to. Again, I feel confronted by the reality that although pulling horses from an auction or dealer changes the outcome for those individuals, it ultimately doesn't stop the movement of animals into the pipeline. It is, at best, as Ali Baker put it, a band aid.

Penny tells me Brian Moore used to be under contract with Canadian slaughterhouses, taking weekly loads over the border to meet a specific quota. Now he takes these animals to feedlots in the Midwest instead, where they live in crowded pens, out in the elements, fighting with each other for food and water. Sometimes, these lots will post the horses for sale, too. By then, the animals typically are close to the point of exhaustion, and Penny doesn't know what is worse—the long trailer ride to a feedlot where life is dire, or a trip directly to the slaughterhouse.

"I'm not saying I'm for slaughter, I'm not against slaughter," says Penny. "I'm just…." She pauses, searching for the right words, and when she speaks again, it is with passion. "I watch Brian Moore do this, and I've had this conversation with him a thousand times—he is animal control. Some of [the horses]—I hate to say it—they either need to be put down right there…or they just need to go. And I don't know how I feel.

"I'd rather they not drive so damn far—the truck ride [to Canada] is pure, freaking hell, 32 hours in the trailer, nonstop. I'd rather we do it in the United States," she continues. "Or even…maybe once a year, offer euthanasia [as an option] to people. Because where do the horses go, for people who don't want to pay, or horse owners who are not able to afford euthanasia? They take them to the auction. If it were not for Brian, and people like him—where would all these horses go?"

Penny scoffs at comments she sees online, alleging that dealers are getting rich shipping horses to feedlots or over the border. In reality, she says, they make only a few hundred dollars per horse.

"This misconception of us lining the kill buyers' pockets so they can buy a whole other round of horses to put on the trailer—they are not making a ton of money…they really aren't," says Penny. "I'm right next to them when they're bidding, and I watch what they pay for them, and I watch what they get for them. Brian's not getting rich doing this, at all. He hates doing it, he really does. He'd rather buy, and sell, and trade—go out west and buy a truckload of horses and bring them to his sale. He'll show them off and make a couple thousand per horse. *That's* where he makes his money."

I think back to my visit to the Lebanon Valley sale, and the obviously quality, well-trained stock horses that sold there for good money. I have no reason to believe Penny is not telling the truth, at least as she understands it and has lived it. Horse dealers are, at the end of it all, businessmen, and livestock is what they trade. But many horse people don't think of their animals as a commodity, and this, perhaps, is the reason why these dealers—and by default, those who associate with them—are so excoriated online.

Penny sees herself as a mediator, someone with the experience to know who to trust and who to avoid; someone who is able to see through dealers' smokescreens, and help buyers find good horses.

"I wish I could educate people all day long, especially at the auctions," she says. "That's why I do what I do. I've learned who to buy from, and who not to buy from. There are lovely horses in the auctions. *Any* horse can end up there. It could be the product of divorce, or something that's lost weight and looks terrible. The 'skinnies'—all I've got to do is feed them, and give them some TLC, and they turn out to be diamonds in the rough, phenomenal horses. But you have to learn to see past that. I've learned to do that, to see them in the pen."

EVERY DAY, RESCUERS ARE GIVING their heart, soul, and energy—and in some cases, their personal financial resources—to create new opportunities for the unwanted, and to try to stem the flow of animals heading into the pipeline. They are the ones who are literally left holding the lead rope when others fail to intervene on these horses' behalf, and their efforts are vital. And yet, after speaking with Penny Parker, I recognize all their efforts are simply not enough.

If we want to stop this—to truly reduce the number of equines ending up with "bad dealers," in kill pens, or in other marginal circumstances—the equine industry needs to do more than just expect rescues to pick up the pieces. No matter the niche we fill within the industry—spectator, participant, official, amateur, professional—we must think more broadly about how to properly care for our animals, across their entire life cycle.

Chapter 4

NEW HOLLAND:
A LAST CHANCE FOR LOST SOULS

IT IS CLEAR THERE IS DIVERSITY of opinion among equine welfare advocates in terms of how best to manage or mitigate the problem of unwanted horses. But when it comes to naming the most notorious equine auction on the East Coast, there is an answer on which everyone can agree.

New Holland.

The buildings are on West Fulton Street, just after you cross a railroad track where freight trains still stop to load grain from the local mill, and a few blocks down from the North American headquarters for the town's signature blue-and-white tractors. The facility's white clapboard siding, the words "New Holland Sales Stables, Inc." emblazoned in red stenciled lettering above livestock loading docks, and the immediate nasal assault of manure mixed with pine bedding all combine to remind one of a vintage fairground, a relic from a bygone era somehow trapped in the present day.

Situated in eastern Lancaster County, Pennsylvania, the auction is located in the heart of one of the largest Amish and Mennonite communities in the United States. For many families living in this rural agricultural region, the frequent auctions at New Holland are a place to come together and socialize as much as to exchange farm supplies and equipment, poultry, and livestock—including horses. But for many of the equines that find themselves tied to the bars lining two aisles on either side of the main auction floor, New Holland will be a last stop, one final bid to get out of a pipeline that flows directly to the slaughterhouse.

The parking lot is already crowded when I leave my car in between two large silver stock trailers and begin to meander through a maze of vendors on a hot July Monday in 2019. Their wares are set up on folding tables or displayed in the backs of small bumper-pull trailers, and include everything from turquoise jewelry to new and used tack, whips, riding apparel, and grooming equipment. Others sell handmade Amish leatherwork, wooden tack boxes, and cabinets.

The pens at New Holland are virtually never empty, and the facility is theoretically kept staffed 24 hours a day, 7 days a week. But that doesn't stop questionable activities from occurring behind the scenes, behavior which ranges from the irresponsible to the downright reprehensible. One morning in March 2016, a gray pony mare was found abandoned in a stall by facility staff. The animal was half blind, lame, malnourished, and covered in what appeared to be over 125 paintball marks. The case drew national media attention when the pony, later named Lily by the staff at the Lancaster County SPCA, was adopted by comedian Jon Stewart and his wife Tracey. Surveillance video from the facility would later lead to the successful conviction of Philip Price, Jr., of Providence, Rhode Island, on three counts of animal cruelty and other charges related to abandoning the injured animal at the sales barn. However, despite raising a $10,000 reward, authorities were ultimately unsuccessful in finding the person or persons responsible for causing Lily's extensive injuries and neglect in the first place.

New Holland's reputation for selling animals no matter their condition caused the sale to become a frequent target of animal welfare advocates and humane officers, who routinely digitally documented atrocities, and then called state police. Even once the sale invoked a ban on any audio or video recording in 2017, conflicts between sales staff and advocates were chronic.

In 1998, veterinarian James "Jim" Holt, VMD, was hired by sales barn management to palpate cows for the dairy sale held each Wednesday and Thursday. Holt is a tall, slender man with soft red hair and a calm affect whose principal work is as a private practitioner for Brandywine Veterinary Services in Coatesville, Pennsylvania. Since 1991, he has practiced veterinary medicine in this pocket of southeastern Pennsylvania, treating everything from Amish- and Mennonite-owned horses to backyard pets to those in Olympic-level training programs at elite Main Line barns. It was impossible for Holt not to hear stories about what was going on at New Holland with the horses. Finally, frustrated by the escalating conflicts between animal advocates and the sale's staff, the sale's upper management asked Holt to see if there was anything he could do to mitigate the situation.

"People would call the police, and since the auctioneer was the person in charge, he basically had to stop the sale and talk to them," says Holt. "It's a sales barn, and they wanted someone to run cover for them. And so, I attended a sale, saw what was going on [that maybe animal advocates had a point], and came to the conclusion that somebody needed to do something."

Holt agreed to help mitigate concerns raised by all parties, but he warned New Holland's upper management he wasn't going to simply sit back and give them *carte blanche* permission to do whatever they wanted. Instead, he planned to implement guidelines that would codify which horses were eligible to run through the sale and which were not, and required absolute authority to remove those horses not meeting the minimum criteria. New Holland leadership agreed to his terms, and in 2000, through a contract supported by both New Holland and the US Department of Agriculture, Holt became the "veterinarian of record" for the sale. Almost immediately, he began actively working to implement change, starting with establishing an on-site Coggins test laboratory. Since taking on the role, Holt has served as an expert witness in court for both sides of the welfare debate at least a half dozen times. Though legally the vet on record doesn't have to be physically present at the sale, Holt has missed only a handful of Mondays in his quarter century of involvement.

On this sunny Monday, horses are still arriving, and Holt will inspect each one before they are given a numerical tag and then brought to the holding area where buyers can inspect the animals. I walk through the front doors of the auction, past a counter selling food, and pause. I am standing directly in front of the chute through which horses will be herded, led, or ridden. It is even narrower than I had imagined—a far tighter space than the chute at Lebanon Valley—barely wide enough for a tractor to drive through. Steep wooden benches double as stairs up each side. The walls are covered in advertorial banners promoting local agricultural businesses. It feels cramped and dingy, and I feel a rise of claustrophobia creeping up my chest.

The auctioneer is already in action, and at the top of the chute nearest to the entrance a man is displaying all manner of new horse equipment. A handful of bidders are purchasing buckets, lead ropes, and pitchforks. A pile of almost out-of-code dewormer is stacked neatly, the next item up for bid. But few are paying much attention, and the tack sale feels like the less-anticipated opening act to a much more exciting main event.

To either side of the chute are narrow hallways that lead to the animals in the sale for the day. I see Holt purposefully walk by; his pale red hair reflects gold in the dim lighting from the exposed lightbulbs, and he clasps a clipboard to his chest.

Not sure of what I am about to see, I take a deep breath and follow him down the aisle.

AS AT LEBANON VALLEY, the types of horse at New Holland run the gamut. Horse breeds are as diverse in their shapes and sizes as dogs, each selectively bred to fill a particular niche in the equine work force. I make my way down the narrow lane, horses tied on either side, and run my eyes over their varied bodies. Tiny ponies, donkeys and mules; big drafts, stock horse types, plenty of Standardbreds, some Thoroughbreds. Some have been bathed and wear hoof oil, the iridescent shine seeming out of place in the cellar-like atmosphere. Most of the horses are calmly eating hay stuffed into the trough ahead of them; others rest a leg and drop their head to nap.

These horses come to the auction from all over the country. Some get off the trailer here for the first time since leaving dealer lots in Texas. Sometimes, the horses lie down to rest, despite the chaotic environment, which can lead some attendees to worry they are sick. But in many cases, they are just exhausted.

The auction may not be able to control the condition of an animal when it arrives on premises, but it can decide which animals it will accept for the sale—and the fact that there are now at least a minimum set of criteria at New Holland is largely thanks to Holt. Knowing that he had to walk a fine line between satisfying the needs of sale management while still addressing animal welfare concerns, Holt turned to Pennsylvania law. He learned that per state statute, it was illegal to sell a horse that couldn't be "worked" or "used." But the law didn't define "work," and it didn't define "use"—meaning that Holt had to establish parameters to determine how lame was too lame, and how thin was too thin.

Over the course of several months, Holt dug into the research, and met with both the sales barn management and humane officers to establish definitions clear enough to help navigate the delicate tight rope between promoting welfare while honoring the purpose of the business— to sell horses. The guidelines, which were influenced by federal legal requirements for slaughter-bound horses, resulted in five parameters Holt could use to assess each equine presented for sale at New Holland: *body condition, lameness, blindness, no debilitating cuts and wounds*, and the last one, a catch-all—*no signs of debilitating disease*. Some 80 to 90 percent of the horses Holt "spins" (rejects) from the auction do not meet minimum criteria in one or both of the first two categories.

The Henneke Body Condition Scoring System is a semi-objective scale used by equine managers and veterinarians to assess the overall *body condition* of a horse. A numerical value from 1 (which means the animal is extremely emaciated) through 9 (extremely fat) is assigned to six different areas of the equine's body. The numbers are added together and divided by 6 to arrive at the animal's Henneke score. Most horses are considered to be in healthy condition with a score ranging from 4.5 to 6. A score of 3 is enough to earn the title of "thin"; it is one point above "emaciated." New Holland sale horses must have a score of 3 or greater. That's still pretty skinny, but when US slaughterhouses were in operation, that was the minimum score required by their delivery standards.

Lameness is another criterion that frequently gets horses spun from the auction. Beyond a horse showing more obvious symptoms of lameness, such as head bobbing or hip-hiking, Holt needed a definition that would exclude a potentially laminitic animal (a horse suffering from acute inflammation of the sensitive tissue layers inside the hoof). What he came up with is that horses must effectively bear weight on all four legs at the walk.

"What that meant to me was they had to put their heel on the ground," explains Holt.

The next two criteria, *blindness* and *no debilitating cuts and wounds*, are less frequently used as reasons for barring a sale but occasionally prove useful. Horses must have sight in at least one eye; this criterion comes straight from federal regulations for slaughter-bound equines. Cuts and wounds are common enough in horses that have been housed with unfamiliar animals that it is difficult to use them alone as a reason to disallow a horse. However, open, draining wounds, or those on the limbs, may be cause for exclusion. And when horses are lame and have a wound, they are out.

When Holt has to use the fifth category—*no signs of debilitating disease*—he knows it is an argument waiting to happen. But when he needs it, he needs it. Its vague, catch-all quality allows Holt to spin horses he feels are unfit, but which don't fall neatly into any of the other categories. Ataxic horses or ones showing signs of other neurological disorders fall into this group; another condition that occurs with some regularity is paraphimosis, which is when a male horse is unable to retract his penis into his sheath.

"I try not to use that category, because that's a gray zone," says Holt. "But I use it when it's necessary."

The New Holland Sales Barn runs several different types of sales—everything from horses to cows to swine—and each sale has a specific manager. But Holt reports only to the company's upper management, which is probably a good thing, as he and the horse sale manager, Malin Zimmerman, frequently clash, particularly over marginal animals Holt has disallowed from the sale.

"We've had those arguments in front of clients, in front of a whole lot of people," says Holt. "We had an argument about one horse—it had multiple problems—it was thin, half blind, and lame, and Malin wanted to sell this horse. I pulled the tags off, and he hand-wrote some new ones and stuck them on the horse."

The horse sold for $10.

In theory, every equine meant to be sold at New Holland is to be inspected by Holt upon arrival. When Holt arrives onsite between 9:00 and 9:30 AM for the 10:00 AM sale, usually about half of the horses have already arrived. The rest show up sometime during the sale; Holt suspects that late-arriving sellers are often hoping to sneak questionable animals in, without giving him an opportunity to evaluate them. Sometimes, these animals actually go through the sales ring before Holt can intervene, and then he must reverse the sale.

Although excluding lame, unhealthy, or otherwise marginal animals from the sale sounds like it should be a good thing, the question that must follow is, what happens to the horse then? When I ask this of Holt, he pauses before answering.

"It varies," he admits. "If the owner is there, and I can talk to them, and if they are in-state, that gives me a lot more ability to try and guide what happens with the horse."

Sometimes, Holt is able to get custody of the horse relinquished to him, and he gets to determine next steps. If the horse's condition is serious enough that it warrants euthanasia, he tries to coordinate with a rescue for funding to cover the costs associated with the procedure. Holt admits that while this is sometimes what he would consider the best scenario, it doesn't happen as often as perhaps it should.

But many of the horses arriving at the sale are delivered by commercial haulers, and the owners are unreachable. In these circumstances, Zimmerman is responsible for making decisions on their behalf.

"I wish I could tell you it was always a good thing, but I'm not convinced it is," admits Holt. "My job is to protect the sales barn from legal liability for selling the horse. But that doesn't mean the horse doesn't get sold in the parking lot. That certainly happens, probably most frequently."

Holt suspects he has lost clients over the years due to his role at New Holland. But he makes no effort to hide what he does there.

"I've identified it as a need," says Holt. "Malin and I do not get along—I'm a pain in his ass, and he's a pain in my ass, but Malin doesn't bother me. I recognize the value I bring to that situation. It's needed—that's not a really great excuse, but it's kind of where I am. I'm 59, and I will not live forever. And my thoughts are, the day I die will be the end of the program."

A MIDDLE-AGED WOMAN with silvery blonde hair swept up in a clip stands in the main entrance sending a text. I can see her bidder's tag tucked under the phone.

When I greet her, she says her name is Brenda, and she lives twenty minutes north of New Holland in Epharata. She has bought a few horses at this auction before, most recently a Thoroughbred who was lovely on the ground but proved too much horse for her under saddle. Now, Brenda tells me she wants a horse to trail ride—something seasoned, something that has "been there, done that."

"Something six or seven years old," she says.

My experience tells me what she needs is a horse 15 years old or older, because it takes that long before they have seen the world a bit and become a reliable, sensible partner. But like many potential horse owners, she is reluctant to buy a slightly older horse, even if he may still have many good years remaining.

She asks me to look at a few of her top choices with her, and we walk back through the animals again. More are arriving as the start time draws near. An elegant small black mare is completely untied, lead rope hanging ineffectually from the bar in front of her. She could wander off if she wanted to, yet she chooses to stand close to her companion, a matching black gelding. I wonder if they are mother and son.

Later I will watch as they are sold to separate bidders.

Suddenly, just ahead of us, a large pinto takes umbrage at the presence of a petite flea-bitten gray on his right side. Panicked, the gray pulls back violently to escape as the pinto double-barrels with both hind feet, full of raw, angry power. *Get away from me.* The gray's red nylon halter doesn't give, but his DNA screams it is imperative to move away from the aggressor. The gray cowers next to the chestnut on his other side. *You didn't move far enough away.* The pinto comes at the gray again; again, the halter holds, and again, the gray tries to make himself invisible next to the chestnut. Many humans watch this micro-drama unfold, but not one goes to move the horses away from each other. I realize I am holding my breath.

A young man, a catch rider, with café au lait skin and a thick, short ponytail, is brushing a few horses. Another catch rider grabs Holt and asks him to check a wound on a horse. He tells her he has already seen it and the horse is fine to ride, but she explains this is a different wound, fresher and on a different leg. Her face reads compassion.

The catch riders might ride dozens of horses during one auction, no idea what to expect from the animals beneath them. I ponder what it would be like to know that you might be the very last rider to sit on a horse in the horse's lifetime…and to do this over and over again, week in, week out.

I tell Brenda she can pay one of these riders $20 to get on a horse for her, to see if the horse is broke and rideable. Despite having purchased horses from the auction before, she is surprised this is an option.

My attention is suddenly arrested by the arrival of a plain bay Thoroughbred, wearing a row of tiny, perfect hunter braids down his neck. He looks youthful and sound and completely perplexed about his surroundings. When they tie him to the rail, he arches his neck in greeting to the horse next to him, who pins his ears in response. Most horse shows are held on the weekend, and I wonder what this horse did or didn't do at this weekend's competition to warrant landing at New Holland on Monday, braids still intact.

When the gelding comes through the chute later, attendees learn he belongs to a local university with an equine degree program. A representative from the college is there at ringside, holding the horse's registration papers. The man seems at ease, but I find myself condemning him and the program for sending a horse here.

None of the horses I see throughout the day are in truly horrendous condition. Holt's standards are holding. But some have the stocked-up legs of an older animal with many miles, the scars of pinfiring, poor feet, or other deformities. These are the marks of a hard life. Yet I find I am most affected by those horses whose sellers have taken the time to bathe and shine them before bringing them to an auction that makes no effort to hide what it is. Perhaps these owners are so desperate, they hope against logic that with a little spit and polish, their horses might get a better outcome when the bidding is done. In a matter of three hours, all these animals are brought into the ring by their owners and sold to strangers. A small pinto pony with blue eyes and a tail braid has clearly been bathed and hoof-oiled. He sells for $275. A larger black-and-white pinto, the top of his tail still showing the purple hue left by a whitening shampoo not completely rinsed out, has a kind eye and rides quietly in the chute despite the chaotic, closed environment. He sells for $750.

These are meat prices.

While walking the aisles with Brenda, I point to several horses that might suit her needs. They aren't flashy or fancy, but do have a calm demeanor and kind eye. However, she has a clear vision of what she is looking for, and she isn't finding that horse here.

I wonder if maybe she is not really ready to buy.

Or perhaps Brenda is remembering her first horse from New Holland, an Appaloosa she purchased when she was in her twenties. The mare ended up being both far older than expected and in foal. Brenda wasn't prepared for a foal, yet she waited until he was two years old and barely handled before she gave him to a 4-H club to be someone's project. She told the club she would take him back if it didn't work out.

The young horse proved to be too much for the 4-H children, too, but the new owners never reached out. Instead, she found out he was sold at New Holland. And not knowing what happened to him haunts her.

I SETTLE IN THE BLEACHERS about halfway up, peering down over the heads of heavy-set dealers in jeans and button downs. I am almost directly across from and slightly above the auctioneer, who sits at a table just a few rows up from the auction floor. He is barely above the eyeline of the dealers down front, an angle from which he can be sure to catch a willing nod or wave in regards to a bid.

The auction begins with minimal fanfare. The first few horses are reluctant to follow Mennonite teenagers down the chute, the next horse coming while the first is going. Bidding is fast and closes low.

Several older animals come through—anywhere from 14 years old to "smooth-mouthed," an old horseman's term to indicate advanced age. Their accepting attitude and the gray-flecked hairs around the eyes and ears also give their years away. They all seem vaguely befuddled about their current circumstances but are so willing—some are ridden by children, including Mennonite girls whose long braids swing behind them to their waists, skirts hiked up to reveal loose-fitting black leggings and sneakers. It breaks my heart as I watch these old veterans sell for less than $1,000 each. No one is buying these animals with the intention of giving them to someone's grandchild or selling them again—at least not to a private home, anyway. These animals are so trusting, so unsuspecting of what is likely to come.

Where are the homes for some of these sweet, older souls?

The truth is they simply do not exist, at least not in the volume they would need to in order to absorb the constant flow of horses in the United States.

As at Lebanon Valley, small horses, mares, the unbroke, all draw little interest and low prices. Three thin horses come in as a group, so skittish they have to be herded, as opposed to led, into the chute. Earlier, I had seen them in a pen together, too feral to be tied to a bar. Supposedly they all had been ridden at one point but "had been turned out for a few years." In those years, they seem to have reverted to a nearly wild state. These animals are bonded to each other and want to stay close for security, but the handlers need them to separate for the bidding. I cringe as the terrified animals are chased apart, their escape blocked with long whips or boards.

Not one sold for more than $800.

A 21-year-old chestnut mare is led in. She is so skinny that her ribs show and her hips protrude. By my eye she must have just barely made the cut for body condition. Her coat and skin are rough, her eyes dull. She stands in the chute, head lowered, the picture of defeat. The auctioneer reads her pedigree and the dealer's assertion that the reason he brought her here is because she is in foal to a prominent stallion whose name I don't recognize.

"I guarantee you she is in foal—due in six weeks!" says a large man wearing a ball cap from somewhere in front of me.

The mare's skin barely covers her own frame. There is clearly no living foal in there. Even he doesn't argue when she sells for just $700.

THE LONGER I SIT IN THE BLEACHERS, the more questions I have. Why are some of these animals still studs? Why is it a good thing that the mare in the chute "has been exposed to a stallion here"? When the only mare-and-foal pair at the sale comes in, the poor foal trotting desperately to keep up with his mother, why should we be happy to hear that this gaunt, roach-backed, awkward-looking mare has been rebred? Do these owners just not understand production for production's sake helps no one?

How do we get ahead of this? How do we change the mentality that any horse that can be bred should be?

Holt compares the situation to dealing with the flow of water from a hose. There are two ways to control the flow of water—you can turn it off at its source, or you can close the nozzle at the end of the hose. The first option stops the flow entirely but leaves you with no water for your garden; the second also stops the flow, but causes pressure to build up along the length of the hose. In extrapolating this analogy to unwanted horses, it comes down to this: closing American slaughterhouses in 2006, followed almost immediately by the 2008 recession, served to turn off the nozzle of the hose and caused unwanted horse numbers to rise. Although some breeders reduced the size of their annual foal crop for several years in response to the recession, in other sectors, production continued almost unabated. And for those animals already "in the hose," there was no where for them to go.

If we want to solve the problem of unwanted horses, and we do not want to reopen American slaughterhouses, it would seem the only feasible option is to turn off the flow at its source—the equestrian industry must find a way to reduce the number of horses being bred. In theory, if this were to happen, prices for horses would rise, breeders and sellers would make a profit, and perhaps, owners would do their utmost to provide high quality care for their animals, given the amount of their investment and high cost of replacement.

Unfortunately, reality isn't quite that black and white. There will always be horses who end up not being capable of doing the job they were originally bred or purchased for, due to temperament, lameness, lack of athleticism, or any of a myriad of other variables. There will always be racehorses and reiners and halter horses who age out of their jobs, and who may or may not be sound enough to continue on into a new performance career. There will always be exceptions, horses that for one reason or another don't fit well into a specific niche. To some degree, there will always be some population of horses considered "unwanted," at least by their current owners.

Further, the laws of supply and demand have taught us that prices only remain high for a desirable commodity (in this case, a horse) when there is sufficient demand to match the available supply. If demand stays high, and supply either stays consistent or drops, prices will remain robust. But as soon as the number of horses on the market exceeds demand—as is the case when the industry overproduces animals, or when the economy slows down—prices plummet, and we end up with more horses than suitable homes.

When the COVID-19 pandemic began in March 2020, the laws of supply and demand hit the horse sale at New Holland in a wholly unexpected way.

Initially, all activity at the business ceased. But as a regional hub for livestock sales, New Holland is intrinsically linked to food production, and although no one is eating horses in the United States, the local Amish and Mennonite communities rely on them for transportation and labor. For these reasons, New Holland was deemed an "essential business" and resumed its weekly sales schedule after a three-week pause. It wasn't long before something happened no one could have predicted—the prices for New Holland horses started to climb.

"We thought they'd be giving away horses," says Holt. "But horses became a relatively popular pastime of people that were social distancing, and there was both a change in the supply and a change in demand."

When the sale resumed, one of the first pairs sent through was a Miniature Horse mare with a foal by her side; they sold together for $4,000. Soon, it was not uncommon for a least a few horses in each sale to bring anywhere from $12,000 to $18,000. Even horses most likely destined to end up on a trailer heading for a foreign slaughterhouse were selling for significantly higher prices, so the number of buyers looking for those horses declined in response. According to Holt, by 2023, there was only one slaughterhouse buyer still coming to the New Holland sale with any regularity.

There was no significant change in the type of animal coming to New Holland—but buyers had a different mentality and were willing to pay more for what was available. It took nearly three years for the average price to return to pre-pandemic levels.

As the cost of keeping horses continues to rise, it remains to be seen what will happen next at New Holland in regards to supply and demand. But perhaps the bigger question is whether the pandemic price surge was an anomaly, or evidence of what could become a "new normal" for unwanted horses, if excessive breeding could be curtailed. With high prices, high demand, and low supply, it suddenly becomes pretty motivating to make good decisions around the care and well-being of the animals you already own.

IN 2022, HOLT WAS APPOINTED to the Pennsylvania Department of Agriculture's Animal Health and Diagnostic Commission, and he now serves as its vice chair. He believes he was appointed to the role at least in part because of his work at New Holland, but it is also because of his awareness of current economic trends within the equine industry. I ask him, after all he has seen and experienced at New Holland, if he thinks we can ever get ahead of the unwanted horse problem without re-opening American slaughterhouses. He sighs before answering.

"My opinion is that banning slaughter in the United States actually increased the amount of suffering that the horse had to go through to get there," says Holt. "Instead of a five-hour truck ride, it became a ten-hour truck ride, plus one additional step."

He is referring to the fact that any slaughter-bound horse must be held for a minimum of 24 to 48 hours to receive federal endorsement of the paperwork required for export.

Several years ago, Holt visited a Canadian slaughter plant for his own education. He saw horses there that he had seen at New Holland; he felt the animals were well handled by the plant. He says he can get behind slaughter as a method of managing unwanted horses, *if* the animals are handled humanely. He has never witnessed the process across the southern border, in Mexico, but admits he has heard rumors the methods used there are less humane.

Making the case that we should re-open American equine slaughterhouses is not a popular argument. Those who support this idea point out that doing so would return control of the process to the auspices of the US Department of Agriculture, an agency that, in theory, could ensure humane treatment and processing of animals. But perhaps more importantly, re-opening American plants would reduce the need for long-distance transport and holding, conditions which unequivocally contribute to increased suffering for the equines involved.

Horses that end up at New Holland may have been shipped hundreds of miles prior to arriving at the sale. They must then endure the stress of the sale itself as well as being in close proximity to dozens of unfamiliar horses. Once sold, they are again loaded onto a tractor trailer and taken to a dealer's lot. Usually, animals are held in pens with as many as twenty other equines, with just one hay feeder and one water source. Horses are social creatures, but they are also hierarchical, and being in tight quarters with limited resources means there is constant friction for position. When the dealer has met their quota, the horses finally get loaded again, this time for a 13-hour (or longer) drive to a plant across the border.

The last weeks of these horses' lives are far worse than any death at a domestic slaughter plant.

But despite all of this, I realize I cannot make peace with the idea of re-opening American slaughter plants—not when there is another option for humanely ending the life of a truly unwanted horse.

AT BOTH THE LEBANON VALLEY and New Holland auctions, I watched horses of all colors, shapes, and sizes run through the chute, while the auctioneers' steady chants served as backing tracks to the thoughts rioting in my mind. As each animal came through, the horseman in me would think, "Oh, that horse just needs shoes, or more groceries, or a little TLC, or training," or "He's clearly terrified," but to solve each of these problems in a horse requires resources and time, which are both in short supply.

But equally heartbreaking were the old souls, kind-looking animals with tired eyes and worn-out bodies, for whom perhaps the best possible outcome would be access to humane euthanasia.

Even among animal advocates, discussions around euthanasia can become charged. The term comes from the Greek for "good death," and its common usage indicates the voluntary termination of life to relieve pain and suffering. In the American Association of Equine Practitioners (AAEP)'s 2019 Care Guidelines for Equine Rescue and Retirement Facilities, the authors acknowledge that humane euthanasia of "unwanted horses or those deemed unfit for adoption is an acceptable procedure once all available alternatives have been explored." Further, "a horse should not have to endure conditions of lack of feed or care erosive of the animal's quality of life."

Of the five specific methods of humane euthanasia cited in the AAEP's 2021 Euthanasia Guidelines, two are only applicable when the animal is under general anesthesia, and for two others, prior sedation "should be considered when possible." One of those latter two methods is the use of a penetrating captive bolt—the same and only method used at a slaughter plant, where it is always performed without sedation.

"We all know it is a whole lot more humane to have a needle put in their neck and go to sleep," says one veterinarian familiar with the captive-bolt procedure. "We need to make more people aware that euthanasia is *not* the worst scenario."

The New Holland horse sale happens every Monday.

Lebanon Valley happens the second Saturday of every month. And there are others—Sugar Creek in Ohio and Bastrop in Louisiana, Unadilla in New York and Kaufman in Texas.

We might not like it, but the horses keep coming, and coming, and coming.

And as long as there are horses that no one wants, because maybe they aren't attractive or are too old or blemished or untrained or there simply aren't enough people looking to own an expensive pet that can live for 30 years—these auctions will continue.

Auctions are a place for livestock to be traded and sold; they are simply a way station along the journey to an inevitable final destination. But attending these auctions proves to me there exists a fundamental disconnect between the traditional definition of livestock and the role the horse actually plays today throughout most of the United States. I begin to wonder if this disconnect is directly responsible for why the question of how best to handle unwanted horses remains largely unresolved.

I determine to turn my focus upstream, toward those groups wading through conflicting beliefs and perspectives in search of common ground.

II

A TANGLED WEB

AFTER VISITING the Lebanon Valley Livestock and New Holland auctions, and learning more about the motivations, experiences, wisdom, and concerns of some of the dedicated equine advocates fully immersed in the day-to-day space of equine rescue, I felt better informed regarding the depth and complexity of the unwanted horse problem, but still unclear how, as a community, equestrians can best move toward resolving it.

Fortunately, there are several national-level equine advocacy organizations working hard to find those answers. Each organization contributes its own unique perspective to the conversation, and collectively, they are drawing disparate stakeholders to the same table, seeking to find common ground and real-world solutions.

Part II explores the conflicting legal, ethical, and value-driven beliefs impacting how equines are perceived, used, and managed in the United States today. Questions regarding their legal classification, historical use, and even food taboos all combine to influence public perception and beliefs about horses, and create such a complex matrix of considerations it is not possible for any single solution to fully resolve the issue. Instead, like untying a knot, we will need to break down the barriers and resolve challenges thread by thread.

Chapter 5

LIVING IN THE GRAY ZONE

*LIVE*STOCK* (NOUN):

> Domestic animals kept on a farm for use or profit; esp., cattle, sheep, and pigs (*Oxford English Dictionary*)

> Animals kept or raised for use or pleasure **especially:** farm animals kept for use or profit (*Merriam-Webster*)

The word *livestock* has been in use since around 1687, and since then has carried a fairly consistent definition. This is evidenced by the similarity in description offered by both Merriam-Webster and the Oxford English dictionaries—this last considered to be *the* authoritative voice of the English language. But by citing other common farmyard species as examples of livestock, and excluding horses, it seems even the esteemed academics at Oxford University in England responsible for managing the venerable publication don't know quite what to do with them. Instead, they offer that the word "horse" is from the Old English, and describe the equine as "a solid-hoofed perissodactyl quadruped (*Equus caballus)*, having a flowing mane and tail, whose voice is a neigh." They go on to state "the animal is well known in the domestic state as a beast of burden and draught, and especially as used for riding upon."

Perhaps it is small wonder, then, that the legal definition of livestock is only marginally less ambiguous. The US Federal Code defines livestock as "cattle, sheep, horses, goats, and other domestic animals ordinarily raised or used on the farm." This definition is inclusive of other types of equines, such as mules or donkeys, and also swine, but it excludes common barnyard residents like turkeys, chickens, ducks, geese, and other types of domesticated fowl, which are all classified as "poultry." Additional species that can be considered "farmed," such as fur-bearing animals like mink, various types of fish, and even laboratory animals like rats, mice, or guinea pigs, are sometimes referred to as "livestock" but excluded from the federal definition.

Back in the late 1960s, a group of stakeholders representing various equine breed and discipline organizations came together to create a first-of-its-kind coalition, with the goal of providing their growing industry with a voice on Capitol Hill in Washington, DC. The result was the formation of the American Horse Council, which since 1969 has served as the only national association responsible for representing every segment of the horse industry. While the American Horse Council maintains a neutral position on the status of equine slaughter, it remains steadfastly, staunchly opposed to any definition of livestock that would exclude the horse.

Julie Broadway has been the American Horse Council's president since 2016, and in that time she has frequently been asked to speak on the importance of the horse's status as a livestock species at various industry conventions and related venues. She acknowledges that although many owners love their horses as they would a cat, dog, or other companion animal species, there are several critical reasons why equines are better left legally classified as livestock—many of them having to do with a complex web of statutes offering both protections to the animals themselves and economic benefits to the industry.

First among these is that with horses categorized as a livestock species, it falls to the US Department of Agriculture to monitor and manage national equine herd health. In addition to providing funding and other resources to conduct equine health-related research, the USDA is responsible for administering both the National Animal Disease Preparedness and Response Program and the National Animal Vaccine and Veterinary Countermeasures Bank. The needs of horses are included under both plans, and collectively, these programs help to keep certain non-endemic equine diseases (such as African Horse Sickness) out of the United States, and monitor the status of certain contagious, endemic diseases (such as equine infectious anemia, equine herpes virus, and vesicular stomatitis—I include resources related to these at the end of this book). If and when outbreaks occur, these programs mobilize to implement protective measures and recommendations to mitigate spread.

"If horses were companion animals or pets, that funding and protection would disappear," explains Broadway.

A second significant benefit to maintaining the designation of horses as livestock is economic in nature—and a change in status could prove financially devastating to equine farm owners, large and small. We know this thanks to the work of the American Horse Council Foundation, the 501(c)3 nonprofit arm of the American Horse Council, established in 1991 to better support educational, research, and charitable initiatives benefiting the industry. Approximately every five years, the AHCF conducts a broad-reaching and deeply researched economic impact study to assess the status, health, and needs of the equine industry. Through data collected by this recurring study, the American Horse Council is better able to analyze how well current laws are working to support the industry, and track trends over time.

In the 2023 edition of the AHCF Economic Impact Study, 62 percent of respondents reported owning or leasing a farm, barn, or stable, representing an estimated 12.5 million acres of United States land dedicated (at least in part) to equine use. As long as the horse remains livestock, certain agricultural-related tax exemptions, allowances for depreciation, and other related laws can be applied to some of these equine properties and businesses. The specific benefits and exemptions permissible under these laws and codes vary from state to state, but often include lucrative incentives to keep land in use for agricultural purposes, and come with a significant reduction in tax liability. The study further revealed that 12.3 percent of all horses in the United States are in some way involved in the breeding industry—and thanks to their livestock status, commercial horse breeders (or owners selling their animals in general) are typically not subject to state sales or excise taxes.

But tax law isn't the only form of legal statute impacted when considering equines as livestock. In many states, husbandry and humane treatment laws dictating minimal acceptable standards of care and management practices for livestock are distinct from those governing companion animals. Whether this is truly a good thing for the horse is hard to say, and to some degree, it depends on where the equine lives. Most humane treatment laws are administered at the state, not federal, level, and the quality of protection for non-human animals varies widely across the country, regardless of each species' legal status.

When it comes to animal welfare law, the distinction between "companion animal" and "livestock" matters, because at times, the difference in the quality of legal protection for a species, based on its status, is staggering. For example, most state statutes exempt "standard agricultural practices" related to animal husbandry from their cruelty laws. When living conditions or activities affecting livestock are called into question, this hazy wording often leaves both law enforcement officials and the judicial system to interpret what actually constitutes a "standard agricultural practice." Meanwhile, there are felony provisions in all 50 states and the District of Columbia for intentionally killing a dog or cat.

Despite their limitations, livestock laws are often written in a way that encourages humane treatment and care while still allowing the use of the animal, and this is perhaps one of the best arguments that in general, livestock statutes do benefit the horse. Further, most livestock protection laws mandate that animals cannot be neglected or abandoned, provide provisions against "overwork," and stipulate sheltering requirements.

One final argument for keeping the horse as a livestock species is also legal in nature; it has to do with state-level limited liability laws. All but two states (California and Maryland) have their own version of a similar law, which generally limits the liability of equine professionals due to the "inherent risk" of equine activities. Broadway says the loss of such protection would greatly impact the manner in which many equine professionals would choose to interact with the general public.

IN FILLING THE AMERICAN HORSE COUNCIL'S role as "the steward of the equine industry," Broadway and her colleagues are constantly on the lookout for any proposed changes to federal law that may impact its diverse interests. This vigilance means at times, they are simultaneously keeping watch on as many as two hundred different bills at various stages of the legislative process. Frequently, the American Horse Council protects the industry's interests through submitting comments to, and holding direct meetings with, congressional members and agency representatives. Many of these legislators and government leaders come to their positions lacking direct experience with agriculture in general and livestock in particular, making the role of the American Horse Council perhaps more critical than ever, especially when it comes to keeping horses legally classified as livestock.

"Some of the work we're involved with now requires us to talk to people who didn't grow up around horses," says Broadway. "They don't understand the issues or the nuances, so our efforts have been more magnified in the educational component of what we do."

Most often, new animal-related legislation or revisions to existing statutes are put forward by a bill's sponsors with the best of intentions. However, the general public's commonly held perception of the horse as a companion animal often filters into the wording of legislative proposals, with no concept of the potential implications.

Several years ago, a congressional member proposed a bill to support victims of domestic violence in maintaining ownership of their pets. The draft wording of the bill included a description of pets that listed horses alongside dogs, cats, and other traditional companion animal species. Broadway says the American Horse Council immediately asked the bill's sponsor for a revision of the wording to ensure horses were listed separately from companion animals, while still including them in the bill.

"That's a slippery slope," says Broadway. "You can say, 'pets—open parenthesis, dogs, cats, rabbits, iguanas, close parenthesis, comma, and horses,' but you can't lump us together, because once we get in a bill, and we are considered a 'pet,' that starts a different conversation."

More recently, another piece of proposed legislation included the use of Miniature Horses in a modified legal definition of "service animal." Although the American Horse Council was generally supportive of the bill's concept, as well as the possibilities such a designation might offer to certain industry stakeholders, Broadway notes they were initially concerned about the implications.

"The question is always, 'Does it start the conversation?'" says Broadway. "If Miniature Horses can be considered service animals—companion animals, if you will—does that 'open the door'? In this case, they did a good job crafting some criteria we were happy about. But it's fascinating, all the nuances that come into play. We are constantly having to correct some people up on the Hill, because when they think of equine-assisted services or therapy programs, they think of those horses as being 'service animals,' or companion animals, and they often refer to them that way…and we have to say, 'No.'"

In its analysis of animal law, the Animal Legal Defense Fund, a California-based organization dedicated to "protecting the lives and advancing the interests of animals through the legal system," acknowledges the blurred lines around the status of the horse. This organization points out that although typically only cats and dogs are considered companion animals for legal purposes, there are some cases in which other species—including horses—may also functionally fall into that category. In his summary of equine-related legal issues for the Michigan State University College of Law's Animal Legal and Historical Center, Craig M. Smith notes horses "occupy a unique place in American law and the narrative that informs it." He goes on to write that because the horse fills many different roles, the treatment of the species in the eyes of the law must cover "a wide spectrum of often competing goals." And thanks to the federal-level 1971 Wild Free-Roaming Horses and Burros Act, the horse is the only species of domesticated livestock also protected as a wild animal on federal lands, and allowed to roam in a "natural state." Smith writes, "This is a type of public and political sentiment that is usually reserved for dogs, cats, and endangered species."

The ambiguity around the horse extends even into wording shared by other federal agencies. On the website for the Centers for Disease Control and Prevention (CDC)—the agency responsible for protecting public health in the United States—a section dedicated to animal health lists horses separately from farm animals. And on the CDC's linked web page dedicated to informing the average American citizen about human health risks specifically related to horses, the agency states, "From pulling a plow over a farmer's field to carrying a cowboy across the open range, horses have always had an important role in society. Today, horses are generally considered companion animals...."

It is truly no wonder our legislators are confused.

"As horses are used less and less for plowing and some of the other agricultural purposes they originally did...I do think it has gotten a little more difficult for people to say they are livestock," admits Broadway. "But there are still plenty of applications. Mennonite and Amish communities use horses as work horses and for farming, as do plenty of ranchers when they are moving cattle and doing other related work."

In the AHCF's 2023 Economic Impact Study, only 8 percent of horses in the United States, just over half a million animals, were determined to be doing "traditional work," which was defined by the authors as farming, ranching, mounted police work, serving in the carriage industry, or providing equine-assisted services. But Broadway suspects this population is being under-reported, despite the authors' extensive efforts to collect data, and the actual numbers of "traditional work" horses are much higher. It can be difficult to convince someone living in an Anabaptist community, for example, or working on a remote ranch, to respond to requests for data collection.

Approximately every five years, the USDA completes a Census of Agriculture, its most recent (at the time of writing) in 2022; among its many data points, the agency attempts to collect information on the size of the horse population in the United States. But the census only counts horses on "working farms," which are defined as farms making over $1,000 annually in "production revenue." And "production revenue," when it comes to horses, is further defined as monies generated from breeding or semen sales. Not boarding. Not training. Not lesson programs or equine-assisted service centers. Only breeding.

"They are leaving out entire segments of the equine population," says Broadway of the USDA census. "The rules for the way they do the census were written seventy years ago, and they have a very narrow definition of what horses 'count.'"

From this admittedly incomplete data, the USDA's 2022 census estimated the United States horse population at only 2.4 million animals. Equine numbers can be found cited in a table sandwiched between a chart summarizing the status of goats, kids, and mohair, and one reporting on poultry. Meanwhile, the 2023 AHCF Economic Impact Study, which collected data over a similar period of time, determined the total population was around *6.65 million* horses.

The discrepancy in reported population size is significant in more ways than one. Most importantly, it is their own census number that the USDA uses to determine its budgetary allocations for all facets of its equine programming. And perhaps because the horse is not truly considered a food species—even by the USDA—the needs of the equine industry simply do not seem to garner full agency attention.

One of the many items on the American Horse Council's agenda is continuing to lobby the USDA to fund a true equine census in the next iteration of the Farm Bill. The American Horse Council also wants to ensure the needs of the equine industry receive due consideration when it comes to important issues affecting agriculture at large—such as the growing shortage of large animal veterinarians. Advocates know they face a future of continued vigilance to ensure maintaining even the status quo.

IN THE FEDERAL 1971 Wild Free-Roaming Horses and Burros Act, Congress described these descendants of once domesticated animals as "living symbols of the historic and pioneer spirit of the West." This poetic description reveals the continued evolution of attitudes toward the horse in American society, some 35 years *before* the last United States-based equine slaughterhouses would find their doors shuttered.

Many Americans probably don't realize that, strictly speaking, equine slaughter is still legal in most states. Only seven—California, Georgia, Florida, Illinois, New Jersey, New York, and Texas—have enacted state-level equine slaughter prohibitions, and in an eighth, Arizona, equine slaughter is only legal with a license. There is no federal-level ban on equine slaughter *per se*; however, beginning with the defunding of USDA inspectors in 2005, the sale or export of horse meat for human consumption (once the primary market) functionally became illegal in the United States.

But the truth is, by that time, it had been decades since there was any domestic market for horse meat to speak of. Even many zoos, which once fed horse meat to certain resident species, had largely moved away from the practice, initially due to public backlash, and later, due to lack of availability. A 2022 poll commissioned by the American Society for the Prevention of Cruelty to Animals and conducted by Lake Research Partners determined that 83 percent of Americans oppose the slaughter of horses in the United States for human consumption (the question specifically asked). Survey analysts further determined "this opposition extends across political party, race, gender, and regardless of whether the respondent lived in a rural or urban setting."

The reasons why so many Americans share this perspective weren't clarified by the ASPCA survey. However, one can perhaps assume it is the logical result of a combination of factors, ranging from the iconography of the horse in popular culture to his current dominant use as a partner in leisure activities. But there is also one other reason—for the most part, to Americans, eating horse meat is considered taboo.

There is a whole field of study—*ethnography*—which examines how the customs of individual people and cultures develop. Food taboos are an accepted part of this field and are documented all over the world. A food taboo exists when a cultural group avoids a certain food for reasons other than simple dislike. Where they occur, food taboos typically have a long history and can often be traced to something ecological (such as conserving a limited resource) or medical (avoiding certain foods that are unhealthy or harmful). Once a society has declared a certain food off limits, the shared avoidance serves the purpose of maintaining group cohesion and identity. Sometimes the original reason for the taboo is long since forgotten, the relic of a time and circumstance generations in the past. Finnish ethnographer Victor Benno Meyer-Rochow writes that when it comes to food taboos, "Rational explanations are not always possible and what to one group is strictly taboo to another may be totally okay."

One of the most common and powerful reasons for the emergence of animal-related food taboos is empathy for the "about to be eaten" species. This empathy can extend to all animals or only to particular species. Meyer-Rochow writes, "In many societies, pet animals enjoy a greater degree of protection and are more likely to be given 'taboo' status…it is almost as if humanness rubs off and the pet becomes regarded as an 'honorary human.'" For example, most Americans find the idea of eating dogs or cats, which are far and away the most popular pets in the United States, repulsive. But in other countries, such as China, there is no such aversion.

Paleolithic era cave art shows humans hunting horses over 30,000 years BCE, and most scientists believe they were first domesticated 6,000 years ago in Asia. Horses and humans have enjoyed a rather cooperative relationship in the centuries since, one which allowed both species to spread farther and be more successful than either would likely have been alone. Horses have been used as direct transport and draft strength; they have been an implement of settlement and civilization of wild places, and a tool of war. Some societies used their flesh, milk, and blood as food sources, but often the animals were more valued for their strength, stamina, and speed.

There are many examples of civilizations with a reluctance to eat horses. The practice was taboo in the ancient Middle East, possibly because of the horse's association with companionship, royalty, and war. Native Americans relied on their horses and mules for hunting and war; they wouldn't eat them except in times of famine. Horses, being single-hooved, are not kosher. Even the Book of Leviticus in the Bible "rules out eating horse." In 732, Pope Gregory III told his subjects to stop eating horse because it was an "impure and detestable" pagan meat.

But there are other examples where eating horses was and is the norm. Among the nomadic tribes of the Asian steppe, covering lands now belonging to Uzbekistan, Kazakhstan, and Mongolia, the horse still serves as both a mode of transport and a source of food (*kazy*, or horse sausage, is a popular treat in this region). In Europe, it is perhaps France that is most closely associated with a culture of eating horse meat. During the French

Revolution in the late 1700s, horses seized from the aristocracy were used to feed a starving population; the act became symbolic of the oppression the society had overcome. And as Napoleon's influence spread throughout Europe in the early 1800s, accompanied with an increase in the urban working horse population, more nations experimented with eating horse meat. Only in Great Britain did the taboo stand, perhaps because across its vast empire, enough other sources of red meat were available.

Yet, the horse was still distinguished from other types of livestock when it came to slaughter practices. Horses were killed in specialist abattoirs, and their meat sold separately from that of other animals. It was the "knacker," not the butcher, who broke down horses into their edible components.

When early American settlers seeking religious freedom arrived in the New World, some brought beliefs against eating horse meat with them. The vastness of the new continent, and the eventual western expansion, meant that other types of meat production were much more efficient than using horses for food. Additionally, horses played a much more significant role in the creation of what would become the United States than they had in the development of most European nations, particularly when it came to the settlement of the West and in major conflicts such as the American Revolution and the Civil War. In fact, in what was an early form of patriotism, eating horse meat was considered "un-American." Its consumption was equated with poverty, war, and the breakdown of society.

But progress in the United States is nothing if not relentless, and the arrival of the Industrial Revolution, with its electric street cars and internal combustion engines, signaled the end of the reign of the horse as a young nation's main mode of transport. Almost overnight, thousands of animals became unneeded, and enterprising American businessmen proposed canning the meat of unwanted horses to sell in Europe. But the United States already had a reputation for being averse to regulations when it came to food, thanks to a history of scares around unsafe or even poisoned meat. By 1896, Belgium had banned the import of meat from the United States, and the price for horse meat in particular had fallen so much that it was being fed to chickens because it was cheaper than corn.

It wasn't until World War I that Americans finally began to truly consider consuming horse meat, and it was out of necessity, not desire. Beef prices rose sharply as canners sent all available supply to troops fighting abroad, and Americans turned to horse steak as an alternative. In 1919, Congress authorized the US Department of Agriculture to officially inspect and stamp horse meat. However, most Americans abandoned it as soon as beef once again became readily available after the war. Instead, Philip Mitchell (PM) Chappel began using the meat for a new enterprise—the first commercial canned dog food, Ken-L-Ration, which soon became so popular that suppliers couldn't keep up with demand.

Horse meat stayed largely off American tables until World War II, when once again food shortages forced "poor man's beef" back onto the menu. During this era, it was even served at the prestigious Harvard Faculty Club in Cambridge, Massachusetts. But at the war's conclusion, backlash against horse meat was strong. The term "horse meat" became a political insult, a booming economy provided a greater degree of wealth and material comfort, and the ownership of horses became more of a leisure pursuit than a necessity. Horses once again came to acquire a status in the American culture which meant that their consumption was anathema to an affluent populace.

It is perhaps this unique and deeply entwined history that makes defining the role of the horse in modern America so challenging. The horse is certainly more resource-intensive, longer lived, and requires a greater financial investment than most companion animal species. But in a culture where horses generally no longer serve their owners in a traditional working capacity, nor are they considered a food species, the livestock mantle doesn't seem to neatly fit either. No one seems to be willing to actually propose that horses belong in a category of their own, something between livestock and companion animals; yet, this is perhaps the most accurate way to define them—a species living in the gray zone.

Regardless of how the horse is classified, it seems clear the sometimes floated idea of re-opening United States equine slaughter plants as a means of managing unwanted horses is one not likely to receive widespread public support. However, accepting this reality puts the onus right back onto the equine industry to come up with its own solutions—because if 83 percent of Americans care enough about horses to be opposed to equine slaughter, one can't imagine they are in favor of simply turning a blind eye to the needs of neglected, discarded, or otherwise unwanted animals either.

Chapter 6

MOVING TOWARD A COMMON GOAL

AS A REMINDER, the late aughts were a somewhat turbulent time for the equine industry. Before the last three equine slaughterhouses in the United States closed in 2007, they collectively processed as many as 100,000 equines annually; it wasn't immediately clear what would happen to this volume of animals once domestic slaughter was no longer an option. Industry leaders were just beginning to grapple with that question when the Global Financial Crisis of 2008 hit, causing the United States labor market to lose 8.4 million jobs, with a concurrent decrease in spending across all facets of the consumer economy.

Nowhere was this reduction felt more acutely than in the fields of leisure and recreation. The equine industry in particular experienced a sharp decline in participation. Membership numbers in even the two largest North American equestrian organizations—the American Quarter Horse Association and the United States Equestrian Federation—dropped precipitously, while horse shows saw plunging entry numbers. Meanwhile, drought conditions in hay-producing states caused feed prices to surge, making providing even basic maintenance rations for pastured horses challenging. Unable to sell or even give away horses, desperate owners began abandoning them at boarding stables, on public lands, and even on deserted coal mines throughout Appalachia. Agricultural auctions turned horses away, certain of their no-sale status.

Amid this swirling uncertainty, industry stakeholders held a summit at the American Horse Council's 2008 annual meeting to discuss the question of how to manage the growing number of horses with nowhere to go. The end result was the creation of a new organization, the Unwanted Horse Coalition, with the mission of drawing all interested parties to the table— regardless of their positions on various issues—to better help horses in transition or at risk. Eventually rebranded as the United Horse Coalition, but with the same mission, at the time of writing the organization is nestled under the auspices of the American Horse Council Foundation and is funded by its 209 members (190 of which are equine rescues or sanctuaries).

Initially, the United Horse Coalition created several "boots on the ground" programs of its own, each developed to address a particular facet of the unwanted horse problem. But more recently, its leaders determined the organization's efforts would be better spent on industry-wide educational initiatives, each supported by hard data—not just anecdotal stories—around why, how, and from where at-risk horses originate. To this end, in 2018, the United Horse Coalition collaborated with several other organizations—including the American Horse Council, the American Society for the Prevention of Cruelty to Animals' Right Horse Program, and the American Association of Equine Practitioners' Foundation for the Horse—to create the Equine Welfare Data Collective (EWDC), a unique program which remains the only data collection service solely focusing on horses. Until the EWDC began its work, equine industry leaders interested in helping horses at risk were making decisions around program creation and funding based on anecdotal stories and "best guess" scenarios.

"These groups came together and said, 'We need to know what is actually happening in the horse rescue and welfare industry,'" explains Kelsey Buckley, EWDC program administrator. "Hard facts can make a huge difference in shifting the way we think about and talk about the programming for the horse."

Since its inception, the EWDC has conducted an annual survey of equine welfare and rescue organizations. So far, nearly 400 groups—some 35 percent of all recorded organizations—have submitted data sets to the EWDC around both quantitative and qualitative points, such as total organizational capacity, average length of stay per equine, and types of services provided. Organizations like the United Horse Coalition now use this aggregated data to, first, better support the already existing efforts of rescues and sanctuaries; second, to create targeted—and therefore hopefully more effective—programming; and finally, to address gaps in coverage or service for horses at risk.

In just six years, data analysis has already revealed some interesting and fairly consistent trends. For example, in a report released in 2024 and reflecting analysis of data collected in 2022, the EWDC determined that over 70 percent of equines entering rescues or sanctuaries did so because of reasons related to the owners—not problems with the horses themselves. In fact, the top two reasons owners asked for assistance in rehoming their animals were, first, the owner's financial situation, and second, issues with the owner's health.

"When you compare that to the reasons why cats and dogs are ending up in shelters, it's very different," says Ashley Harkins, who was the director of the United Horse Coalition until spring 2024 and is now the operations manager for the American Horse Council. "It is telling us as an industry that we need to take a different approach. To help these at-risk horses, the best thing we can do is get ahead of why they are entering rescues and sanctuaries in the first place. We need to tackle the source, and offer direct programming to help owners, both short- and long-term."

With this goal, one of the first projects the United Horse Coalition started was an online database of educational materials promoting the importance of "owning responsibly," and intended for both current and prospective horse owners. This free resource was designed to help equestrians fully evaluate their ability to care for a horse long-term, ideally before they commit to the responsibility and expense of horse ownership. For example, prospective owners are encouraged to seek the assistance of an experienced trainer, and to work with an established rescue, to ensure their new horse is a good match. Additional materials help to spell out the costs of horse ownership, including ballpark figures for both routine and emergency medical care, training, and feed and facility costs.

"People often think with their emotions, and not their heads," says Harkins with a laugh. "We are trying to ask horse enthusiasts and owners to think more proactively, before they make that decision to get into horse ownership, because they do have to take responsibility for that animal's care, or find a solution if it's not going to be a perfect scenario."

Other resources help owners to think about making a plan for the unexpected events in their own lives—anything from an owner losing a job to an untimely death. Owners are encouraged to include their horses in estate planning, as well as build a personal financial safety net for unexpected equine expenditures.

"One bad day can be all it takes for your horse to go from being safe with you to put into a situation where they need to be rehomed," says Harkins. "We are trying to get people to think about these unplanned scenarios. It can happen to anybody—nobody in the industry is immune."

And when an owner needs help, the United Horse Coalition wants to be sure they can find available resources efficiently. The UHC Equine Resource Database is a free-to-access and fairly comprehensive online list of the services offered by nearly 1,500 rescues, sanctuaries, and other equine welfare-related organizations distributed across the country. Whether an owner is in need of short-term solutions, such as financial assistance to cover feed or routine farrier or veterinary care during a time of hardship, or a more permanent placement for a horse, the database's search feature allows users to dial in on exactly what services are available in a given area. The database also indicates those organizations which have undergone an accreditation process, such as that offered by the Global Federation of Animal Sanctuaries, the Thoroughbred Aftercare Alliance, and the Standardbred Transition Alliance, or are affiliated with the ASPCA's Right Horse Program (this last is not an accrediting body, but membership does ensure a high standard in care and policy). If an organization is not accredited, the United Horse Coalition provides resources around the types of questions an owner should ask to determine if a rescue or sanctuary is in good standing.

In a recent annual audit of organizations helping horses at risk, the EWDC determined that just over 1,000 groups currently offer "custodial services"—meaning they have the capability to take physical custody of an equine in need. An additional 408 groups provide *non*-custodial services, such as safety net programs, direct placement assistance, training or behavioral modification programs, and funding for specific services such as euthanasia or castration. Out of the nearly 1,500 total organizations offering support to horses at risk, 365 offer some combination of the two service types.

Knowing that an owner's finances are the single most common cause of a horse ending up at a rescue, the EWDC has been particularly interested in learning more about the availability and capacity of safety net programs for horse owners in need. Theoretically, some of these owners would prefer to not rehome their animals, so finding ways to offer support during times of financial challenge could both ease the burden on rescues offering custodial services and prevent animals from ending up at auction.

"So much of our industry is tied into the economy," says Harkins. "When things are going great, we're doing great. When things are bad— that's when you start to see more people needing to transition their horse. If we can help owners to keep their horses at home with them, and out of the rescue and sanctuary system, then we're doing our jobs."

In 2022, the most common request was for feed assistance, at 31 percent, followed by veterinary assistance at 28 percent; safety net organizations reported they were able to fill 44 percent and 55 percent of those requests, respectively. The only request for aid fulfilled 100 percent of the time was for euthanasia assistance; this support typically helps with both the cost of the procedure and disposition of the remains.

Although Buckley is encouraged by the number of requests being filled, she acknowledges there is more work to be done in this area. "There is some support out there, but we still need to take a step back and think, 'Where do we go next?'"

Harkins notes that an increasing number of requests for assistance is actually a positive sign, because it means that some of the stigma around asking for help has decreased.

"The atmosphere is so different now than it used to be, in terms of asking for help. People felt so judged, and now, it's encouraged," says Harkins. "It's better to reach out before it becomes a problem. It's much easier for a rescue to place a horse that's in good condition than it is to spend six months of time and resources to get the horse from A to B."

ALTHOUGH THE COMBINED work of the United Horse Coalition and the Equine Welfare Data Collective has helped to better inform current efforts to support horses at risk or in transition, there are still gaps in the data that need to be filled. In particular, we need to confirm the actual number of equines still being exported annually for the purpose of slaughter, as well as identify the total national capacity of our existing equine rescues and sanctuaries. Defining these numbers with verifiable data is critical; only once we know exactly how many at-risk horses we have the ability to care for with our existing resources can productive efforts be made toward further growth in these areas.

When it comes to calculating the number of equines in the United States still being shipped abroad for slaughter, most organizations rely on a combination of their own observations, anecdotal reports, incomplete data shared by individual auctions, and information provided by the US Department of Agriculture's Animal and Plant Health Inspection Service (APHIS)—this last frequently heavily redacted and obtained through Freedom of Information Act requests. By most accounts, it is believed that just over 20,000 equines are exported annually. But for some equine advocates, any number of US-based horses still meeting this fate is too many, and they are working hard to close that loophole by lobbying for the passage of the SAFE Act.

The "Save America's Forgotten Equines" Act, or SAFE Act, would make it *illegal* to slaughter horses in the United States for human consumption (remember, any existing bans are only at the state level), as well as prohibit the export of live equines for the same purpose. Originally proposed as the Safeguard American Food Exports Act, the acronym is also a somewhat clever play on a common argument made by the bill's advocates—that domestic horse meat is not safe for human consumption due to the variety of commonly used medications which might be present in a horse's body. A version of the Act was first proposed in 2013 by Senators Mary Landrieu (D-LA) and Lindsey Graham (R-SC), and Representatives Patrick Meehan (R-PA) and Jan Schakowsky (D-IL); since then, some variant of the legislation has been put forward almost annually, but it has yet to make it out of committee for a floor vote.

When it comes to the SAFE Act, not knowing the exact number of horses still being shipped or the true national capacity of our rescues makes some industry leaders a little nervous. The truth is, if the bill should become law, we don't know for certain if our existing rescues and sanctuaries could easily absorb the animals that would be impacted—and if additional resources should prove necessary, we don't know what type or how many. This could put horses already at risk in further danger of not receiving the help they need.

Another variable to consider when it comes to determining the capacity of our rescues is the average "length of stay" for an intake. When an animal must stay in the care of a rescue for a longer period of time, that horse will use more consumable resources, and his presence will preclude another animal from entering. That's not to say horses requiring more resources or time shouldn't be helped—but when an organization is dedicating their efforts toward helping these types of horses, their overall capacity will be lower. This is another reason why safety net services have become so valuable—first, because they keep horses that don't truly need rehoming out of the shelter system, and secondly, if these horses do later on end up needing further help, they tend to arrive in better condition, making them more readily rehomed and reducing their length of stay.

Unfortunately, accurately determining an average length of stay per horse nationally is difficult, because frankly, many equine rescues and sanctuaries are operating with a small, overextended staff, and that kind of record keeping simply isn't a top priority. In short, these individuals are too busy doing the actual work to document and report on it—and it's not clear how a more robust data set would impact the findings. The United Horse Coalition is currently actively pursuing ways to better support organizations with their record keeping, including providing training on the use of simple software programs, and developing basic, easy-to-fill-in automated tables.

"Although we can get a sense of what is going on based on the data we're being given, there is a big question mark," says Harkins. "There are other organizations that periodically will collect on-the-spot polls and other data, and it does track with what we are collecting."

What we do know is that rescue survey respondents are caring for an average of 38 equines at once, in some combination of foster homes or direct shelter services. And for those groups able to keep track, we know that the average length of stay for each animal is 302 days.

Since EWDC began its annual audits in 2019, they have recorded a net gain of 61 new organizations offering services to help horses at risk, bringing the grand total of custodial providers to 1,063. Collectively, these organization report they are 73 percent full. At least in theory, there is room for more animals within our existing system. But when pressed, nearly all rescues report they would need to find additional resources, including both staff and funding, to handle anything beyond their current population numbers.

"We are asked frequently if our organizations could handle a sudden influx of animals," says Buckley. "Right now, theoretically, they have the space. But, in reality, our rescues would need funding, networking, and help from the larger industry to handle anything more."

SHORTLY BEFORE the United Horse Coalition began its work, two other national-level animal advocacy groups—the Animal Welfare Institute and the Humane Society of the United States (now Humane World for Animals)—joined forces to create an equine rescue alliance of their own. Officially established in 2007 and dubbed the Homes for Horses Coalition, the original goal of its founders was to bring together equine rescues and sanctuaries as a united voice of opposition in the fight to end slaughter. But they soon realized there was a need for these groups to have an easier way to share ideas with one another, and the organization's role quickly expanded. Although the Homes for Horses Coalition remains committed to lobbying at both the state and federal level in support of a range of initiatives to better legally protect both domestic and wild equines, today the organization also provides networking, collaboration, and community-building opportunities to nonprofits working within the equine welfare space. Now operating under the auspices of the Animal Welfare Institute and American Wild Horse

Conservation, as of 2024, the Homes for Horses Coalition boasts over 500 member organizations, located in 48 states and 7 countries.

To join the Homes for Horses Coalition, nonprofits must self-report on a range of criteria, including the condition of their property, their general care and welfare practices, re-feeding standards (for emaciated or extremely thin horses), and their adoption policies. To be eligible for membership, organizations must require that the shelter has first right of refusal to take back an adopted animal when one needs to be rehomed again; they must have a stated policy against breeding animals under their care; and they may only use humane euthanasia to end suffering, not as a population management tool. Veterinary and farrier references are checked by the Homes for Horses Coalition before an organization is accepted for membership. It should be noted that not all Homes for Horses Coalition members are working in the realm of adoption; advocacy groups, safety net organizations, sanctuaries, and others also support its mission.

In return, the Homes for Horses Coalition has compiled a comprehensive online resource library for its member organizations, as well as curated several unique opportunities for them to share ideas and network with other members. In addition to an annual in-person conference held each fall, the Homes for Horses Coalition offers regular educational webinars and monthly "Coffee Hours"—informal, virtual gatherings at which nonprofit leaders can share victories, challenges, and frustrations, as well as brainstorm new ideas and initiatives.

"It's about connecting organizations, so they are not siloed," explains Tessa Archibald, Homes for Horses Coalition manager and equine policy associate for the Animal Welfare Institute. "We have members in our Coalition who have extremely successful organizations, who have been running for twenty years—and rescues just starting out. There's a lot to learn in any industry from folks who have already been there, and there's no exception in terms of this work as well. There's always more to learn with horses, as we all know."

Although its members enjoy the professionalization and networking opportunities the HHC provides, many also join the organization in support of the legal and advocacy work it undertakes. Unlike the United

Horse Coalition and its parent organization, the American Horse Council, which have both chosen to take a neutral stance on the status of equine slaughter, the Homes for Horses Coalition strongly opposes the practice, and continues to actively lobby for its legal prohibition.

"Our members run organizations dedicated to saving equines and participate in the interception of horses ending up in the slaughter pipeline each year," explains Archibald. "Those horses are not broken horses. Oftentimes they're sound, they're healthy, they're young. They might be racehorses, family pets, wild horses. Rescues in our coalition are able to place these horses in loving homes, every day."

And although it doesn't have a specific published statement on the legal classification of the horse as livestock, Archibald says the Homes for Horses Coalition would be supportive of a broader definition that better takes into account the reality of how horses function in our modern society.

"They are treated as pets, and that's how many Americans view them," says Archibald. "They are seen as individuals, and most often, they are kept for pleasure, not strictly for commerce. In our view, 'horses as livestock' creates challenges for law enforcement to actually protect horses, and to intervene and prosecute for cruelty in a humane and just way."

The issue of slaughter is a divisive one, even among advocacy groups. When bills come forward that might legally end the practice, horse lovers can be found arguing on both sides of the issue. From the Homes for Horses Coalition's perspective, this lack of unity is not only damaging to the industry, it promotes the further suffering of horses.

"Slaughter is not talked about in traditional equine spheres, because it makes people feel uncomfortable," says Archibald. "But if we love horses, and then turn a blind eye to how they can be treated—there is a lot of room for growth in that space, among all horse people."

The Homes for Horses Coalition also believes that the continued availability of equine slaughter—even if it happens over the border—is perpetuating what Archibald calls the "predatory kill-buyer industry."

"It's a cruel system that can take advantage of horses and people," says Archibald. "That system can financially cripple individuals and equine rescues, and ultimately, that reduces the number of horses that can be helped. Sometimes, those horses being 'bailed out' don't have a safe place to land, and the kill buyers—the reality is, they are going to ship a certain number of horses no matter what, no matter which ones get pulled. And that can be a hard thing for folks to accept.

"These kill buyers are just exploiting people and taking their money. It is a horrible thing to see, and the only reason that can happen is because slaughter, and shipping horses to slaughter specifically, is still legal. They wouldn't be able to pull this scheme if it wasn't."

Which leads us back to the SAFE Act, the passage of which is one of the Homes for Horses Coalition's main advocacy goals. When speaking to members of Congress, they use the strength of their diverse membership to argue that advancing the bill is the right thing to do for both America's horses and their constituents.

Another way the Homes for Horses Coalition hopes to move the needle on this and related issues is through education and outreach to the greater horse loving community. Specifically, they encourage prospective horse owners to consider finding new horses at reputable rescues, where there is generally more transparency than at an auction or a kill buyer's lot. To make finding a rescue easier, each of the Homes for Horses Coalition's member organizations is listed under their online directory, sortable by type and location.

"They will work with you closely to find the right fit, even more than a sales barn," says Archibald. "They truly have the horse's best interest at heart. Any horse is just a few sales, or even one sale, away from being a 'rescue' or 'in transition.' They are not specific horses; they are *just horses.* They can fit into any type—any sport you like to do, there is a horse in transition who can do that job or maybe has even done that job before."

WHEN IT COMES TO reducing the number of horses ending up at risk, the Homes for Horses Coalition believes the equine industry needs to work toward cultivating a mindset that sees horses as a lifelong commitment, and to promote compassion across all facets of equine activities and phases of life. This doesn't necessarily mean that one owner will keep a horse for the duration of his life, but rather that she thinks broadly about what the arc of her horse's life will look like.

"Being part of the horse community and loving horses, I personally believe you should have an interest in protecting them, even if you aren't specifically involved in rescue," says Archibald. "Where are the horses you use coming from? Where do they go when they are no longer a good fit? How are the other horses in your barn, your community, your discipline, treated? It's about setting new horse people up for success, to instill in them the fact this is not a disposable commodity or item. This is a living being, and you should have a vested interest in their life, and how that looks and how it relates to your own life."

Many of Homes for Horses Coalition's member organizations are uniquely poised to help support the industry in this evolution, while the Homes for Horses Coalition itself is there to support its members in doing their work. In fact, they believe that uniting and collaborating in this effort may be the only path forward.

"It's definitely trickle down, but if we can disburse information that can ultimately result in more donations for a rescue, they can make decisions that will help more horses," says Archibald. "There is a lot of money in the horse world—if some of that was given back to support horses in transition, or to create better retirement options or sanctuaries, there would be more resources to prop up that part of the horse industry. By supporting the improvements and success of our rescue organizations, we can improve the lives of horses in transition."

Expanding the availability and financial support for safety net services is another opportunity both for growth and greater industry involvement within the equine welfare space. But concurrently, the Homes for Horses Coalition sees a need to increase awareness of the availability of these types of services, as well as ensure that those individuals who receive them feel supported, not judged.

"It is about reducing the stigma around using those resources," says Archibald. "People wait until they really desperately need help, and that's challenging. For people with horses who are going through a tough time, how can we support those horses in their current homes, to reduce the number in transition that need new homes? If there is somebody who already cares for them, and we can support the human-animal bond, that's important. But people need to know these programs exist, and how to access them."

Archibald shares she has heard reports that safety net services are sometimes being underutilized by those who might need them the most.

"It's disappointing to hear," she acknowledges. "Even in places where there are resources available, no one is using them. Whether it's marketing, or stigma, how can we change that? Because there are people out there who need the funding—how do you get them connected with the right resources?"

Even if they are not able to be ridden or driven, the Homes for Horses Coalition does not believe in the use of euthanasia for horses who can still maintain an adequate quality of life. But Archibald notes accepting its use for horses who are truly suffering, or for whom a transition would cause extreme distress, needs to become more common. Too often, owners are unwilling or unable to face the reality of declining animals, and sometimes attempt to rehome them instead, whether they do it directly, at an auction, or through a rescue organization.

"Our human interests should not be placed above the life of that animal, and maybe that is controversial to say," says Archibald. "It is about asking ourselves, how can we create an atmosphere and environment where those decisions can be made for the best interest of the horse, and not for any other reason? Rescues often have to take on that burden, whether it is actually taking on the horse and the cost of the euthanasia, or taking on the emotional toll of counseling people through these decisions. It's wonderful they are there to do that, but I don't think it should solely fall on them. They already do so much soul-challenging work, and 'compassion fatigue' is real."

Instead, Archibald hopes the new industry standard can be teaching owners how to recognize quality of life markers in a horse, instilling an expectation that owners need to plan ahead for end-of-life expenses and protocols (or connect owners with financial support), and cultivating a nurturing, supportive attitude toward owners making this final decision.

"Knowledge of welfare indicators and end-of-life preparation should be more prevalent within the industry, and a discussion people are willing to have," says Archibald. "It's knowledge that needs to be provided in a thoughtful, educated manner, in all sectors of the industry."

WHEN IT COMES TO advocating for animal welfare, few groups are as well known to the general public as the American Society for the Prevention of Cruelty to Animals (ASPCA). Established by former diplomat Henry Bergh in 1866 with the guiding belief that all animals are entitled to kind and respectful treatment and must be legally protected, today the ASPCA's wide-reaching programs address everything from humane education to lobbying to direct boots-on-the-ground support. In 2016, the ASPCA was one of the stakeholders involved in the creation of the Right Horse Initiative, a collaborative program dedicated to promoting the adoption of equines from shelters and rescues. The program was publicly launched in 2017 by, and nurtured with support from, the Arnall Family Foundation until late 2019, when it officially found its permanent home with the ASPCA. Now known as ASPCA Right Horse, its goal remains the same: "to massively increase horse adoption in the United States."

Drawing on lessons learned from helping shelter cats and dogs find homes, ASCPA Right Horse seeks to normalize the idea that not only can adopting from an equine rescue result in a perfect match, visiting shelters should become a normal and routine part of finding a new equine partner.

"Previously, people didn't necessarily look to adoption when they're looking for a horse, so equines could enter a shelter or rescue, and languish there for a long time," explains Christie Schulte Kappert. She is the ASPCA's Senior Director of Equine Welfare, and has spent a lot of time thinking about how to make progress in terms of finding new homes for horses at risk or in transition.

"At the same time, there is a lack of direct participation from the horse industry in seeing this as an issue they could impact, and understanding how they could make an impact," she continues. "When I say equine welfare, there's a million things that could come up, and not everyone agrees on every issue. But adoption is something we can all agree on, and there's a way for everybody to contribute, whether that be one percent of their time, or more than that."

To that end, ASCPA Right Horse is attempting to increase national equine adoption rates with a three-pronged strategy. First, in collaboration with their industry partners, ASCPA Right Horse creates wide-reaching marketing around the idea that amazing horses can be found at shelters and rescues, and that there is a "right horse" for every person (and for that matter, a right person for every horse). Secondly, ASPCA Right Horse seeks to help shelters and rescues to increase their capacity by efficiently helping new intakes transition to their new homes, thereby freeing up space for the next horse in need. Finally, ASPCA Right Horse works to increase industry collaboration around these collective efforts, including connecting resources with the groups and people who need them the most.

To be successful in achieving their goals, changing industry attitudes about rescue horses is, perhaps, one of ASPCA Right Horse's top priorities.

"For many years, there's been a deeply held stigma that if a horse is at a rescue, it's because there's something wrong with him, and therefore he is not a good option for whatever I am looking for in a companion or partner," says Schulte Kappert. "That was a vicious cycle, turning people away from shelters, and causing horses to sit there for longer."

But she points to evolved attitudes around the adoption of companion animals as evidence that change is possible.

"Decades ago, people didn't go to a shelter to adopt a dog," says Schulte Kappert. "Now, people are proud of their rescue dogs; they say, 'Rescued is my favorite breed,' and very often, a shelter is the first place you go to get a dog or a cat. We are seeing signs of a shift for horses now, as well. There is so much social support for that, and that landscape is changing all the time."

ASCPA Right Horse is helping to spread the word about the statistics gleaned from EWDC research, particularly emphasizing the fact that the vast majority of horses in shelters arrive there due to issues in their previous owner's life, not because of a problem with the animal himself. To further combat the stereotype of "rescue horse as something less-than," ASPCA Right Horse focuses on sharing stories about horses that have found their homes through adoption. These kinds of stories serve to further break down the belief that when horses end up at a rescue, they now have some sort of black mark that will follow them into their future. Instead, they spotlight the fact that rescue horses are really just regular horses who ended up needing some extra help.

"Because horses are big, and can be expensive and live a long time, it's highly likely they will be subject to one of these transitions throughout their life," says Schulte Kappert. "Each horse has the potential, at some point in their life, to need a safety net service. I say that not as a fear tactic, but to underscore this is something we need everyone's involvement in. It's about integrating these horses into every piece of the industry."

But changing perceptions around rescue horses isn't the only place where ASPCA Right Horse would like to see some evolution. To help these animals more readily get into homes, ASPCA Right Horse also advocates for less restrictive adoption protocols at rescues and shelters, thereby making the option to adopt more accessible to more people.

"It comes from a place of great intention, of wanting to say, 'Let's do everything we can to make sure this person is going to take good care of this horse,'" says Schulte Kappert of overly rigorous adoption policies. "We care about the welfare of every horse, but really excessive applications, lots of questions making adopters prove they are good enough for the horse—what that does is it turns away a huge portion of good people who would be otherwise interested in adopting. It's too much work, it's complicated, it's intimidating, and sometimes, it's straight up disrespectful. We don't even believe it results in better adoptions, and there are other, easier, ways to get a horse." She pauses, then continues, "It's so important for shelters to see themselves as rehomers. They are the ones that have the expertise to say, 'Here's the horse on day one, here's what he needs to get from point A to point B, to get into a home'— whether that is training and behavioral support, medical care, or that matchmaking to help find the very right person."

Extrapolating from data gathered in the cat and dog adoption field, ASPCA Right Horse believes that overly restrictive adoption policies don't actually lead to better outcomes for the animals. As an alternative, they promote the use of what Schulte Kappert calls a "conversational style of adoption."

"Instead of me saying to you, 'Are you experienced with horses?' I could say, 'Tell me about your experience with horses,'" she explains. "One person might say they train wild Mustangs, and another that they went to horse camp as a kid. Those answers are going to guide you down a different path. It's not that one or the other is more 'worthy' of a horse, but those conversations open the door to learn more, they build a positive relationship, and it lays a foundation for matchmaking. And should that person need help in the future, they are going to come back to the shelter."

It can be challenging for the leadership of an organization to change their way of thinking around adoption policies, particularly when they have invested significant time and resources in preparing animals for rehoming and feel protective of their future. But Schulte Kappert believes this shift is essential if we are going to increase adoption numbers, thereby maximizing the number of horses we can help.

"These processes are utterly critical to welcoming more people to adoption, and saving more horses' lives," says Schulte Kappert. "And they will cultivate other types of support—volunteers, donors, social media fans, everything. It's a big shift, but we've been working a lot on it. It can be scary, and we understand that. But we know that it works."

CURRENTLY, ASCPA RIGHT HORSE has 41 "adoption partners"—rescues, shelters, and other custodial organizations whose vision and mission regarding increasing capacity and decreasing length of stay for their equine intakes is in alignment with that of the ASPCA. Just over 20 additional groups are in the "warm-up ring," meaning they are in the process of becoming a partner. Approval is competitive, and requires a rigorous and time-consuming evaluation of the organization to determine if it is a good fit for the program.

"It's very relationship-based, and we take the time to get to know each other," says Schulte Kappert. "It's different from an accreditation process, where they get a set of requirements, go out and fulfill them, and come back. It's a two-way relationship, and we want to make sure we can give each group adequate attention."

For those groups who do partner with ASPCA Right Horse, the benefits are significant. Not only does the ASPCA provide approximately $1 million annually in grant funding to their adoption partners, members become integrated into a network of supportive collaborators committed to finding practical solutions to the real-world challenges of equine rescue.

"We encourage groups to get together and say, 'here's what we think will work,' then they try it, gather some data, and come back and share results," says Schulte Kappert. "Most ideas work in at least some capacity, but if it didn't work, we talk about what we can learn from that. If we want different results, we have to try things differently. We create a space where these groups can take risks, and be innovative, and we can all learn."

One important note is that to be considered as an ASPCA Right Horse adoption partner, each organization must demonstrate a strong commitment to increase both their capacity and adoption rates. This means organizations offering primarily sanctuary services (which generally entails providing lifetime care for an animal) are not eligible to become adoption partners. The reasoning is partially practical—after all, even the ASPCA does not have unlimited resources—and partially philosophical.

"There are 6.6 million horses in the United States, and one of the things that is challenging is we don't know exactly how many of those are at risk—and most horses are just one sale away from becoming at risk," explains Schulte Kappert. "Horses can be at risk for anything from benign neglect, languishing in a pasture, all the way to entering the slaughter pipeline, to simply needing a new home. Horses in any of these categories need support in some way. The only way we can ensure all those horses have support is if the organizations and shelters that are here to support them increase their capacity to do so.

"When a horse goes into a sanctuary, they are typically not leaving," she continues. "That is perfectly fine and great—for those horses. If you have space for 20 horses at a sanctuary, and those horses come in and never leave, those 20 horses are safe. But, if those horses come in, and after six months, they are adopted, that's 40 horses a year, every year, and over time, it's hundreds of horses. It is utterly critical that horses that go into rehoming programs get back out the door and into a private home to make space for others in need."

In 2017, the ASPCA conducted a study that concluded that at least 2.3 million American adults had both the interest and ability to adopt a horse. ASPCA Right Horse uses this (admittedly aging) data to argue that plenty of homes for horses at risk exist, but collectively, rescues need to do a much better job of connecting these horses with those homes. Yet ASCPA Right Horse adoption partners are not exclusively high-capacity adoption groups. Some organizations currently place as few as 10 animals annually—but because they know 10 more are waiting to take those stalls, they remain strongly focused on getting those animals rehomed efficiently, with the additional goal of gently increasing their capacity in the future.

"Increasing capacity doesn't mean an organization must [take in] 300 horses annually," says Schulte Kappert. "It means, for an organization of any size, when a horse comes in, they are creating a plan for him to go from the rescue into a new home efficiently."

ASPCA Right Horse also benefits from the support of its nearly 100 industry partners, a mix of both for-profit and nonprofit organizations and businesses, who collectively provide services, products, guidance, access to resources, and broader community outreach than ASPCA Right Horse could offer on its own. The composition of ASPCA Right Horse industry partners represents the breadth of the equine world, and when it comes to animal welfare, they may not necessarily see eye to eye on all issues. Yet when it comes to promoting equine adoptions, they can find common ground.

"We really facilitate and welcome conversations with our industry partners, because every group comes in with a different perspective and background," notes Schulte Kappert. "We need everyone's involvement—

first, because it's the right thing to do for the horse. Second, because it's what most people want to do. They want there to be enough support for people who have horses.

"At the ASPCA, we are very practical, and celebrate the horse-human relationship," she emphasizes. "Horses have many different, wonderful uses—riding, competition, companionship—and that should not change. At the same time, there is discourse on the fact we have to do better for animal welfare. Within the Right Horse program, we leave some of the more controversial things at the door. Focusing on adoption in this way is something really powerful for everybody, and we're hoping to encourage more folks to lock hands with us in that effort."

IN LATE 2021, the ASPCA opened its Equine Transition and Adoption Center in the Oklahoma City, Oklahoma, suburb of El Reno. Designed as a pilot program dedicated to "developing solutions to the barriers that get in the way of at-risk horses finding homes," the ASPCA Equine Transition and Adoption Center works directly with owners in need to determine best next steps for their horses. When an owner contacts the ASPCA Equine Transition and Adoption Center, a mobile team (including a local veterinarian) first assesses the horse at home. Based on what they find, they will either provide subsidized or free medical care onsite and leave the horse with his owner, or if it is determined that rehoming is a better option, bring the horse to the El Reno facility. Once there, a skilled team, including a training and behavior specialist, works with each animal in preparation for adoption. At least in part, the goal of the ASPCA's Equine Transition and Adoption Center program is to create a replicable blueprint to help horses—particularly those with issues that traditionally make them harder to place—get into new homes efficiently.

Given the level of support they were prepared to provide, the team behind the ASPCA Equine Transition and Adoption Center assumed they would be overrun with requests for assistance—and since its inception, the program has helped over 400 at-risk horses. But they also uncovered a rather shocking piece of information: on average, owners in need had been seeking help for their horses for anywhere from 18 months to 2 years before finally connecting with their program.

"That's a long time for a person to be struggling, and for a horse to maybe be declining if they are not able to get the care they need," says Schulte Kappert. "One of the things we learned is the existence of slaughter causes owners to delay seeking care. People are, rightfully, concerned about where their horse is going to go and whether they are going to be taken care of, if they offer them to a program. We've had to put a dedicated marketing campaign behind the Equine Transition and Adoption Center, to share what we offer and why it's a safe thing.

"There are safety net services that exist, but people don't know they exist, and there's not enough yet. It's a chicken-egg problem. You have to not only provide the programs, but promote them."

The ASPCA takes a slightly broader definition of the term "safety net organization" than some other national groups. They consider any organization offering services to horses at risk, or those animals likely to become so, to belong under the "safety net" umbrella—anything from providing short-term financial assistance with basic care, to offering behavioral/training support, to covering unique requests, such as supplying assistance with building better physical shelters for privately owned animals. At the far end of the safety net spectrum are those organizations offering custodial services.

"We would consider a horse entering the shelter a part of safety net services in the sense that it's preventing him from falling into a bad situation," explains Schulte Kappert.

But in the ASPCA's experience—based on data gathered from their Oklahoma facility, and other data collected from partners across the country—as many as 60 percent of the calls for help shelters receive come from owners who don't actually need to rehome their horses. What they need is judgment-free assistance in covering the costs of their animals' basic care during times of personal hardship, before their animal's health problems become so significant they require more advanced services and interventions.

With this in mind, in 2018 the ASPCA's Equine Welfare department piloted the Vet Direct Safety Net program, which helped local veterinarians to identify and assist at-risk horses within their service areas. In 2020, the American Association of Equine Practitioners (AAEP) and its philanthropic arm, the Foundation for the Horse, partnered with the ASPCA to further expand the program. Today, the AAEP'S Vet Direct Safety Net program offers participating veterinarians up to $600 toward the cost of emergency care for horses and owners in need. "Emergency care" is somewhat broadly defined; the AAEP provides a list of approved services, up to and including humane euthanasia.

"The Vet Direct Safety Net has been over 95 percent successful in keeping those horses in their homes," notes Schulte Kappert. "They don't need to go anywhere—so let's leave them where they are and make sure they are well cared for."

It is in supporting safety net programs that, perhaps, broader industry involvement could make the greatest impact.

"It's the whole metaphor of instead of pulling drowning people out of the river, let's go up the river and prevent them from falling in in the first place," says Schulte Kappert. "We need to get help to these at-risk horses earlier. Increasing the availability and awareness of safety net programs could be one way to do that, along with greater industry collaboration.

"We think there will always be a need for some horses to go somewhere, and that's why it's so important for shelters to see themselves as rehomers." She repeats a point made earlier for emphasis. "This is something we need everyone's involvement in, whether that looks like, 'I'm a professional horse trainer, and of the 50 horses I train a year, one I do as a volunteer for a rescue.' Or, 'I'm a vet, and of all the cases I see in a year, three are under the Vet Direct Safety Net program.' It's media companies figuring out how to incorporate these stories, and breed and discipline organizations that provide special incentives for adopted horses."

But equally important—at least from the ASCPA's perspective—is the need to both legally end domestic equine slaughter, and pass the SAFE Act to prevent horses from being shipped abroad. Like the Homes for Horses Coalition, the ASPCA is staunchly anti-slaughter, and the organization's advocacy efforts are focused toward supporting the SAFE Act's passage, as well as promoting other anti-cruelty initiatives.

"Slaughter exists because there is international demand for the meat, and because it's still legal to export [horses]," says Schulte Kappert. "We know those horses who are shipped to slaughter could be given a positive outcome in the United States, whether they are healthy enough to be rehomed, or if not, they are given compassionate euthanasia by a vet in their home, or as close to their home as possible. We know from market dynamics that as long as there is a foreign demand for horsemeat, some number of horses will be purchased and sent to slaughter. We need to do both—we have to plug the hole in the ship, while we are bailing the ship out. As long as the slaughter pipeline remains open, people will find ways to get horses, honestly or dishonestly, from people who don't know any better, or don't have the ability to access one of these safety net programs."

It is the vision of ASPCA Right Horse that by helping shelters increase their capacity and ability to efficiently rehome adoptable horses, and by boosting the number of safety net services and promoting their accessibility, more at-risk horses will stay safe and find new homes.

"The number of horses going to slaughter has been declining really steadily over the past few years," says Schulte Kappert. "It's not a method of population control. It's simply not, and the fact slaughter exists causes some powerful dynamics—owners delaying seeking care because they're worried where the horse is going to go, and the whole cycle of kill-pen/bailout rackets, which are a huge distraction and a drain on resources. The only way we get rid of that is passing the SAFE Act.

"Slaughter isn't coming back, and it doesn't need to," emphasizes Schulte Kappert with iron in her voice. "We're beyond that."

ALTHOUGH EACH OF THESE national-level organizations clearly has some distinct differences in perspective around how to best help horses at risk, a few common themes also emerged. First, collaboration across the entire breadth of the industry is essential if we want to move the needle when it comes to helping these equines. We need to mobilize resources, which include goods, services, funding, and facilities, to better support those rescues and sanctuaries already doing the work, and perhaps, to help new programs evolve. We need to normalize the expectation that when it comes to horses, long-range thinking is key, and to better support owners, first, in choosing the right horse for their needs, and second, in making plans before the unexpected occurs. Finally, we need to accept that despite good intentions, resources are finite and sometimes horses and their owners are going to fall into unfortunate circumstances. When this happens, equine enthusiasts need to withhold judgment and instead prioritize getting those animals (and people) the help they need.

With 6.6 million horses in the United States and a diverse industry, there likely will always be more work to be done in the realm of protecting the well-being of equines across their life cycle. But key stakeholders are working collaboratively to find realistic solutions and practical outcomes. As a group, horsemen tend to be wedded to tradition, doing things the way they've always been done; change in the industry comes slowly. Yet I can now see that not only is a change in industry attitudes and practices coming—it has already begun.

TRANSFORMATION

ALTHOUGH VARIOUS ORGANIZATIONS within the equine industry may disagree on the best path forward, or even if the problem of "unwanted horses" can truly be solved, they appear to be united in their belief that doing *something* is better than doing nothing at all. With nearly 1,500 organizations dedicating their efforts toward helping horses at risk or in transition, unique and creative ideas are being implemented to help us move toward a cohesive solution.

Many leaders of these organizations are advocating for a different paradigm, one in which the equine industry itself becomes responsible for ensuring the well-being of *all horses,* from each responsibly planned breeding through a humane death. In Part III, we will explore the work of several of these organizations, which—through their creative programming—are changing the future for unwanted horses while simultaneously proving there are better options than the slaughter pipeline.

Some of these programs evolved thanks to the collaboration and networking promoted by regional and national coalitions; others began as a tiny seed of an idea, nourished and supported by passionate people, eventually growing into a solution greater than anyone had originally dreamed possible. And in learning about the impact of these programs on the horses and people they serve, another truth emerges, perhaps explaining why resuming equine slaughter will never be acceptable in the United States—for many Americans, the horse's true role is that of healer.

Chapter 7

AFTER THE FINISH LINE:
THE RISE OF THOROUGHBRED AFTERCARE

ONE OF THE MOST NOTABLE of Hall of Fame jockey Bill Shoemaker's 8,833 career wins came on the back of a flame-colored colt named Ferdinand in the 1986 Kentucky Derby. Shoemaker, 54, piloted the 17–1 shot around a seemingly impenetrable wall of horseflesh to become the oldest jockey to ever capture the famous garland of red roses presented to the race's winner.

Ferdinand's win was also emotional for his Hall of Fame trainer Charlie Whittingham. Despite saddling winners at top tracks from coast to coast during his nearly five-decade career, Whittingham had never before won the crown jewel of racing, and "Ferdy" had also made him, at 73 years of age, the oldest trainer to ever do so. The 1986 Kentucky Derby fairy tale became the stuff of racing legend.

In a four-year career, the gentle colt with a golden forelock and white star won only 8 of 29 starts, but he seemed to save his best performances for when it counted the most. Ferdy's final win was in the 1987 Breeder's Cup Classic, at the time the richest purse in racing at $3 million. In that race, he defeated 1987 Kentucky Derby winner Alysheba by a nose; he went on to be awarded the 1987 Eclipse Award for Horse of the Year. By the time of his retirement late in 1988, Ferdinand had amassed nearly $4 million in career earnings, making him the fifth-leading money winner of all time.

Starting in 1989, Ferdinand stood at stud at Claiborne Farm, near Paris, Kentucky, with an initial stud fee of $30,000, live foal guaranteed. But after his first few crops failed to produce any notable winners, in 1994, he was sold to Japan's JS Company. He stood at Arrow Stud, on the island of Hokkaido, Japan, from 1995 through 2000.

While he was initially popular with Japanese breeders (Ferdy covered 77 mares in his first year abroad), interest steadily waned, and he bred just 10 mares in his final season.

In 2003, Ferdinand's breeders, the Keck family, inquired about his status. Barbara Bayer, the Japan correspondent for *Bloodhorse* magazine, searched for Ferdinand on the family's behalf. She ultimately traced him to Japanese horse dealer Yoshikazo Watanabe, who told her the 18-year-old stallion had been sold to him on February 3, 2001. Bayer asked to see Ferdinand.

"Actually, he isn't around anymore," Watanabe told her. "He was disposed of late last year."

In Japan, the term "disposed of" is a euphemism for "sent to slaughter." While the specifics have never been uncovered, all evidence indicates that sometime in 2002, the Eclipse Award winner was slaughtered for pet food.

Disturbingly, racing fans realized it wasn't the first time in recent memory that a former top American racehorse had met his end in a foreign slaughterhouse.

The striking bay stallion Exceller—coincidentally also trained by Whittingham and ridden by Shoemaker—made history as a five-year-old when he won the 1978 Jockey Club Gold Cup, becoming the only horse to ever defeat two Triple Crown winners (Affirmed and Seattle Slew) in the same race. After amassing 15 career wins and earning over $1.6 million in lifetime earnings (this value not adjusted for inflation), Exceller stood at stud for several years at Gainesway Farm in Lexington, Kentucky. He was sold to a Swedish buyer in 1991; a combination of poor results in the breeding shed and his owner's bankruptcy led to Exceller's slaughterhouse death in April 1997.

Although news of Exceller's death caused a ripple of concern among racing enthusiasts (and, perhaps in response, he was posthumously inducted into the US Racing Hall of Fame in 1999), it was Ferdinand's ignoble ending that truly stunned the American Thoroughbred community. Whittingham passed away in 1999, but Shoemaker was still alive and reeled from the news.

"It's very disturbing," Shoemaker said in a July 2003 *New York Times* article. "He was a real good horse…I guess he wasn't reproducing well and ended up in a slaughterhouse. It wouldn't have happened over here."

Perhaps not for a horse like Ferdinand, who played such a pivotal role in the careers of racing royalty. But at the time, only a handful of organizations were seeking to provide alternative options for those horses running lower on the race card—particularly geldings, who had no future value in the breeding shed. Planning for a Thoroughbred's post-track career simply wasn't part of the culture; in fact, of the 62,000 horses slaughtered in the United States in 2001, an estimated 10 percent were former Thoroughbred racehorses. Although some American racing fans didn't want to acknowledge it, washed up racehorses were still being tossed aside like a losing ticket on a $2 bet.

But the slaughterhouse deaths of first Exceller and later Ferdinand—two well-bred, highly regarded stallions—proved that no Thoroughbred was immune from suffering such a fate, and racing enthusiasts began to demand change. From this outcry, the world of Thoroughbred aftercare emerged, tentatively at first, but in the years to come, with growing momentum and industry-wide support. Defined by the Thoroughbred Aftercare Alliance as the "care, retraining, and rehoming of a racehorse once the horse leaves the racetrack," the word "aftercare" has gone from needing explanation to being an everyday part of racing vocabulary. Today, planning for a racehorse's post-track career (or careers) is not only expected, it has become normalized, and in some racing jurisdictions, the once-common practice of discarding ex-racehorses at a low-end auction can lose you your license.

Currently, the Thoroughbred Aftercare Alliance, an industry-supported nonprofit organization dedicated to funding and accrediting aftercare programs, endorses the work of 86 distinct groups, each specializing in meeting a different facet of a racehorse's post-track needs. Since 2012, Thoroughbred Aftercare Alliance accredited organizations have assisted nearly 18,000 former racehorses, whether that be through providing permanent sanctuary, rehabilitation, retraining, and rehoming services, or managing incentive programs to make the adoption of former racehorses more appealing to the greater equestrian community.

There are many lessons to be learned from the success story of Thoroughbred aftercare, ranging from the massive sea change in industry attitudes toward the practice to the recognition of work yet to be done. But perhaps the most important of these is proving that tremendous evolution is possible when the horse community unites for the good of the animal they love.

THE POPULARITY OF HORSE RACING has ebbed and flowed in the United States. In the late 1800s, just over 300 tracks existed across the country; however, a rising tide of anti-gambling sentiment left only 25 still in operation by 1908. But when the Great Depression hit in the 1930s, pari-mutuel gambling was legalized in hopes of boosting the economy, and the sport was suddenly reborn. Famous tracks like Santa Anita, Del Mar, and Hollywood Park in California, Suffolk Downs in Massachusetts, Keeneland in Kentucky, and Gulfstream Park in Florida were all built between 1934 and 1939. Triple Crown winners Gallant Fox, Omaha, and War Admiral drew crowds in the thousands—citizens looking for something to cheer for—and the victories of underdogs like Seabiscuit gave hope to the desperate masses.

World War II effectively ended the Great Depression and also quelled the popularity of racing for several decades. But the sport experienced a resurgence in the 1970s, thanks largely to the success of a powerful copper-colored colt named Secretariat. After a 25-year gap, Secretariat captured the Triple Crown and the covers of *Time, Newsweek,* and *Sports Illustrated*; he was a runner-up for the 1973 *Sports Illustrated* Sportsman of the Year. His dominance drew fans back to racetracks across the country, and when Seattle Slew and Affirmed both netted the Triple Crown in back-to-back seasons at the end of the decade, the sport's popularity seemed secure.

However, for those who loved the tradition of horse racing—standing trackside to view the favorites, watching trainers saddle their charges in the paddock area, handicappers and fans alike anxiously rolling the *Daily Racing Forum* in hand while the animals were led to post—racing had changed. In a 1987 *Boston Globe* article, the horses are referred to as "byproducts" of the racing industry, and with simulcasting, bettors could gather in remote locations to wager on meets across the country, never once setting foot at a racing venue. At the same time, increased legalization of casinos and slot machines gave patrons options besides the horses on which to exercise their luck in games of chance.

In 1980, total attendance at North American Thoroughbred tracks was just over 55 million. By 1986, when Ferdinand won the Kentucky Derby, it was down 5.1 percent, to roughly 52 million. One year later, it was down another 3 million. In the years to follow, this downward trend in attendance continued, and industry leaders grew increasingly concerned. For all of horse racing's history and pageantry—after all, it is still dubbed "the sport of kings"—it seemed to be losing widespread appeal.

Industry insiders believe this is due, at least in part, to the general public's increasing concern for the welfare of the animals themselves. The well-broadcast stories of Exceller and Ferdinand's deaths were followed by several nationally televised breakdowns of famous horses at premier events. In 2006, Kentucky Derby winner Barbaro shattered his right hind leg in the Preakness Stakes, and despite aggressive attempts to save him, was ultimately euthanized; two years later, the filly Eight Belles suffered catastrophic fractures in both front legs after finishing second in the 2008 Kentucky Derby and was euthanized on the track. Equally significant was the rise of social media in the 2000s; suddenly, photos and information about down-on-their-luck former racehorses was available to the masses at the click of a mouse.

In 2011, The Jockey Club (which maintains the official American Thoroughbred studbook and generally provides cohesion to the nation's racing industry) commissioned the management consulting firm McKinsey and Company to "analyze racing's economics for the next 10 years and recommend initiatives that could significantly improve the outlook for the sport." In the resulting report, analysts noted racing attendance had declined by 30 percent in the previous decade, and even more chilling for the sport's longevity, it was losing fans at the rate of 4 percent a year. Further, their analysis indicated one of the major reasons for this decline was related to "brand perception"—only 19 percent of the general public had a "positive impression of Thoroughbred racing," and even among racing fans, only 46 percent would recommend the sport to others.

A January 2016 Harris poll showed that only 1 percent of Americans listed horse racing as their favorite sport, and it ranked thirteenth overall, behind arguably less dramatic athletic pursuits, like swimming or track and field. And although premier racing events—such as the Kentucky Derby and Breeder's Cup—remained popular, even American Pharaoh's 2015 Triple Crown victory, which ended a 37-year drought, did little to boost spectator attendance at the series.

In a 2018 follow-up analysis, McKinsey and Company found fairly similar results in regards to public perception of horse racing—this, despite several years of concerted effort to reframe the sport's image. In a presentation that year, The Jockey Club's President and Chief Operating Officer, James L. Gagliano, said, "One of the big issues in racing's public perception continues to be on the matter of animal welfare." He went on to state that in a survey of the entire fanbase, "the top concern was treatment of horses after retirement."

"When horses end up in a risky situation, Thoroughbreds are easily identifiable, because of their tattoos [and now microchips], which makes us more susceptible to criticism," explains Stacie Clark Rogers, operations consultant with the Thoroughbred Aftercare Alliance. "Other breeds are not as easily identifiable, so other equine sports are not called out as often."

Clark Rogers has been a fixture in the world of Thoroughbred aftercare since the early 2000s. For nearly a decade, she worked for the Eclipse Award-winning Stronach family, who breed and race Thoroughbreds out of their Adena Springs Farms, with facilities located in Ontario, Canada, Kentucky, and Florida. In 2004, Clark Rogers helped to establish a first-of-its-kind, in-house retirement program at Adena Springs North in Ontario, which during her tenure successfully let down, rehabilitated, and rehomed nearly 500 animals from the Stronach program. She was also involved in developing aftercare programs at the Stronach Group's Santa Anita and Gulfstream Parks. The daughter of Thoroughbred owners and trainers and herself a former jockey, Clark Rogers is passionate about Thoroughbred racing in general, and aftercare in particular.

"At first, it was like the Wild West," she says with a chuckle about the early years of aftercare, which experienced an upsurge in the mid to late aughts. "There wasn't a cohesive, collective thing going on. At the time, it was sort of sporadic, and it was all over the map."

It was in 2011 that trainer Jack Wolf invited Clark Rogers to participate in a gathering of industry leaders—including representatives from The Jockey Club, the National Thoroughbred Racing Association, and a star-studded collection of top trainers, owners, and breeders, as well as other major industry stakeholders—to discuss the public's growing concerns around equine welfare in racing, and other related topics. That initial gathering grew into more talks and more brainstorming, and eventually, the formation of a board. With seed money provided by the Breeder's Cup, The Jockey Club, and the Keeneland Association, the Thoroughbred Aftercare Alliance was officially launched in February 2012 with two main goals: first, to serve as an accrediting body for existing and future aftercare groups, and second, to coordinate fundraising efforts to support them.

"The idea was, if we could get funding from every touch point of a Thoroughbred's life, from conception to retirement, that would become the horse's '401k,'" explains Clark Rogers, who has remained involved with the Thoroughbred Aftercare Alliance since its inception. "Unfortunately, that did not amass to the amount we had predicted or hoped for, because if people contributed in one place they did not feel obligated to contribute at another touch point. But that's how it started, and it has grown from giving out $1 million and accrediting 21 organizations to 86 accredited organizations and giving out over $4.5 million this year."

The Thoroughbred Aftercare Alliance serves as an umbrella organization, helping to support the efforts of individual aftercare programs of varying sizes, across all racing jurisdictions. Obtaining Thoroughbred Aftercare Alliance accreditation is a rigorous process and includes a complete review of the organization's general management practices, financial history and records, governance structure, adoption policies and procedures (if applicable), and herd health management practices. After this material is reviewed and approved by the Thoroughbred Aftercare Alliance board, the applicant's facility is visited by an inspector before official accreditation is granted. Accreditation is good for two years, although organizations are re-inspected annually and must provide quarterly updates on their inventory.

For those organizations receiving accreditation, it is an accolade displayed with pride. The now-familiar blue-and-white "Thoroughbred Aftercare Alliance Accredited" logo shows both adopters and donors that the organization is dedicated to upholding the highest standards of excellence in aftercare. And in addition to providing funding to each of its accredited organizations, the Thoroughbred Aftercare Alliance assists with marketing, networking, and unifying the messaging around aftercare as a whole.

"A rising tide floats all boats," says Clark Rogers. "When an organization becomes accredited, they become part of the family, and they lose some of that competitiveness with other organizations. We meet about once a month, and our groups have evolved for the better by getting to know, and learning from, each other.

"Being accredited gets these organizations to be part of a greater good," she continues. "We need one voice, so it's really clear in all of our racing jurisdictions what aftercare is and why it matters. We can tick away at the big ones, but to get to the smaller tracks, the smaller horsemen's groups, the smaller breeders, and help them understand this is important— we need this collective voice."

Since its inception, the Thoroughbred Aftercare Alliance has disbursed nearly $32 million to its accredited organizations, despite the original pathway to sustainable funding conceived by its founders not coming to fruition as intended. However, with the number of accredited organizations steadily increasing, the Thoroughbred Aftercare Alliance must also keep pace in its fundraising efforts to maintain a high level of grant support. Today, it relies on a combination of industry-based and private donations.

On the industry side of things, financial contributions come from several pillars of the racing community, which has brought increased validity to the Thoroughbred Aftercare Alliance's work. The Jockey Club remains one of the organization's biggest financial supporters, largely through the collection of fees in conjunction with certain mandatory registry-related transactions. Several racetracks (including Keeneland, Churchill Downs, 1/ ST Racing, and NYRA) all make an annual contribution, and several sales companies (such as Fasig-Tipton, Ocala Breeders' Sales, Keeneland, Texas Thoroughbred Association, Wanamaker's, and Canadian Thoroughbred Horse Society Ontario) match the fees paid by buyers and consignors who agree to donate a small percentage of monies from their sales. Funding also comes from several top breeding farms, who commit to donating a percentage of their stallions' stud fees.

Thoroughbred Aftercare Alliance leaders are grateful for the loyal support of these industry principals, but note it is essential for all levels and facets of the racing industry to become involved in funding the aftercare effort.

"The mindset has to change," says Clark Rogers. "This isn't fundraising; it's a part of doing business in the industry. That attitude change came very quickly for some, while others are still dragging their heels. We are talking about the change in consciousness and the right to social license. If we want people to like our industry, and want to support it, we need to show we are doing right by the horses.

"We wouldn't exist without sustainable funding. It's better than it was, but it can be much better. When Thoroughbred Aftercare Alliance started, it wasn't going to be a fundraising model, it was going to be an industry-initiative supported model. It has had to evolve."

To that end, Thoroughbred Aftercare Alliance staff coordinates events and marketing campaigns dedicated to promoting aftercare awareness, as well as creative fundraising efforts in support of its accredited organizations.

"While the racing industry is a key supporter, we are constantly having to work on fundraising to sustain supporting the organizations we provide grants to," explains Samantha Smith, director of marketing and communications for the organization. "We offer ways to set up recurring donations, trainer pledges, donations from fans, or in honor of or in memory of a special horse. There are many ways to support."

In an effort to share ideas and find creative solutions, the Thoroughbred Aftercare Alliance is a member of the International Forum for the Aftercare of Racehorses (IFAR). Members include regulatory bodies, aftercare organizations, racetracks, industry groups, media companies, and individuals from around the world, all with an interest in promoting the aftercare movement. From this worldwide network, ideas and inspiration flow in all directions.

"We have changed as a society, for the better," says Clark Rogers. "There has been a change in consciousness toward how we treat other sentient beings. There is a change in tolerance for what we expect animals should be enduring for us. Racing is a great sport—it's fun, it's exciting, and we love to see horses race. But at the end of the day, we are a fan-based industry, and in order to have a fan of the sport, they have to feel good about it."

OVER 30 YEARS AGO, New Vocations Racehorse Adoption Program founder and executive director Dot Morgan realized she was facing the prospect of needing a new career. Her two daughters were young adults and required less support from her; although she kept busy enough managing her family's broodmares and running their farm in Laura, Ohio, she felt as if she still had more to give.

"I had a teaching certificate in agriculture, and I knew I could go to work for a feed company, or teach," says Dot. "But I wanted God's direction for my life, and I spent serious time praying. If I'd known what was coming, I would have turned and run the other way—it would have scared me to death," she adds with a laugh. "But that, I believe, is one of the reasons God doesn't show us the future."

At the time, Dot didn't know anything about kill buyers or the slaughter industry, and she didn't think too much about what happened to a racehorse when he was no longer suitable for racing. She and her husband Charley Morgan, a fifth-generation Standardbred breeder and trainer, were proud members of the Ohio Harness Horsemen's Association and the Ohio Harness Horse Breeders Association, and people in these organizations weren't talking about those kinds of things, either.

But one fall day in 1991, Dot went with Charley to the local fairgrounds where he trained their youngsters and watched while a dealer loaded horse after horse into his stock trailer. She assumed these Standardbreds must be injured or lame, but when she asked, the man told her there was nothing wrong with them—just that they were done racing, and he was hauling them to auction.

"He told me by the time he would get to the sale, two or three of them would have fallen on the floor, and the rest would be walking all over them," remembers Dot. "Then he said, 'Who would want such a crazy horse?' Well, I knew better than that. They'd been treated like hot house orchids, and they'd never been hauled like that in their lives, in a stock trailer with no mats, slipping in their feces. They were terrified.

"When I started delving into what was going on, I learned that was what most people did—sent them off to the dealer's if they were done with them," she continues. "These owners and breeders were part of that generation where horses were livestock, and when livestock is through with its productiveness, it goes to never-never land, and you never worry about them again. But it was pretty much swept under the carpet."

Dot began researching other options for retired racehorses. She came up with only two organizations working to fill that niche—the Thoroughbred Retirement Foundation and the Standardbred Retirement Foundation (although they have similar names, the two groups are totally independent of one another). At the time, both organizations were more focused on providing sanctuary than on rehoming efforts, and between the two of them, were caring for several hundred animals.

"Once they were full, they couldn't take any more horses, and they weren't trying to adopt the horses they had," says Dot. "It was a dead-end business model. I thought, 'There needs to be a sustainable business model,' because you can't 'warehouse' these horses for the rest of their lives. The horses needed an intermediary to stand in the gap for them, to get them into homes."

Dot—whose extensive equestrian experience included work with both Standardbreds and Thoroughbreds, as well as traditional ridden disciplines—realized she could be what these horses needed, someone who could link the broader equestrian community with the racing community. Not only did she have extensive connections within the world of racing, she knew retiring racehorses were well-cared for, well-trained athletes, and with some reschooling, would be suitable for most equestrian pursuits. She also knew that with their generally more sensitive temperaments, Thoroughbreds were especially likely to find themselves in trouble once their racing days were over.

"I learned that if Standardbreds were basically sound, the Amish were taking quite a few of them to use for transportation," says Dot. "But the Thoroughbreds didn't have an outlet like that, and they were a lot more spirited and took a more experienced person to handle than the Standardbreds did. So they were more at risk."

Dot hung copies of a handwritten, 12-inch by 14-inch poster at tracks in Ohio and Kentucky in 1992. She doesn't remember the exact wording, but it said something like "Don't let your horse go to the killers—call me and I'll find a good home for it." She also took out a small ad in the *Bloodhorse*, saying basically the same thing. Almost immediately, her phone began to ring—and it hasn't stopped since.

The first horses to arrive came from the barn of a forward-thinking Eclipse Award winning trainer in Louisiana.

"They were relatively sound," remembers Dot. "They had some old injuries—tendons and ankles and knees—but they were sound enough to be ridden. I rode them, my daughter rode them, and we took pictures and put them in the local newspapers."

Once those horses found new homes, a few more came in to take their place.

"It was just my personal mission at that point," says Dot.

And for the better part of five years, that was how things remained. Horses (mostly Thoroughbreds, but some Standardbreds as well) came to Dot directly from their owners, and she committed to finding them good homes, usually by placing print ads in local and regional publications or via word of mouth. Adopters paid a small fee and were required to send Dot regular updates on their horse's progress, complete with photos. As this was the early days of the internet, most of that communication happened via snail mail, and Dot still has a drawer full of old progress photos from her nascent efforts in racehorse adoption.

"It worked out very well, and the owners of the horses loved what we were doing," says Dot.

At the same time, Dot tried to raise awareness that not only did retiring racehorses deserve a second career, most were ready to step into almost any niche people could imagine. She began attending trade fairs, including the first ever Equine Affaire in Ohio in 1994 (they haven't missed one since), where they spoke to attendees, sold swag with adoption-themed logos, and generally promoted the idea of using an adopted ex-racehorse as a recreational mount.

"I had to prove the Standardbreds make good riding horses," remembers Dot. "The Thoroughbreds were proven as riding horses, but they started to fall out of favor when Warmbloods came on the scene—they were big, fancy, and quieter than a Thoroughbred. So both Standardbreds and Thoroughbreds needed to be promoted for what they can do.

"The equestrian world accepted us a bit better than the racing world, at first," she continues with a chuckle. "But then, as the racing world saw these horses being successful in the equestrian world, it tugged on their heartstrings—that this is the alternative to not knowing where they're going. This is the alternative to them maybe going to slaughter, that horse who made you so proud in the winner's circle, who won trophies and awards for you. We had to grow their awareness."

Eventually (and thanks to an influential conversation with a "prominent Thoroughbred owner"), Dot agreed to transform her "personal mission" into a registered 501(c)3 nonprofit, primarily so owners could write off the donation of their horse. New Vocations Racehorse Adoption Program received its legal nonprofit status in 1999, and was one of the first organizations to be awarded Thoroughbred Aftercare Alliance accreditation in 2013, making it one of the earliest leaders in the field of aftercare.

"I was really quite happy with the way it was going, and I didn't want to deal with the red tape," says Dot with a laugh about her initial reluctance to become a registered nonprofit organization. "But he twisted my arm when he said, 'You'll be able to help a lot more horses.' And once the process was complete, the horses just started flooding in."

New Vocations quickly evolved from what had begun as essentially a one-woman show to a wide-reaching network, including a main base at Merewith Farm in Lexington, Kentucky, eight satellite facilities, and four rehabs, all overseen by a team of independent contractors and paid staff. Both of Dot's now adult daughters, Winnie Nemeth and Anna Ford, are involved with the program as the Standardbred and Thoroughbred program directors, respectively. To date, New Vocations has placed over 9,000 former racehorses into new homes, and that number is still growing every year. They call themselves the "nation's largest racehorse adoption program," and have garnered a sterling reputation in the world of aftercare.

"These horses are *not* unwanted—they are unneeded," Dot clarifies. "Their owners care a lot about them, or they wouldn't send them to us. One of the keys that has made us so successful, besides our faith in God—and I truly believe He has His hand on this program and on every single horse— is we not only knew the racing side of things, we knew the equestrian side of things," she continues. "We understood what it took to be a nice pleasure horse or a show horse, and we understood all the different injuries because we dealt with them all the time in our own racehorses."

New Vocations still places both Thoroughbreds and Standardbreds, in about an 80–20 split. When new animals come into their program, they are immediately evaluated by a New Vocations trainer, who assesses the horse's temperament, suitability for a purpose other than racing, and soundness. Adopters frequently cite the ability of the New Vocations team to select just the right horse for their needs and abilities as one of the many reasons they would recommend the program.

"Our trainers start evaluating them from the second they step off that horse trailer," says Dot. "If they have an injury, we'll have our vets come and do what needs to be done, and if they need to go to rehab, each of our facilities either has a rehab nearby, or they have rehab stalls on their premises. The horses get the time off they need—whether it's a month, four months, six months, or occasionally, even as much as a year."

Even horses with injuries serious enough to generally preclude future soundness are given several months to rest and heal. If they don't come sound, first, the animal's donor is given the opportunity to resume ownership; otherwise, New Vocations finds him a sanctuary home, provided the horse's condition will not set him up for a lifetime of pain and suffering.

"The ones that will be in pain the rest of their lives, we are not going to try to put them anywhere else," says Dot. "We think that's the most humane thing to do. If they are comfortable but unrideable, we can usually find them a place to go."

AS WORD ABOUT NEW VOCATIONS spread, and especially once social media made sharing news about its work easier, horses and adopters alike began coming from farther and farther afield. In 2023, New Vocations accepted horses from 40 different tracks across the country—and animals went to new homes in 34 states.

Dot doesn't necessarily expect an adopter to keep her horse for the rest of his life; she appreciates that horses live a long time, and that goals and circumstances change. But all New Vocations horses are sent to their new homes with a copy of a conditional bill of sale, letting future owners know the horse will always have a home with the program.

"We keep our adoption fees low, because we know that acquiring the horse is the cheapest part," says Dot. "But we have strings attached— they cannot sell the horse for 12 months, and during that time, they have to update us at three, six, and nine months with current pictures and a paragraph telling us what they're doing. If an adopter has problems they can't work through, the horse has to come back to us."

Although the organization won't adopt to a first-time horse owner or a complete beginner—in the application, potential adopters must demonstrate they have previous experience with green horses—applicants otherwise represent the breadth of equestrian sport, from riders with top competitive aspirations to those simply looking for a pleasant and willing pleasure mount. And as it turns out, there are plenty of Thoroughbreds who can fill any and all of these niches.

When Dr. Jenna Encheff's beloved but aging Quarter Horse gelding needed to reduce his workload in 2009, she only had a handful of criteria for her next mount. First, because she didn't own a trailer, the animal needed to be located close enough to her home outside of Toledo, Ohio, that she could convince a friend to pick him up. Second, the horse needed to enjoy trail riding, preferably in a Western saddle—she wasn't interested in a fancy, overly athletic, show horse type. And finally, the horse needed to be available for adoption. Encheff was familiar with the world of kill buyers and slaughterhouses, and because she "didn't have lofty goals," she was committed to offering a home to a horse that might not suit a rider with greater ambitions.

Encheff learned to ride on Quarter Horses; her first horse, TG, whom she purchased with her own money when she was a teenager, was a Quarter Horse, and she admits she sort of assumed she would always own Quarter Horses. She had never considered adopting a Thoroughbred, but when she found New Vocations through an online search and saw they had a farm in Marysville, Ohio, she decided it was worth a look.

"I didn't know much about Thoroughbreds at the time, except from racing," says Encheff. "I knew they were beautiful. I had a chat with the adoption manager, told her I wanted a horse that was going to be safe and quiet, and decided to put in an application."

Encheff was heading home from work when she got the call she had been approved. She was so excited she had to pull over to the side of the road to celebrate the news. The adoption manager had matched her with two potential horses, and a short time later, she went to meet them in person.

"They were both bays, and I love my plain bays," says Encheff with a chuckle.

Ultimately, she went with the adoption manager's recommendation and picked a six-year-old gelding registered with The Jockey Club as A Little Elusive, but known around the barn as Shorty. At 15.3 hands, he had a build similar to her Quarter Horse and an easy-going temperament. Because he had raced in New Orleans, Encheff renamed her new horse Jazz.

"She seemed to really know what I wanted," says Encheff of the adoption manager. "The process, and transition, was super easy—and that's why I went back for two more!"

In 2013, Encheff added a gray gelding named Rat Like Cunning to her herd; called The Rat at the track, she renamed him Mishka (which means "mouse" in Bulgarian, a nod to both his original name and her own ethnic heritage). A member of the first foal crop from Kentucky Derby and Preakness Stakes winner Silver Charm, Mishka raced until he was 13 years old.

"I was looking for an older horse that I could still ride if I wanted to, who needed a softer landing," says Encheff. "Crazily enough, he's now my go-to trail horse. He's definitely a blue-collar horse; he worked hard on the track, and he's still working now."

Then, late in 2019, she adopted a third New Vocations horse—Nevis Peak, a three-year-old chestnut son of the famous Bluegrass Cat, who never made it to the track due to his petite size and a bone chip in a fetlock. She calls him Keno, in honor of her late grandfather.

Encheff's trio of Thoroughbred geldings live in a field with a huge run-in shed at her house; they are all barefoot (she trims them herself), completely sound, and rarely even require blanketing in winter.

"You hear that all Thoroughbreds are hot, and crazy, and all they want to do is run," says Encheff. "But Jazz and Keno are the laziest horses ever. Thoroughbreds have their quirks, but if you have patience and time—like with any other horse—you work through it."

Today, Encheff knows more about Thoroughbred bloodlines than Quarter Horses, and proudly volunteers at the New Vocations booth at the Kentucky Three-Day Event every April, where she tells anyone who will listen about her experience with adopting ex-racehorses.

"There are so many quality horses, and I think adopting is the way to go," says Encheff. "Where could I ever get a son of Silver Charm for $400? You get these quality bloodlines, for a reasonable cost—and make space for new ones to come into the organization."

Pleasure rider and lifelong horsewoman Pat Robinson subscribes to a similar philosophy. Originally from the mid-Atlantic region, 40 years ago she moved to her 80-acre Moonshadow Farm in Tyrone, Missouri, a town in the Ozark foothills so small it isn't on most maps. For many years, Robinson visited the local auctions and bought down-on-their-luck horses for the purpose of rehabilitating, training, and rehoming; she estimates she's helped as many as 70 horses at risk, mostly Quarter Horses, find new homes. But along the way, she also picked up a handful of Thoroughbreds, often still wearing racing plates, and has always admired the breed.

"I didn't keep many of them for myself," says Robinson of her rescues, whom she supported by working two or three jobs at once. "But when I'd lose a horse or place a horse, I got another horse, as long as I had the room."

Robinson first learned of New Vocations "sometime around 2011" when she stopped by their booth at an event at the Kentucky Horse Park. She had always wanted a Standardbred for use as a trail horse, and when Robinson found out the organization would adopt to her in Missouri, she put in her application.

"After my first experience, I was in love with the program," she continues. "[New Vocations] was outstanding to work with."

Her first Standardbred, Medal Play, proved to be a wonderful trail mount—reliable and steady—but ultimately, Robinson decided he was too tall. At close to 17 hands, it was impossible for Robinson to mount him from the ground, and she knew she couldn't always count on having a handy rock or stump nearby.

"I ride out in the middle of nowhere, by myself," says Robinson. "And it could be miles to walk back to the trailer."

But one of Robinson's trainers had always admired Medal Play, so the gelding moved to his farm and became a mount for his three young children. And as it turned out, when Robinson let New Vocations know the horse had been rehomed, they had recently acquired a Standardbred in need of a unique placement—and they hoped Robinson might be his match. At 15 years old and with a lifetime of use leading to chronic issues, Rome Warrior was deemed only suitable as a pasture pet or for light riding. After Robinson heard his backstory—treasured by his late breeder/trainer, the horse had changed hands more than 15 times since the man's death— Robinson moved Rome Warrior to what would become his final home at Moonshadow Farm.

"He was an absolute delight—he was one of the most fun horses I've ever had," says Robinson with a catch in her voice. "Just because you don't ride them, it doesn't mean they won't be the best thing that ever happened to you."

Robinson got into the habit of keeping an eye on the New Vocations page, looking for horses with quirks, or those who otherwise needed a special situation—and she learned that New Vocations had the habit of not giving up on these types of horses. Over the years, Robinson and the team at New Vocations developed an unofficial partnership of sorts, and the mutual respect between them is palpable.

Robinson has adopted a total of 10 New Vocations horses (six Standardbreds and four Thoroughbreds), almost of all of which fell into the "difficult to adopt" category. Her first Thoroughbred from the program was a gelding named Sonny's Circus, who had trailering issues; her second was a mare named Pal's First Lady, who had been adopted and returned to the program twice.

"We love Pat [Robinson]," says Dot. "She is extremely conscientious, and offers to take some of the horses that are with us a long time, usually due to physical limitations or temperament. She lovingly works with them, within their capacity, and then after a year or more if she finds the perfect home, she transfers them and takes another that needs her patient attention."

"I'm 73 years old, and I need a horse that's reasonably quiet and is a good trail horse," says Robinson. "And every time, that's exactly what they've found for me. And I've emailed them about some horse I thought would be perfect for me, and they've said, 'No, maybe not.' I admire that. They're not just trying to find a home for a horse, they're trying to make a lifelong placement for that horse, and I think that's important. I certainly feel now when they say, 'Yeah, he's probably going to be a good trail horse,' he's probably going to be a good trail horse."

But third generation professional horsewoman Katie Gardner was looking for a true equine athlete when she contacted New Vocations. Both her late grandmother, the legendary show pony breeder Eileen Beckman, and her mother, Randee Beckman, taught Gardner from an early age that not only are Thoroughbreds the original sport horse, they are truly a *horseman's* horse.

"Thoroughbreds care about the relationship," says Gardner, who is based at her family's Otteridge Farm in Bedford, Virginia. "They are more sensitive than Warmbloods, they're a lot smarter, and things matter more to them, as individuals."

As a teenager, Gardner showed in the hunters on her first Thoroughbred, Silver Screen, under the watchful eye of coaches Olin and Sally Armstrong. She credits her time with that horse and those trainers with turning her from being "a bit of a cowboy" on horseback to a softer, more educated rider. But it was an unexpected, longtime partnership with a special off-track Thoroughbred that sealed her passion for the breed.

Struggler's Legend raced sporadically, with modest results, until he was six. He was striking, with a beautiful bay coat, two white socks, a broad blaze, and elegant movement; in 2008, his previous owners gave him to Gardner's mother, saying the gelding had been kicked around a bit and needed a break. They thought he might make a nice pleasure mount for her use.

"I never laid eyes on him until I went to unload him," remembers Gardner. "By the time we got down the ramp together, he was no longer my mother's horse. That horse is who put me on the map with Thoroughbreds."

Gardner—who has a degree in musical theater from Lynchburg College and a deep love of old Hollywood—renamed her new horse Frankly My Dear (a nod to *Gone With the Wind*), and for the next 15 years, the pair earned countless tri-color ribbons at horse shows up and down the East Coast. Although primarily a hunter, "Frank" and Gardner also experienced success in the jumper ring and on the line. When they weren't competing, they were foxhunting with Deep Run Hunt, trying out sidesaddle, or jumping courses at home without a bridle.

"You name it, I've done it with him," says Gardner. "He is once in a lifetime. I will never have another Frank."

But in May 2021, the year he turned 20, Frank needed some time off due to an injury. Although he eventually made a complete recovery, Gardner acknowledged it might be time to look for a younger prospect to bring along—and she knew exactly what breed that horse would be.

"For me, there has never been any option but a Thoroughbred, ever," says Gardner. "And that's because of Frank. Never say never, but I can't imagine myself with a personal horse that isn't a Thoroughbred. I love them, I understand them, I ride them well, and I know how to train them."

She was committed to adopting, not purchasing, her next Thoroughbred, and put in an application with New Vocations. One day in October 2021, Gardner was scrolling her social media when her eye was caught by the photo of a striking black three-year-old gelding by More Than Ready, available at the program's Lexington, Kentucky, facility. The youngster had been in race training but never made a start. Instantly, she knew she had found her next horse.

"I didn't see a video or anything, just this one photo on Instagram," Gardner admits with a laugh. "But he was put together great. I sent the email saying I wanted to adopt him, and *then* I went looking for his videos."

Gardner was on a tour of Thomas Jefferson's Monticello when she got the call from the adoption manager; she sprinted down the mountain to get her credit card to pay the adoption fee on the spot. In another ode to Hollywood, she rechristened her new horse Sunset Boulevard, with a barn name of Max.

"He is a fantastic mover, and a fantastic jumper," says Gardner. "He showed eight times his four-year-old year, and came home champion six times, and reserve twice."

Since then, Gardner has helped several of her amateur clients select and produce New Vocations Thoroughbreds of their own. And while other young professionals may steer their clients toward Warmbloods, Gardner finds Thoroughbreds suit her clientele just fine.

"The thing is, there is less commission money to be made, obtaining an American Thoroughbred for your customer versus importing a six-figure horse from Europe," says Gardner. "But when you treat these Thoroughbreds like quality horses, you get a quality horse. They perform like quality horses."

Gardner admits she will always be a huge advocate for racehorse adoption, and praises the work done by aftercare organizations like New Vocations to find new purpose for these animals.

"We hear about the 5 percent of racing owners or trainers who will dump at auctions, but I think that's not the norm," says Gardner. "What programs like New Vocations and others have done is made aftercare a viable option. They've gotten the racing connection, and the tracks, and The Jockey Club, and all these big entities in Thoroughbred racing to believe it's the thing to do now. Which is amazing, because it didn't used to be like that." She pauses.

"It shows the horse community can do some great stuff—if we make up our minds to work together."

IN THE LATE 1970s, a young advertising executive from New Jersey read a magazine article detailing the uncertain and frequently traumatic fate many Thoroughbreds faced when they were no longer suitable for racing. It would have been easy to put down the magazine and walk away. Instead, Monique Koehler decided to do something about it. She was going to establish a program "to save Thoroughbred horses no longer able to compete on the racetrack from possible neglect, abuse, and slaughter." Over four decades later, and despite a few hiccups along the way, the Thoroughbred Retirement Foundation remains committed to its original mission.

By the early 80s, Koehler had managed to garner support for her idea but was struggling to find an affordable facility suitable to house retired racehorses. Enter her friend New York State Senator Howard Nolan, a racing enthusiast and Thoroughbred owner who later in his career went on to become president of the New York Thoroughbred Breeder's Association and chairman of the Breeder's Cup. One day, Nolan noticed an abandoned dairy barn adjacent to the New York State Department of Corrections detention center in Wallkill, a rural hamlet about two hours north of New York City. At one time, the Department ran beef and dairy farms at many of its prisons, but the program had been suspended; Nolan recognized that the idyllic 100-acre property could be converted for horses.

That was in 1983, and it took nearly a year and a half to complete the necessary logistical, legal, and facility infrastructure required to support the TRF Second Chances Program, a unique collaboration between Koehler's Thoroughbred Retirement Foundation and the state of New York's Department of Corrections. The state agreed to provide the land and labor; the Thoroughbred Retirement Foundation, using its horses and staff, would create, implement, and maintain an equine management-focused vocational training program for incarcerated people approaching parole eligibility.

In some ways, both ideas were well ahead of their time. In the early eighties, not only was the concept of planning for aftercare virtually unheard of within the racing industry, this kind of collaborative vocational training program was a complete unknown.

"We still have the original contract, written on a typewriter," says Chelsea O'Reilly, director of equine programs for the Thoroughbred Retirement Foundation, now headquartered in Saratoga Springs, New York. "It says, 'This is an untried vocational training system.' I've never seen anything like that in a contract before—basically saying, 'Everyone, take a breath, it will be okay. If there are issues, let's talk about it.' They would never allow something like that now.

"Most organizations start with horses and grow into something around the healing of people," she continues. "This did it from the get-go."

The first horse to take up residence at the Wallkill Correctional Facility was Promised Road, a nine-year-old gelding whose nine wins in 64 starts all came in claiming races. His generally undistinguished racing career became somewhat emblematic of the type of horses that would find their way into Thoroughbred Retirement Foundation care. With few alternative options at the time and a pervasive mindset within the racing industry that they were not responsible for the animals past their racing days, initially, horses coming to the Foundation were a mixed bag. Some were rideable, some were only pasture sound; all needed a safe place to land. In the years to come, as organizations like New Vocations began to offer retraining and placement programs for rideable ex-racehorses, the Thoroughbred Retirement Foundation began to focus more exclusively on providing lifetime sanctuary for animals unlikely to adjust to a second career.

"If the horse is four to six years old and super sound, we try to steer them elsewhere," says O'Reilly. "But if they are older, or a broodmare who's had five foals, or they have a slab fracture, or kissing spines, or hock arthritis—those are our horses."

Today, the Thoroughbred Retirement Foundation cares for 400 animals, living on 15 farms in 8 states. Eight of those farms are associated with a correctional facility and home to a TRF Second Chances Program; the remainder are private sanctuaries, caring for anywhere from 3 to 60 animals. With an average age in their herd of 22 years, death, whether from natural causes or due to the infirmities of old age, is a not-uncommon occurrence. But new horses can only join the Foundation's herd if an existing member passes away or is adopted. Their waitlist is generally first come, first served, and fluctuates from the single digits to as many as 40 animals.

Although adoption is not the main focus, the Foundation does place a handful of horses into new homes each year; frequently, these are animals who have been part of the herd for an extended period due to performance-limiting injuries or related issues. But thanks to a combination of attentive care from participants in the TRF Second Chances Program and the tincture of time, some animals eventually return to mental and physical soundness.

"We do try to pull the sound horses, because they're using a spot for a horse that truly needs sanctuary," explains O'Reilly. "A fun thing for me is to pull horses from the prisons—who, eight years later, that bowed tendon looks pretty good, or horses that just needed a mental break for five years—and see them go on to second careers.

"There is a honey hole of people who would like teenaged, sound horses, who don't want or need that four-year-old chestnut mare with white socks straight off the track," she continues with a laugh. "What they need is the 16-year-old bay gelding who has been working with the inmates for 10 years."

But if there is any concern at all around long-term soundness, the animal will remain under Foundation care and supervision—and should a former resident require a home in the future, they immediately get bumped to the top of the waitlist.

As aftercare options have become both more available and accessible, the Foundation's staff has noticed a shift in the type of animal requiring their sanctuary services. They consider this change a good thing, because it seems to indicate the racing industry is prioritizing preserving soundness over running a fading horse "one more time."

"States have come up with funnel programs, like Take the Lead in New York, or Beyond the Wire in Maryland, which helps to connect trainers to aftercare programs," says O'Reilly. "Those programs know that sound horses are easier to transition and place, so they are being retired earlier, and sounder. When we do get inquiries from the track, it is usually for horses needing let-down time, or with major, career-ending injuries."

These days, the Foundation gets most of its calls from private individuals looking to responsibly rehome a Thoroughbred whom they can no longer care for. Often these horses are older, or have chronic issues, making them a perfect fit for TRF Second Chances Programs, where they become invaluable teachers for participants who learn how to recognize, manage, and handle various common equine conditions.

"The majority of horses now come from private entities, when the horse is done with their third, fourth, or fifth career," says O'Reilly. "We are taking them later in life."

In general, horses in need of more intense monitoring, care, or support, are sent to a TRF Second Chances Program facility, where participants can manage their daily needs. Horses with fewer requirements tend to be sent to a sanctuary farm, but occasionally, animals transition between the two types of facilities.

"The perfect instance is when I have a sanctuary farm next to a prison, so they can work off each other," says O'Reilly. "And we have that almost everywhere. With a herd of 400, it's interesting to see which types of horses thrive where, or which types of injuries are best overseen at certain places."

CLEARLY, THE FACT AN ORGANIZATION like the Thoroughbred Retirement Foundation exists has benefited thousands of animals in its

40 years. But equally significant is the impact these animals have had on the incarcerated people who care for and learn from them. Currently, the majority of TRF Second Chances Program participants are men; the program at the Lowell Correctional Facility in Florida serves only women, while another in the same state works with juveniles. Most of the time, participants have no previous experience with horses, and despite occasional initial reluctance, ultimately find themselves transformed.

"This is such a game-changer for the guys," says O'Reilly. "The theme I hear from every single farm manager is that when the guys first come out, they are very selfish. There's lots of, 'Poor me…why am I here…it's not my fault…I shouldn't have to be doing this.'

"It's usually at about three months you start to hear the self*less* talk. They say, 'Did so-and-so get their meds today,' or, 'So-and-so looks funny on that foot.' There is a change in mentality that happens, just by getting them out of the prison and onto the farm."

The TRF Second Chances Program is based around the Groom Elite curriculum, which the Thoroughbred Retirement Foundation has licensed for use at each of its facilities. The skills participants acquire range from those related to general horse handling and farm management to developing feeding plans and identifying and treating basic lameness and wounds. Participants successfully completing the program will earn a Groom Elite certificate, and in some states, vocational certification from the Department of Corrections. Many graduates find work on horse farms and racetracks; some go in other related directions, such as employment at tack shops. These credentials also qualify program graduates to work with the Department of Labor to help them find a job upon their release.

"They learn they can do things they never thought they'd be doing," says O'Reilly. "That is one of the biggest things I hear: 'Never did I think I'd be on a tractor, brush-hogging a field, or noticing one of the horses didn't drink that day.' It's so outside of where they thought they would be."

Different states and farms offer participants additional learning opportunities. Women in the Florida program with previous horse experience have the chance to train as exercise riders (this is the only program with a mounted option). Several programs offer instruction in natural horsemanship, and participants learn how navigate an unmounted obstacle course as part of their education. Participants in the Kentucky and South Carolina programs learn to make hay; those in the California program can complete a six-week farrier course. So far, two men have continued on from that experience to attend professional farrier's school.

"One of them now works on a pack train as a blacksmith," says O'Reilly. "And he says, 'If you'd told me I'd be riding a horse and shoeing mules in the mountains of California, I would have laughed my butt off.' We are talking about inner-city people, who have never seen anything other than a dog."

Some participants choose equine management specifically as their vocational training option; others are assigned to the program by their correctional facility. Universally, there are some restrictions on who is eligible to work with the horses; incarcerated people with a conviction related to animal abuse, elder abuse, or physical assault are generally ineligible. The only occasional exception made to this rule is for individuals who have served lengthy sentences on related charges but have shown no further tendencies toward violence.

Enrollment size varies by facility and at times is limited per state regulations; currently, it ranges from 4 to 18 participants per site. At several facilities, there is a waitlist to get into the TRF Second Chances Program—particularly in Kentucky, where local farms are desperate to hire qualified help and are quite happy to give these men an opportunity. In fact, one (quite famous) farm in Lexington will meet graduates at the correctional facility on the day they are released.

"Think about what that does for the guys who are still in the program, to see that," says O'Reilly.

The duration of the program also varies by correctional facility. Generally, the TRF Second Chances Program is considered a "pre-release program"—participants typically enroll when they are within a year to 18 months of parole eligibility, and ideally, they graduate just prior to their release. At the juvenile detention center in Florida, with a capacity of 72 beds, youth typically participate for anywhere from three to eight months, ensuring as many of them have the opportunity to work with the horses as possible.

ALTHOUGH THE TRF Second Chances Program has been in existence for nearly four decades, most evidence of its efficacy is only anecdotal. This is due, at least in part, to the fact that each state tracks the results of its vocational training programs differently; many don't separate out results by specific program, and a bit shockingly, some don't really track results at all.

"It's all about recidivism rates," says O'Reilly, referring to the percentage of previously incarcerated people who re-offend in the future. "The average recidivism rate in the United States is 70 percent within seven years. It's basically a revolving door. But research shows that, on average, people who do a high school diploma while they are in prison, or vocational programming, are 18 to 20 percent less likely to go back to jail."

For those states tracking results for the equine programming specifically, the recidivism rate ranges from as high as 20 to as low as 6 percent—well below the national average.

"It is ridiculous how effective horses are," says O'Reilly. "The horses have done nothing to them. The horse just looks at them every day for breakfast, lunch, and dinner, to be brushed and loved. The horse doesn't judge them, doesn't care what they did or about the tattoos on their arm."

For people who have spent years in prison, leaving its confines to work on the farm also helps to flex mental muscles that may have atrophied during their incarceration and to regain skills they will need to rejoin the world beyond the prison's boundaries.

"The farm has no walls, no fence," says O'Reilly. "It has nothing. The biggest change for them is being able to make decisions as to what they are doing on a daily basis. Inside, there is no decision-making—you are to do as you are told, every day, all day. Out on the farm, they have their tasks, and it is up to them to get them done. That is a huge part of helping them transition back into society. It also teaches them how to shift gears, and change plans—like if it rains, or the vet is unexpectedly coming. That skill is very difficult for some of the guys, coming to the farm from the para-military inside."

But perhaps the best evidence of success are the stories shared by participants themselves. The Thoroughbred Retirement Foundation regularly receives letters and calls from program graduates; sometimes, they are looking for job placement assistance, and sometimes, it is to simply say thank you. Recently, they received a letter from one program alumna who originally worried she would have no marketable skills upon her release; thanks to TRF Second Chances, she was hired within three days.

"Her boss says she is the first one there and the last to leave, every single day," says O'Reilly. "The more I talk about TRF Second Chances, the more I can break the stigma of hiring people who were in prison, and highlight what these horses can do for them," she continues. "You can't care about it if you don't know. And the more people who care, the more people and sanctuary horses we can help."

JULIANNE "JULES" STOWELL now fully owns the consequences of the "poor choices and bad company" she entertained in her late teens and early twenties—but it's been a journey to arrive at this point. At the young age of 17, the one-time honor student found herself caught in a cycle of substance abuse and all that comes with it. A series of arrests, probation violations, and charges ranging from theft to fleeing and eluding ultimately led to her 2017 incarceration at the Lowell Correctional Institution in Ocala, Florida. She was sentenced to 80 months behind bars.

"It feels like your life is over, being sentenced to that amount of time," says Julianne, who was 31 when I spoke with her. "I was in my twenties, and I found myself thinking, 'I should be in school, making something of myself, starting a career, and instead, I'm going to prison.' The life you once knew is over, and you're stuck at a standstill. You go numb; prison will make you that way. You have to redirect your focus from the world you once knew, because that's not your life anymore. Prison is your new reality."

Julianne admits she spent the first year of her sentence angry, mostly at herself, and she struggled with being separated from her family. Her parents, Charles and Barbara Stowell, still live in the house where she grew up in the beach town of Cape Canaveral, Florida, just 20 minutes from the famous Kennedy Space Center. The Stowells are a tight-knit family, and Julianne knew the choices she had made still shocked them.

"I had this great life," says Julianne bluntly. "I was on track to living a prosperous life, but I threw it all away because I was blinded by the temptations of the world. I was disappointed and mad at myself for making those decisions that led me to prison. It took me three years to make that 180-degree change, to get back in a good spiritual, mental, and emotional state of being…to find myself again, to love myself, and to get back on the right track."

From that point on, Julianne decided she would be "strategic" about how she spent the remainder of her sentence. She wanted to focus on bettering herself and gaining skills so she could come out of incarceration with a "jump start." A lifelong animal lover, Julianne dedicated two years to a program that taught her dog handling and training skills. However, working with the horses was her ultimate goal, and the moment she became eligible, Julianne enrolled in the TRF Second Chances Program.

"They're a lot like big dogs, in all honesty," says Julianne with a laugh. "Horses are goofy, with so much personality, and each one is different in their own way. But like all animals, they also have a calming, serene aspect to them. They soothe your soul.

"And the thing about the retired racehorses—I compare them to a lot of people who are incarcerated," she continues. "We are viewed as the discarded members of society…. Racehorses, once they are broken down, or if they're not capable of racing and making earnings, they're discarded. I related to them on that level."

Julianne soon settled into her new routine: wake up at 5:00 AM; begin the required processing to leave the prison at 6:15 AM; arrive at the farm by 7:00 AM. She and the other participants worked until about 2:00 or 2:30 PM, Monday through Friday, with the option to also come out on weekends. Julianne was often at the farm six days a week.

"For a lot of girls, the more they can get out of that gate, and be away from the prison, the better," says Julianne.

It took her two years to complete the 1,200-hour program; after that, Julianne became a teacher's aide, helping staff to educate new participants.

She remained an active presence at the farm until just prior to obtaining work release, with about eight months left to serve of her sentence.

"Being in those programs definitely was the best thing for me," says Julianne. "It gives you purpose, especially having to care for and look after something else. It's not about *you* anymore. If I don't show up, this horse may not eat or may not get cared for. That's rewarding.

"Each person goes through certain trials, and when you look at someone, you don't know what they've been through," she continues. "When you look at that racehorse, it's the same thing. You don't know what that horse has endured in his career, or in his lifetime. And then, to experience unconditional love—they look forward to you being there. They get excited to see you. It was amazing, just the best thing ever."

Julianne soon acquired the nickname "The Psych" (short for psychiatrist) for her seemingly intuitive ability to work with quirky or sensitive animals. Although she loved every horse she worked with, she felt particularly drawn to "the broken ones." It would be one of these horses who taught Julianne to understand death in a more spiritual way—a lesson that at the time, she didn't know she needed.

When Mr. Angel arrived at the Thoroughbred Retirement Foundation, he brought with him a reputation for "unsafe" behavior, acquired after hospitalizing his previous owner. Then, not long after his arrival, the aged dark bay gelding needed surgery to remove a fly larva from his eye. Combined with his emotional baggage, the follow-up treatments left Mr. Angel somewhat untrusting and quite headshy. To top it all off, he had terrible feet and needed to wear boots instead of shoes to stay comfortable.

"The girl who handled him before me literally did everything possible to save this horse," says Julianne. "And he was just progressively getting worse. For months, I would sit and watch him in the field, struggling. He was just declining."

Finally, one day she went to the program director and told him she felt it was Mr. Angel's time. On the day of the scheduled procedure, Julianne spent the morning with the gelding, giving him a bath and extra attention. Later, she warned the vet to be careful as she approached with the syringe, as Mr. Angel could still be unpredictable around his head. But instead, the aged gelding remained calm, even softening his eye and releasing a sigh.

"It's like he knew what was coming, accepted his fate, and was okay with that," says Julianne. "That was a life-changing, touching moment for me, because it helped me to understand and view death in a different way. Being there for six years, I started experiencing the loss of family members, which was a big struggle for me. That horse touched my life."

TWO WEEKS PRIOR to Julianne's release, her mother Barbara received a phone call from Stephanie Brennan, a Thoroughbred Retirement Foundation board member and Director of Sales and Marketing for Niall Brennan Stables in Ocala. Brennan had met Julianne during her time at TRF Second Chances, and wanted to interview her for an opening at their farm.

Julianne was released on April 12, 2023. Five days later, she started working as the Client Relations Specialist for Niall Brennan Stables.

"I often find myself getting caught in the beauty of this gorgeous, 160-acre farm, and thinking, 'This isn't real,'" says Julianne of her position. "It's still surreal to me, and it was definitely a blessing. The farm schedule is very similar to the prison schedule. I was already conditioned for the schedule, and the structure of it. It was the best thing for me, and exactly what I needed, because I like to say, 'Idle hands are the devil's playground.'"

In her current role, Julianne creates the daily set list and training schedule, assists with administering equine therapies, manages and updates the website, corresponds with clients, and coordinates the maintenance department—along with whatever other additional duties need to be taken care of in the daily management of a large equine operation. Although she is open about her past, she is also looking forward to her future—a future made possible, at least in part, thanks to a herd of retired racehorses.

"I'm the first one to tell you, 'Yeah, I did six years in prison. I was no angel,'" says Julianne. "I *was* an inmate, but I'm no longer an inmate.

When I'm out walking around, I'm no different from the next person. I'm an individual, a person, a thriving member of society."

NO ONE IN THE WORLD of Thoroughbred aftercare would be so bold as to say they have "solved" the problem—but most agree huge strides have been made and are hopeful for even greater progress in the years to come.

"This is part of the lifecycle of a racehorse now, and it never was 15, 20, 25 years before," says Dot Morgan.

She points to the Thoroughbred Aftercare Alliance's accreditation process as a significant positive step, as it gives donors and owners confidence in the organizations they choose to work with. Additionally, she credits programs such as the Retired Racehorse Project and The Jockey Club's Thoroughbred Incentive Program for positively promoting the use of Thoroughbreds beyond the track in both competitive and non-competitive ways.

"These incentive programs give people a goal, something to target and work toward, and encourage them to go out and enjoy their horse," says Dot. "They have really helped raise the visibility of what Thoroughbreds can do, and in turn, enhanced their value and appeal.

"I truly believe there are enough charities and aftercare organizations in operation that no Thoroughbred or Standardbred should fall through the cracks, as long as owners and trainers look for an option," she continues. "Sometimes there's a waitlist, and the owner might have to pay the board bill for that horse until they can get him in. But I think we've made great headway in that area."

Nevertheless, opportunities for further growth remain. For example, there is currently minimal tracking around exactly what happens, long-term, to each of the approximately 18,000 Thoroughbred foals registered with The Jockey Club each year. In Australia, on the other hand, a Thoroughbred is tracked from 48 hours after birth until two years after retirement. This information could help industry leaders, breeders, trainers, and owners prevent animals from unwittingly falling into less-than-ideal circumstances. And of course, funding is always an issue.

"It's a constant evolution of best practices, and recognizing the things that are working," says Clark Rogers. "It's about getting owners to start thinking about the eventual retirement of their racehorse and knowing what their options are. When we know what we know, we need to do the right thing. If the Thoroughbred industry fails because they aren't taking care of their horses, I think you will find that other equine sports will fail. We have to become more sincere about what we are practicing here, if we are going around saying we love horses."

*"I truly believe there are enough charities
and aftercare organizations in operation that no
Thoroughbred or Standardbred should fall through the cracks,
as long as owners and trainers look for an option."*

DOT MORGAN
FOUNDER, NEW VOCATIONS RACEHORSE ADOPTION

Chapter 8

SAVING THE HORSES OF APPALACHIA:
A MODEL FOR SUCCESS

ON A HOT AND MUGGY AFTERNOON in late August 2021, I climb toward the top of a crowded set of dusty wooden bleachers, my eye on a possible seat next to a woman wearing a cowboy hat, button-down blouse, and tight jeans, none of which seems like the most comfortable attire for the day's conditions. She is talking on her cell and swigging from a bottle of beer, and simply tips her head in acknowledgment of my query as to whether the space beside her is open.

I take a moment to survey the still-gathering crowd; ongoing pandemic and social distancing be damned, hundreds of spectators are either jockeying for space along the fence bordering the large covered arena, or like myself, are trying to cram into the few remaining open seats on bleachers arranged along the edge. Despite the thick air and cramped conditions, the atmosphere is festive, and the crowd so energetic it is far easier to simply sit and take it all in than try to carry on a conversation.

In fact, it seems as if most of the residents of tiny Winfield, West Virginia—population 2,300—have turned out this afternoon to enjoy the highly anticipated finale to the 2021 Appalachian Trainer Face Off (ATFO). Over the preceding two days, competitors have already completed the technical and trail phases of the event with their equine partners. On this third and final night of competition, the top 10 pairs in each division will perform their freestyles—a no-holds-barred, anything-goes performance by horse and rider, all set to music. With several previous ATFO winners in the lineup and a history of freestyle performances featuring everything from totally tackless riding to parading through rings of fire, tonight's show is certain to be a crowd-pleaser.

But perhaps the most emotional and tension-filled component of tonight's agenda will begin after the final ATFO champions are crowned.

Mixed among the casual enthusiasts in tonight's crowd are eager, hopeful shoppers clutching programs and holding bidding paddles made of plates and tongue depressors. In the months and weeks leading up to this competition, these individuals and families have completed a lengthy and rigorous application process to become "pre-approved" to adopt selected horses being exhibited tonight. However, unlike a traditional shelter adoption, where there is generally a set fee dictated by the species, age, gender, and special needs of the animal in question, these equines will find their new homes through a minimum-bid-required live auction.

Some of the animals being auctioned tonight are part of the official ATFO competition, while others are being exhibited through the non-competitive "Showcase" event. But all the equines—nearly 60 in total—share one thing in common: they were each saved from a life of suffering, neglect, or simply bad luck thanks to a West Virginia-based equine rescue called Heart of Phoenix.

In just over a decade, Heart of Phoenix has rescued over 1,200 equines at risk, established the largest equine event in West Virginia in the ATFO, and through education, outreach, and innovation, has completely altered the trajectory of life for the average unwanted horse in rural Appalachia. For her efforts, Heart of Phoenix founder and president Tinia Creamer was presented with the ASPCA's Equine Welfare Award in 2019.

From the beginning, Heart of Phoenix's journey has been strewn with obstacles that could justifiably have caused the organization to fold—but today, it serves as one model of how perseverance and out-of-the-box thinking can effect change, even in the face of seemingly insurmountable odds. Throughout its existence, Heart of Phoenix has pursued a dual mission: to not only actively engage in saving suffering horses, but also to pursue actions that might change the regional culture such that it reduces the incidence of neglect altogether. While this dichotomy may seem impossible to achieve, to paraphrase Creamer—if Heart of Phoenix can make a difference to the equines of Appalachia, then positive change can occur anywhere.

APPALACHIA IS A REGION of the United States defined not by borders but by culture and a cycle of profound poverty; it is a place where both animals and humans suffer in ways not easily understood by those who don't witness it. In the past, several organizations have tried to address pervasive equine neglect within this economically impoverished region, which covers 420 counties in 13 states. But it is fair to say until Heart of Phoenix was founded in 2012, none had succeeded on a large scale.

However, Creamer never intended to found an equine rescue. A native West Virginian, Creamer rode horses with friends throughout her teen years, but once she hit adulthood, life took her in new directions. She moved away from home, spending several years in Florida and giving birth to her first child before returning to West Virginia late in 2006.

But on January 13, 2007, the trajectory of Creamer's life would change forever.

That day, Creamer's three younger siblings—aged 19, 17, and 14—were killed in a horrific apartment fire in Huntington, West Virginia, the deadliest of its kind in 50 years. The tragedy left Creamer, just 24 at the time, reeling in shock and pain. For nearly a year, she was bereft, desolate and filled with despair. Then, in 2008, the Global Financial Crisis hit, impacting Appalachia disproportionately compared to the rest of the country in terms of both a reduction in median household income and an increased incidence of poverty across the region.

As economic conditions worsened, Creamer noticed a rapid increase in the number of horses offered for free on Craigslist. She began answering ads and independently rehabilitated a few horses whose owners could no longer support them. Helping these horses in need gave Creamer the sense of purpose she had been missing.

One fateful stormy day, she responded to a call about a horse tied to a tree in a flash-flood-prone area. With storm waters rising, it seemed Creamer had arrived just in time. But the mare was in terrible shape. Her body was little more than a skeleton draped with skin; she had hollow, sunken eyes, and her untended hooves had grown so long they curled upward like elf shoes. She could barely walk.

Although Creamer successfully led the unnamed mare through floodwaters to safety, ultimately, her efforts would prove insufficient to offset years of neglect. The entire experience—from the mare's dramatic rescue to her failed rehabilitation and eventual death—proved pivotal for Creamer. On the day she laid the mare to rest, Creamer decided she was going to prevent this situation from happening to as many other horses as possible.

Late in 2011, Creamer filed the required paperwork to establish a new nonprofit dedicated to saving the horses of Appalachia, and it became official as she approached her thirtieth birthday the next April. She named her new rescue Heart of Phoenix, the symbolism of a bird reborn from the ashes of flame a tribute to both the mare she couldn't save and her own personal journey through loss and grief. But in the early years, with limited resources, the sheer massive scope of equine neglect and suffering throughout Appalachia in general, and West Virginia in particular, seemed a problem almost too huge to tackle.

"When you consider that you're living in an area where children suffer extreme neglect and go without food, it seemed impossible to make any progress," says Creamer, her deep, husky voice revealing just a hint of southern drawl. "You're fighting a constant animal control crisis and cases of gross neglect, where you're trying to get animal control to come in and take a horse that isn't going to survive much longer, in counties that don't have the money to prosecute child abuse cases."

Creamer's strategy to overcome these challenges was inspired by a well-known quote from one of her early idols, Fred Rogers: "Look for the helpers." Slowly, at first, but later with increasing momentum, Heart of Phoenix grew from a core group of volunteers to a network spanning the country, thanks largely to a constant willingness to ask for help and an active presence on social media (Creamer, who pens many of the organization's posts, studied English literature at Marshall University and is an eloquent, poetic, and at times passionate writer). With their combined efforts, enthusiasm, and support, overcoming seemingly insurmountable odds became a possibility.

But particularly at first, Heart of Phoenix's volunteers needed to develop a fairly thick skin. Due to a combination of lack of owner education, profound poverty, and limited resources, animals coming to the rescue were routinely severely emaciated, and sometimes also bore scars of extreme trauma such as improperly healed injuries or active infections. Frequently, they also lacked training, which could range from a completely unhandled animal to one simply requiring a "refresher" of previous work with a skilled horseman. One of the first challenges facing Heart of Phoenix was to find a way to not only rehabilitate their intakes' bodies, but their minds.

In small animal rescue, utilizing foster homes to care for homeless animals is a common and well-accepted model, but in Heart of Phoenix's early years, it was virtually unheard of for larger species like equines. Despite this, due to its limited budget and lack of a facility, Creamer believed recruiting volunteer foster homes was the only way for Heart of Phoenix to maximize the number of horses it could help. They put the word out to their network, and even Creamer couldn't have predicted the result—owners and managers at training programs, lesson facilities, and boarding barns throughout the East Coast and into the Midwest not only offered to foster Heart of Phoenix's animals, but provide training at little or no cost. Today, nearly two-thirds of Heart of Phoenix's approximately 125 equines are rehabilitating in foster homes.

"It was out of desperation and need that we adopted the foster model," admits Creamer. "But now it is a model that many, if not all, organizations follow. And we were able to say yes to the typical horse that ends up in rescue—that horse is usually untrained or poorly trained."

In 2016, Heart of Phoenix finally acquired a home base of its own when it signed the lease on Mulligan Farm, located just outside of Huntington, West Virginia. Today, most new intakes come to Mulligan for evaluation, where an expert team of veterinarians, farriers, and horse trainers determines the foster situation best equipped to manage each animal's care moving forward. Those horses remaining at Mulligan long term are generally those requiring more intensive TLC.

One hard topic that Creamer is more than willing to discuss is the need to truly normalize the use of humane euthanasia in cases where horses' age, health issues, or unsoundness means they cannot have a high quality of life. In reality, making that call—particularly for a younger animal with a low-grade but chronic condition—can be difficult, not just for owners but for those working in rescue organizations.

"A lot of rescues will not accept horses that just need euthanasia, but I think that's the way to solve so many problems," says Creamer. "It's not cruel—the animal doesn't give one hoot about tomorrow. Make a good, ethical decision for this horse, don't let it have another bad day, and that horse is now out of the equation."

Starting in 2019, but escalating in the years that followed, Heart of Phoenix has seen an increase in the number of owner-surrendered horses coming into the rescue simply requiring end-of-life care. And that is just fine with Creamer—in fact, Heart of Phoenix prioritizes assisting these cases, knowing that offering this critical support will protect both horse and human in the long run.

"We are more apt to accept a horse knowing that is the likely outcome," says Creamer. "Those are horses you can take out of the cycle, and make sure nothing else bad happens."

It is important to understand this *isn't* euthanasia for population control. It is used to end the suffering of an animal with no prospects for a better future. It also allows the rescue to dedicate the majority of its resources to helping animals with a realistic chance of finding a home by resolving whatever barriers stand in the way.

Each year, Heart of Phoenix receives hundreds of applications from prospective adopters, all looking for healthy, sane, rideable horses. But many of the animals Heart of Phoenix takes into their care do not meet this criteria, at least not at first. If a horse arrives with a treatable health or soundness issue, Heart of Phoenix will invest in any necessary diagnostics and medical care, so long as doing so does not leave the animal in unmanageable or chronic pain. Almost as often, Heart of Phoenix's intakes lack proper training, and resolving that problem was, at least in part, responsible for the genesis of the ATFO, and also one of the main motivations for establishing enduring partnerships with trainers within their foster network.

But of the hundreds of equines Heart of Phoenix has helped lift up from bad circumstances, a select few fall into a special category. These are the ones they call "Appalachian Brumbies"—feral horses descended from domesticated animals turned out on Appalachia's hundreds of thousands of acres of abandoned coal mines. Typically small, sturdy, and gaited, these feral horses remain a source of controversy within the region today. To understand why, one must learn a little bit about the history of central Appalachia and the self-reliant culture of its people.

FOR DECADES, the dominant industry in Appalachia has been coal mining, and now-abandoned mines are particularly prevalent in the mountains of West Virginia and eastern Kentucky. Initially, mining operations were conducted mostly underground, but today, surface mining techniques such as contouring and mountaintop removal are more common. Although safer for those involved in the extraction process than other methods, surface mining techniques leave significant scars behind on the landscape. Since the 1970s, federal regulations require mining companies to pay a bond as a deposit of good faith that, when they close a mine, they will implement reclamation practices to restore habitat for native species. Only once new vegetation has fully taken root, and the native habitat restored, is the company's bond released.

As recently as the eighties, horses were still an important part of life in this mountainous region, where the topography is dominated by steep hillsides and plunging valleys. One woman I spoke with, who grew up in eastern Kentucky in the seventies, told me there were no paved roads in her community when she was a child. The surrounding terrain was so vast and so remote, getting around on horseback was the only reasonable option. Another woman from the same area explained that owning horses was a point of pride for locals, and only the poorest families didn't have at least one. Both women agreed to share with me their experiences of growing up with horses in rural Appalachia, but declined to be identified by name for this book. I would learn this wariness of outsiders is still a common trait to residents in the area.

Compared to the surrounding terrain, reclaimed minelands are often fairly flat, hard to access by the general public, and grow lushly once seeded with native grasses. For these reasons, local residents found them to be ideal for free-grazing livestock, and it became common practice to release animals on the former minelands each spring, and gather them up again come fall. Most everyone knew which horses belonged to whom, and the community kept a collective eye on their well-being. Further, there was an unspoken "gentleman's agreement" that stallions were not to be turned out with the loose horses, and stud colts foaled out on the mines were gathered at weaning and gelded. According to locals, for several decades herd sizes remained stable, the minelands were not overgrazed, and the horses seemed to do well enough free-roaming on reclaimed mountaintops. Although utilizing the land in this way wasn't technically legal, by most accounts, mining companies and private landowners alike generally turned a blind eye to the practice.

Depending on who you ask, the situation began to change sometime in the early 2000s. Thanks to the combined effects of easier access through an increased number of paved roads and improved connectivity through the nascent internet, non-locals became aware of the practice of grazing horses on reclaimed minelands and took advantage of the opportunity. Soon, herd numbers increased exponentially, stallions were introduced, and when the recession hit in 2008, the situation reached crisis level. With an equine population numbering far beyond what could be sustained by available native forage, herds began wandering down from the minelands in search of food, water, and salt. Frequently, they ended up in roadways, where they were a hazard to themselves and drivers.

No single entity—government or otherwise—can provide a fully accurate accounting of the total number of feral horses living on central Appalachia's coal mines, either in the past or the present, partially because the population grew in such an insidious way, and partially because of the rugged nature of the area. Creamer guesses by the mid 2000s, there were as many as 4,000 feral horses living in central Appalachia, and most were not thriving—as was evidenced by an escalating number of witness accounts reporting emaciated animals wandering into yards and congregating in roadways.

To be clear, these equines are not "wild"—they are "feral." Feral animals belong to domesticated species deliberately released or escaped from containment; wild animals are species native to the ecosystem of an area and fully evolved to live within it. Of course, the longer feral animals remain on their own, the more "wild-like" they become, and for multi-generational mineland horses, nearly any attempts to capture or handle them fail, largely because of the highly unique skill set required. Meanwhile, life on the minelands for recently released domesticated horses is a hardscrabble existence; many starve to death, or are hit by cars, deliberately run down on ATVs, or even hunted for sport.

As the feral horse problem escalated, governmental agencies and local animal control officers in central Appalachia were ill-equipped to make any moves toward addressing it. Further, some local residents believed the horses to be a tourist attraction, even advertising visits to see "West Virginia's wild horses," and resisting any suggestion of reducing herd numbers (this is still a challenge today). Late in 2019, at least 15 mineland horses were found shot to death in eastern Kentucky, and reports of the slaughter made national news; nearly $20,000 was raised as a reward for any information leading to the prosecution of the person or persons responsible.

For several years in the late 2010s, Heart of Phoenix dedicated significant time and resources to assisting with gathers of these feral animals. Once caught, most were quite literally untouchable, having reverted to an inner, wild nature in order to survive. Their behavior could be defensive, aggressive, fearful—or some combination of all three. Only the most experienced of trainers had the patience and skill set to reach the once-domesticated animal within.

It was in trying to save these horses that in 2017, the Appalachian Trainer Face Off (ATFO) came to be. Modeled on the Extreme Mustang Makeover, a highly successful program partnering trainers with range-gathered mustangs, the ATFO combines a Heart of Phoenix horse with a skilled trainer, who is given 100 days to work with the animal. Trainers pick up their horses in May, and in late August, they return to West Virginia for a three-phase public demonstration, with performances judged by a panel of top industry experts.

Since its inception, over 220 equines have gone through the program, and over 150 trainers have offered their services. Top competitors win a coveted belt buckle, an array of sponsored prizes, and bragging rights; in addition, if their animal is successfully sold at auction to one of those pre-approved bidders, the trainer will split the proceeds with Heart of Phoenix. The event has become the organization's marquee fundraiser, adding over $350,000 to the organization's coffers as of 2023.

"When I started doing this, you couldn't even charge an adoption fee," says Creamer. "If you were going to put someone through an adoption process, they sure weren't going to pay. It's been a big struggle to convince people these horses *are* valuable. They are sound, sane, trainable horses with so much potential. The ATFO really shows that—the trainers come from all disciplines and do some incredible things."

The trainers competing in the 2021 ATFO are divided into two categories, amateur and professional, which I learn has more to do with their overall level of experience in working with feral and semi-feral horses than it does with actually making a living as a horse trainer. The most challenging animals are assigned to trainers qualified for the pro division, while those drawn by amateurs are expected to be more straightforward in terms of their training needs.

The same policy applies to potential ATFO adopters—based on their equine experience, skill level, and access to further training and support, each applicant is approved to bid only on those horses in alignment with their personal circumstances. It is not unusual for some of the most challenging horses to have only a handful of qualified adopters in their queue; if they are not adopted at competition's end, frequently, these horses will stay with their current trainer for further education. Occasionally, the trainers themselves will even put in an adoption application for the horse they are working with; others will encourage friends and clients to do so instead, hoping the newly adopted horse might stay within their sphere of influence.

Jordyn Dominguez, 19, was a 2021 ATFO rookie competing in the

Amateur Division. She traveled five hours each way from her home in South Whitley, Indiana, to participate.

"I totally fell in love with the program, that they take the horses from unwanted, from skin and bones, to making them a horse that somebody would want," explains Dominguez, who first attended the event as a spectator in 2020. "I watched the freestyle last year and thought, 'This is something I have to do.'"

For her ATFO partner, Dominguez selected a three-year-old mare named Paprika, who is no doubt named in honor of her bright chestnut coat. Paprika was surrendered by her owner to Heart of Phoenix as a baby, and fortunately never suffered from neglect or rough handling. When Dominguez started working with her, Paprika knew basic handling skills and how to stand quietly for the farrier, but beyond that, she was pretty much a clean slate. She became one of the first horses Dominguez started under saddle on her own.

"I would like to be a professional trainer one day, but I don't consider myself a pro right now," she says. "I am doing this for the experience, and I love that it gives an unwanted horse a chance at life. I like what it stands for. I don't have any problem volunteering my time to give a horse a good home. Plus, every horse will teach you something different, so as many different horses I can work with, the better I am."

Dominguez already has three horses of her own at home, and she deliberately did not put in an application to adopt Paprika herself. But she knows tonight's auction will still be tough.

"I think I'm going to cry, but it'll be happy in the long run," she admits. "The applications are really extensive, and the horses are going to a good home. And if somebody takes a horse then says, 'Hey, this horse doesn't mesh with me,' they go back to the rescue. I'm not worried about where she ends up at all."

Dominguez is referring to the thorough screening process Heart of Phoenix puts its potential adopters through, which goes a long way toward weeding out tire-kickers, casual shoppers, and those perhaps not financially stable enough to take on horse ownership. For those meeting the organization's stringent criteria, there is still a clause in the adoption contract indicating that the animal is never to be traded, sold, or rehomed; if the owner's circumstances or needs should change, the animal must be returned to Heart of Phoenix.

The organization makes every effort to keep track of the equines they have placed in adoptive homes, but occasionally, animals fall through the cracks, and this is why all Heart of Phoenix horses are branded on their left shoulder with the organization's distinctive mark: a capital "P" encircled by a heart. Should a Heart of Phoenix horse ever end up in an unsavory situation, the brand is a virtually unalterable verification of the horse's original provenance and can help the rescue reclaim a lost animal.

The brand is a bit harder to see on Professional Division competitor Samara Manich's horse, Ysera. Most likely a draft cross, this big-bodied, snow-white, pink-skinned mare ran through an auction in Oklahoma with nine similar animals, all totally feral. A Texas rescue picked them up, but when no one there could make any progress with the group's training, Creamer drove out to collect them, believing that the ATFO was perhaps their best shot at a new life. Manich, who specializes in working with feral or "problem" horses at her NGU Horse Training and Stables in Indiana, Pennsylvania, is competing at the ATFO for the second time. She chose Ysera specifically for her size—16.2 hands.

"One of the things I saw last year was that the horses coming through were much smaller, and I heard a couple of people saying how if the horse was bigger, they'd bid on it," says 35-year-old Manich. "I had my fiancé Matt with me when we got to pick our horses, and when he saw her, he said, 'She is big and white; people are going to love her.'"

Once she got Ysera home, Manich learned she might have her work cut out for her; it took eight days before she could even touch the cautious mare. But she soon learned Ysera loved treats, and used that as a tool to begin to earn her trust. As she spent more time with Ysera, Manich found her to be an intelligent horse in need of positive reinforcement when faced with new challenges. They systematically progressed through a training program, until Ysera was calmly working under saddle. Manich felt a trail-riding home might suit her best.

But training feral horses rarely goes according to plan, and while schooling at the competition venue after her arrival at the ATFO, Ysera did something she had never done even once during her 100 days of training—she bucked under saddle. In fact, she bucked several times in a row, ultimately sending Manich to the ground, stepping on her hand and leaving her with a severely bruised tail bone.

"There were no warning signs," Manich says with a resigned sigh. "I was told I survived four or five bucks. I remember looking down at one point, and just seeing her mane flowing and I thought, 'Oh, gosh, this is really pretty good.'"

Because of her injuries, Manich decides to compete Ysera in hand instead of under saddle the weekend I am there. She believes the mare's uncharacteristic behavior is because the atmosphere at the show grounds is simply too much for her to handle at this stage of her training; she hopes any prospective adopters in the audience will overlook this recent setback. (Unfortunately, they would not—Ysera was one of several horses not sold at the auction.)

Like Dominguez, Colby O'Connor, 19, was also making her ATFO debut in the Amateur Division. She had been working with a four-year-old mare named Juniper, who certainly stands out among the other entrants due to her stunning grulla coat. The pair didn't perform as well as O'Connor had hoped in the technical phase, but they finished second in the trail portion and stood in fourth place overall, heading into the freestyle, scheduled to start in just a few hours.

"I'm not going to lie to you—I haven't practiced nothing for the freestyle, and that's what we are stressing about—what are we going to do," says O'Connor, who holds her hands together tightly and shifts her weight from foot to foot.

I am struck by both her modesty and obvious discomfort with being interviewed. But put O'Connor on a horse, and it is clear she is at home. Over the past several days, I have watched O'Connor work not just with Juniper, but also Pistachio, a 12-year-old mare being exhibited in the Showcase—just a few of the Heart of Phoenix horses that have found their way to her family's Rockin H Stables in LaGrange, Kentucky. She admits she has lost count of exactly how many Heart of Phoenix horses they have fostered and helped transition into new homes since she first learned about the program. But working with Juniper in the ATFO has been a special experience.

"It is possibly my last day with her," says O'Connor. She pauses and blinks back tears before continuing. "I love that horse, and I don't want to get rid of her. She was an owner surrender, and during the draw, they told us the previous owner said she was bratty and a little bit crazy. I didn't see that in her at all. The first month, she seemed like maybe she'd been abused in the past, and we had to show her it's okay, and we love you. Today is the day I've been dreading. I think she's taught me a lot. Now, I know what I'm capable of—starting a horse that knew nothing, to where she is at now. It built my confidence quite a bit in my training skills."

It seems like Juniper and O'Connor each have a fan base at the ATFO. While watching the trail competition, I sit with a family of four wearing matching purple "Team Juniper" t-shirts. They previously adopted a Showcase horse trained by O'Connor and have traveled all the way from their home near Louisville, Kentucky, to cheer her on. During Juniper's turn on the trail course—which included navigating zigzag poles, crossing a wooden bridge, stepping into a kiddie pool filled with water, and even moving a huge stuffed teddy bear from one barrel to another—each family member has a phone out to take photos or video of the round.

O'Connor tells me there have been a lot of inquiries about Juniper— at least one prospective adopter drove eight hours from her home in North Carolina to Kentucky to meet the mare in person. I suspect the auction will be a difficult experience for this young trainer, even as she tries to comfort herself with the fact that Heart of Phoenix's screening process virtually ensures the animal's long-term well-being.

"What I hope for her is she gets a home where she is loved like she is at my house, and cared for like she is my personal horse," says O'Connor. "I hope whoever gets her continues that, because she didn't know love, and that people aren't there to hurt you."

One trainer who is more than prepared for the night's freestyle is Brenda Hanson, 30, who comes from Andover, Ohio. Hanson is a full-time professional trainer, and for years, she specialized specifically in colt-starting, although now she prefers to do finishing work. Her experience has paid off at the ATFO—she won the entire competition at her debut in 2018, and was the reserve champion in both 2019 and 2020. All of which is sort of ironic, considering that Hanson admits she has become increasingly conservative when it comes to working with "outlaw" horses.

"Feral horses have never been my thing," says Hanson with a laugh. "I like nice, gentle horses, and easy-going colts. It makes your job a lot easier, and it's safer. I have a farm and a lot of training horses, and I can't be getting hurt. But I've always been a sucker for down-on-their-luck horses. I go to the sales barn all the time, and I pluck out something I think doesn't deserve to be there. It's nice to take a horse that knows absolutely nothing and turn it into something."

It was thanks to her friendship with Creamer that Hanson first became aware of feral horses living on abandoned minelands in Appalachia, and although she wanted to help, she always felt too busy with her own business to become more actively involved. When she finally applied to be a part of the ATFO in 2018, Hanson chose a palomino Appalachian Brumby named Sansa. When this mare was first gathered, the vets scored her body condition at less than a 1, and euthanasia seemed like the most reasonable option. But the team at Heart of Phoenix still gave her a chance, and thanks to their care—and Hanson's training—Sansa became a healthy, usable horse, and was adopted by a Heart of Phoenix volunteer for $8,000. Hanson points out with a fair degree of pride that it is Sansa's image on the promotional banner hanging outside the barn.

"I know she has a good forever home," says Hanson. "You know when you take them home, that they are going to go somewhere and find a different home. You know you did the right thing, but it's hard to not get attached, especially when you've put in so much time."

Hanson is competing this year with a chestnut gelding named Shauny, and she told Creamer he was one of the most difficult horses she's ever worked with. Compared to her previous ATFO projects, he has taken more time and more patience—and perhaps has pushed Hanson closest to the point of giving up.

"When I brought this horse home, I thought I'd made a big mistake," admits Hanson. "I thought I should take him back, and that I should quit this year. He didn't like people, he was quite aggressive, and if you got too close to him, he'd try to bite your face off. He was not a pet."

Shauny is straight-up Appalachian Brumby. Although he isn't gaited, he looks like he could be. Shauny is small, perhaps 14.2 hands, and sturdy, with a long, wavy, flaxen-colored mane and tail. He belonged to one of the most desperate-looking herds ever gathered by Heart of Phoenix; located in Grant County, West Virginia, the animals were described as "skeletal" upon intake, and rescuers found the decaying corpse of the herd stallion nearby. The herd was gathered just the previous winter, and Shauny was still regaining weight when Hanson met him in May. On horse selection day, she thought the colt (now gelded) looked like he had a good brain and didn't seem too scared. But once she got him back to her own farm, Shauny tested her resolve, her skills, and her willpower.

"I don't think he went out of my barn for the first 50 days," says Hanson. "I taught him how to lead in the barn aisle way before I even got him to the round pen and started working him. But for whatever reason, I just didn't quit. I kept going, kept going, kept going, and eventually, he figured me out. I've learned if you want to be patient, and take your time, and don't push the horse past what it can do, that's the faster way to get there."

Shauny's success at ATFO is perhaps a testament to both Hanson's skill and her dedication to doing what's best for the horse. The pair placed fourth in the technical phase and won the trail class, leaving him in second place going into the freestyle. Hanson has a "pretty decent" freestyle planned, but despite Shauny's consistency this weekend, she doesn't really think he stands a strong chance of being adopted.

"He's been quite the challenge," she says with a sigh. "He needs to go to someone who knows what they're doing—I think a lot of people got that."

AS THE START TIME for the ATFO freestyle performances draws near, both the energy in the arena and size of the crowd grow larger (later, I would learn over 2,000 spectators attended the 2021 event). The evening begins with a demonstration by professional trainer Eric Potraffke of Circle P Horsemanship in Williamstown, Kentucky, who is riding an eight-year-old roan Mustang named Bastille. Although he is listed in the show program as being part of the night's auction, Heart of Phoenix leadership has decided to withdraw Bastille from the bill. Unlike the other animals performing tonight, Bastille has been in training with Potraffke for a full year and even now, is not quite ready to be adopted. Creamer, who is serving as the evening's emcee, explains all of this prior to the pair's performance.

"Bastille was purchased by someone at auction in Pennsylvania," Creamer explains, her deep voice and charisma working together to settle the crowd. "He was still a stallion, and he got loose and was living free in West Virginia before he ended up with Heart of Phoenix. Not every horse can be a 100-day horse, so if they need a year, they get a year."

When I'd spoken with Potraffke about the gelding earlier in the day, he'd told me it had taken a lot of time and patience to earn Bastille's trust, and although the horse had come a long way, he still demanded his trainer's full attention whenever they worked together. Although Potraffke had exposed Bastille to a plethora of unusual stimuli and ridden him extensively both in and out of the arena at home, he'd confided he was worried about their freestyle performance—that the crowd and commotion might prove to be too much for both of them.

"I'm just going to go out there and show what he can do," Potraffke had told me. "I'm just gonna go in there and keep him calm, make it a good experience, and move on." He'd paused, and I'd sensed he was almost perceiving the scene to come in his mind. "I hate being in front of people," he'd continued with a sheepish smile, adjusting the worn cowboy hat on his head and sinking deeper into the hay bale he'd been sitting on. "I can do 10, but not 200. I'm just going to concentrate, and just ride, and hopefully I don't look up. Hopefully, we can help each other out."

Thinking of this conversation, I can't help but smile as I watch horse and rider in the arena before me. True to Potraffke's prediction, neither one looks wholly comfortable—Bastille's ears are swiveling and his eyes a little wide, while his rider's gaze is focused toward his horse's neck. But Potraffke's attention appears to be wholly concentrated on his mount, not the crowd, and in return, Bastille is clearly trying to stay attentive to his rider.

Next, the top ten entrants in the Amateur Division of the ATFO begin performing their freestyles, in reverse order of standing. As each animal prepares to enter the arena, Creamer shares a little of their backstory with the crowd. First there is Sumo, a thickly built pony gelding, who is resplendent with blue and silver tinsel in his mane and tail. He came to Heart of Phoenix after his elderly owner passed away, leaving him homeless. Riddle, a delicate skewbald mare, comes next—saved from a feral breeding herd, she had a Body Condition Score of only 2.5 when her ATFO trainer picked her up, but tonight, there is not a rib to be seen and she truly shines, from the purple ribbons in her braids to the pink sparkles on her hooves. Four other animals, each with an equally unique history and proud trainer, enter and leave the ring before it is time for Juniper and O'Connor to perform.

Knowing she felt ill-prepared just a few hours earlier, I am excited to see what O'Connor and her team have come up with for tonight's performance, and my curiosity is further piqued when a stock trailer is backed up to the far end of the arena. Each freestyle ride is timed, and O'Connor uses her first few moments to simply demonstrate Juniper's rideability. But suddenly, the trailer's back door slides open, and a calf jumps out, racing down the length of the arena. O'Connor spins Juniper and like a shot, they are in pursuit, O'Connor swinging a lariat over her head. I realize I am holding my breath as she throws, and when she misses, I groan in disappointment along with the rest of the audience. With time running out, O'Connor instead uses Juniper to herd the calf back out of the arena toward the waiting trailer.

The Professional Division begins with an unmounted demonstration featuring Manich and Ysera. The sun is setting, and the big mare's coat reflects the shine of the arena lights; Manich looks ethereal, her long, straight, honey-brown hair shining too and framing her face, her movements elegant and graceful. She longes Ysera for a few moments, then hands her off to a second handler, highlighting that this once-feral mare now has the capacity to believe that not all humans mean her harm. The performance is brief, the mare well-behaved, and I'm sure Manich breathed a sigh of relief to have completed all three phases of the competition, given how their weekend had begun.

The professional performances quickly increase in intensity. Mavis the mule goes next—with only one month of under-saddle training on the mule's resume, Mavis's trainer tosses balls into a basin, blasts a leafblower, and drags a tree behind them. Two horses later, a chestnut stock-type mare named Jerrika comes in, towing a small wagon containing her trainer's baby girl, who is turning a year old. As horse and rider slow-jog around the arena, a recording of rap artist 50 Cent chants, "It's ya birthday," the song's deep base punctuating the rhythm of the horse's feet striking the ground. Four more performances follow, featuring fancy costumes, flying capes, waving tarps, and even a working equitation demonstration, before it is time for Hanson and Shauny to take their turn.

As Creamer recounts the hard-luck start to Shauny's life out on the mines, a black draft horse driven by a heavy-set man and hauling a long, low flatbed begins slowly circling the edge of the arena. Then Hanson enters, mounted on a dun and ponying a fully tacked Shauny. The trio perform a side-pass, eight legs carefully moving in choreographed harmony, before Hanson switches mounts from horseback. She hands off the dun, rides directly past the draft horse (still circling the arena), then turns and rides Shauny right up and onto the moving flatbed. The pair allow themselves to be towed around as if Hanson is the master of ceremonies and this is a perfectly normal thing to do; Shauny stands like a rock. The draft horse's steady, cadenced rhythm never varies, not when the pair first got on board, nor later when Hanson finally asks Shauny to back off the still-moving drag. Even this modest trainer can't hide her obvious and deserved satisfaction with this recently feral animal's cooperation during their performance.

By the time the freestyles are done, the crowd's energy is positively electric. When Creamer announces the winners for each division a short time later, O'Connor finishes fifth in the Amateur Division, and Hanson captures the Professional Division reserve championship, her fourth top-two finish in four tries. As the winners pose for photographs with each other and their many donated prizes, the tenor of the audience changes. Some spectators have drifted away, while those with bidding paddles have moved closer to the rail and into the lower tiers of the bleachers.

It is time for the auction to begin.

"WEST VIRGINIA NEVER HAS ANYTHING to be proud of—but I can say, without a doubt, we have the best equine advocacy agency in the world!" Creamer, facing the remaining crowd, is acting almost like a barker, firing them up and inspiring their imaginations, and in response, they cheer, clap, and stomp their feet on the wooden bleachers.

The woman standing next to her also commands attention, and Creamer hands the mic over. The new speaker is petite, with sharply styled and vibrantly colored strawberry-red hair, dark boot-cut jeans, and a white blouse embellished with intricate braiding across the top. She is the auctioneer, and the first horse up, a five-year-old Haflinger mare named Mary Jane, is already entering the arena. With authority, the fiery auctioneer begins her captivating fast-talk, a hint of West Virginian twang punctuating her words. Unlike the other auctions I have attended, this one feels more like a carnival, and in what seems like an impossibly short period of time, she has run the bidding up to $3,800, snaps her fingers, and points at a bidder on the rail.

"Sold!" she cries, and we realize the night's prices are going to be high and its bidders sharp.

In rapid succession, she sells the next several horses: Marcus, a professional ATFO entry, for $4,000; Comet, from the Amateur Division, for $3,000; Jolie, a true black Gypsy Vanner, replete with feathers, from the Showcase category, is next.

"You could put her in your garden and just look at her," the auctioneer says, just before selling the mare for $1,500. Jolie's new owners jump up and down and hug each other in excitement.

Juniper is next up for auction. O'Connor stands beside her, and tears are streaming down her cheeks as the $800 starting bid is quickly snapped up by a woman on the rail. It is immediately countered by a proxy bidder holding a cell phone to his ear, and shortly, a lightning-fast bidding war ensues. The price soars all the way to $9,750; when the auctioneer asks for $10,000, the crestfallen woman on the rail shakes her head no, ceding victory to the proxy. Creamer takes the paddle from the proxy bidder, walks over to O'Connor, and turns it around so she can see the winner.

"She's yours," says Creamer.

O'Connor stands there in utter shock for a beat, before throwing her arms around the mare's neck.

Unbeknownst to her, O'Connor's family had put in an application to adopt Juniper and secured the winning bid. But as she returned Juniper to her stall, O'Connor knew the night's outcome didn't feel right—the other bidder was the woman from North Carolina who had been so committed to Juniper's entire journey, and who she knew was willing to give the horse a lifelong home.

The next day, O'Connor would put the wheels in motion to transfer ownership to the other bidder, saying on her social media that she is "a true believer that everything happens for a reason."

Prices for the next several horses range from a low of $600 to a high of $4,400, but Juniper's sale would remain the highest ticket of the night. Dominguez was also in tears, sitting on Paprika bareback, when the mare sold for $3,300. She's not the only one—trainers and new owners alike are caught up in the emotion and charged atmosphere of the night's proceedings, with tears and hugs, and cheers chorusing around the arena.

Shanuy is one of the last to come up for bid. Hanson is standing next to him, gently stroking his neck, as the auctioneer works to drum up interest. She accepts a minimum starting bid of $1,000 from someone on the rail, but despite her best efforts, she is unable to drum up any further bids. Despite his impressive performance this weekend, perhaps Shauny's unsettled history has preceded him, and few bidders remain with the requisite skills or experience to continue his training. People seem to be squirming uncomfortably under the auctioneer's powerful gaze.

"I'm gonna sell him," the auctioneer threatens, but no one answers her call, and she points her finger again. "Sold, for $1,000."

"That's to Brenda," Creamer chimes in, and it is as if the crowd makes a collective exhale, and they begin to applaud. Hanson smiles broadly and fairly floats out of the arena…with her new horse.

MORE THAN ONCE, Creamer has said the ATFO is an event borne out of desperation and need, because people are inherently more likely to adopt a sane, rideable horse, and when the average horse coming into your rescue lacks training and you have no funds, you have to get creative. When I caught up with her recently, she admitted that although every grand idea eventually runs its course, she doesn't think the ATFO is a concept ready for retirement just yet—but it does require constant evolution to suit changing times.

Since its inception, the demographics of the average Heart of Phoenix intake have shifted from "feral and recently gathered" to mostly owner surrenders. Creamer attributes this to a challenging economy, soaring prices on everything horse-related, and in some cases, an aging owner population. Horses still live much longer than cats or dogs, and we still don't do the best job planning for their end-of-life care. And although annual attendance at the ATFO has declined slightly since my visit in 2021, average prices at the sale have increased to around $3,700 a horse.

"We get over 10,000 inquiries a year from people looking for a horse," says Creamer. "Are all of those good? No. But there are people looking for horses constantly. We don't have a horse overpopulation problem. We have horses with bad outcomes, because they live so much longer than cats and dogs, and they are so much more fragile."

I'm not sure I totally agree with Creamer, but I can see Creamer's point. If we as a community—horse owners, trainers, veterinarians, rescuers, all of us—can do a better job making humane decisions for those horses living a truly *poor* quality of life, there will be more space for those animals who have the potential to live a truly *good* quality of life, with just a little (or sometimes, a lot) of help. It's not about saying "no" to the hardest cases, but rather about being realistic regarding animals' long-term well-being, after analyzing the cards they've been dealt.

For a reluctant rescuer, Creamer, and the organization she founded, have made an immeasurable impact within a region almost paralyzed for lack of resources. For many years, she was perhaps seeking to fill the void or numb the pain from her own unspeakable loss, but eventually, Creamer came to believe that "rescuing the horses of Appalachia is why God put her on this earth."

"In that we save horses, we save people," says Creamer. "People came far to change things for horses in Appalachia."

Chapter 9

THE PROFESSOR IS IN:
LIFE LESSONS THROUGH HORSEMANSHIP

DURING HER YOUNGER YEARS, Jordan Altman's family moved around quite a bit, spending time in New York and Kentucky before eventually landing in Lynchburg, Virginia, a medium-sized city located just east of the state's famed Blue Ridge Mountains. Altman faced the prospect of starting her final year of middle school in yet another new town, but for her, coping with change was a familiar challenge. In fact, throughout Altman's 14 years, instability had become practically the only constant.

Altman's parents both struggled with substance abuse, ultimately leaving her in the custody of her grandparents. But far from offering her nurturing care and comfort, they verbally abused her, and soon she was struggling with a myriad of mental health issues, including anxiety, depression, and panic attacks severe enough they required hospitalization. Most of the time, Altman kept to herself; she didn't want people to feel badly for her or treat her any differently. Besides, life had taught her that in the end, people were just going to let you down.

"It was not a healthy environment for a young kid," says Altman of her home life as a teen. Now approaching her twenty-fifth birthday, Altman is petite, with long, slender limbs, light-brown hair pulled back into a ponytail, and an aura of barely restrained energy. She is a young woman who likes to be on the move, to be actively doing something—including sharing the story of how being part of Brook Hill Farm in Forest, Virginia, where she now works as the barn manager, saved her life.

"If it wasn't for here, I don't think I'd be here, in all honesty," Altman confesses. "Coming out here helped keep me on a direct path, instead of veering off and ending up in a very bad place. This was my safe haven. My 14-year-old self would not believe how life has turned out."

BROOK HILL FARM'S founder Jo Anne Miller had no intention of turning her family's farm, located on 45 acres in the Bellevue Historic District in Bedford County, into the home of a nonprofit dedicated to improving the lives of horses and people. In fact, it all started fairly innocuously, when over dinner one evening, her good friend and veterinarian Dr. Ron Fessler suggested she bring in lame horses for rehabilitation and sanctuary. A lifelong horsewoman, initially she laughed at the notion. *Who would want to take in a bunch of lame horses?* she thought to herself.

"But in this county, you had to have one grazing animal for every 5 acres to be taxed as a farm," explains Miller. "He said, 'Let me just bring in some unwanted horses.' It started as a horse rescue."

In 2001, Brook Hill Retirement Center for Horses was officially established, and Miller drew on her own experience, plus time spent working as Fessler's vet tech, to rehabilitate horses with serious injury, or provide sanctuary to those unable to continue working in traditional roles. The need was so great, and the program so successful, that it wasn't long before Miller had more horses to care for than time. She needed either more help or fewer horses; she opted for the help.

"I started bringing inner-city kids to the farm, because I thought it would be good for them," explains Miller. "I realized they were failing school, and I told them they had to pass their classes before they could work with the horses."

Miller—an educator turned corporate manager turned educator—set up an on-site tutoring program for the young people coming to help on the farm. It wasn't long before she saw there was a special alchemy between a horse in need and a young person facing personal challenges. In 2010, she quit her "real job" to manage the program full time.

Today, Brook Hill offers programming 50 weeks of the year, with activities ranging from traditional therapeutic riding lessons (they are a PATH International Premier Accredited Center) to United Neigh, an alternative school program (Altman is an alumna), to Gates 4 Change, a program for youth-at-risk serving those who might otherwise fall through the cracks. The young people who participate in the latter two programs tend to fit a certain demographic—their families live well below the poverty line, they are struggling with a mental health diagnosis, and they have already "failed out" of traditional therapy programs.

For most of these young people, Brook Hill is their last hope.

Miller is the first to admit that mental health therapy is not the focus of the work at Brook Hill, but despite this, connecting youth-at-risk with horses offers a therapeutic effect. Lessons focusing on horsemanship skills give participants the opportunity to view their own challenges through a new lens. And although the majority of participants have never even been near a horse before coming to Brook Hill—and some are quite skeptical they will enjoy the experience—for those willing to step out of their comfort zone, the benefits are life-changing.

"I think the reason we are so successful is because everyone else is going at it from a psychological perspective," says Miller. "We go at it from an educational perspective. I tell this to the kids: [I] don't care how you feel—I'm going to give you a coping skill so you can survive and have appropriate behavior."

Brook Hill's approach seems to be just the bandage wounded young people need in order to separate themselves from life experiences often too horrific to verbalize. Although Miller doesn't ask her students to share their history, in time, they often do. One young woman, a refugee, was brutally raped before her family fled their homeland. A young man facing a felony assault and battery charge was himself a victim of serious abuse; upon arrival at Brook Hill, he was also anorexic and regularly cutting himself. Most—like Altman—lack parents or other adult role models in their lives to turn to. None are interested in re-living their trauma by discussing it in depth.

"We are not beating around the bush about what is going on," says Miller. "But I'm willing to sit with them and tell them what I'm going to do to help them. Our kids have been able to be successful, but I think they have chosen a different manner to do it. We are about learning coping skills and being able to deal with what's happened by moving forward."

But perhaps equally remarkable is that the majority of the horses helping Brook Hill's students to develop these crucial, life-saving skills were also once cast away themselves—neglected, thrown off, or otherwise discarded by conventional equestrians. When horses arrive at Brook Hill, most require patience, care, and special attention to restore their health and return to being their best selves. The horses begin their rehabilitation with Miller's most advanced students, and when ready, continue into a training program overseen by Brook Hill staff but implemented by the young people in the program. Some of the horses will remain with the program long-term, but others—almost 540 of them, since the program's inception—go on to new adoptive homes, thanks to the hard work put in by Brook Hill students.

It is a marvelous symbiosis—two beings wounded and hurting, often due to factors beyond their control, being given the time, space, and support to heal. But neither can do it alone. Working with Brook Hill's horses can't change what these youth have experienced, but in helping the horses, students learn how to regulate their own emotions, reactions, and behavior. These young adults develop positive qualities like self-confidence, self-belief, and the ability to ground in the present, that will help them move beyond the challenges they have faced. With all their attention and creative energy focused on helping the horses, most of the time, the youth don't realize they are also helping themselves.

Like the bumper stickers proudly displayed by adopters of rescue dogs, the question becomes, "Who saved who?"

An older mare with a sweet expression stands patiently at the gate; she is barefoot, her mane is long, and her coat has turned completely white. This is Saucy, a former 3'6" show horse who is now 27 years old and living in the Brook Hill Farm Sanctuary. But for several years, Saucy worked as a riding horse at Brook Hill, and she is also the first horse Altman felt deeply connected to. She considers Saucy to be her "heart horse."

"I really attached myself to her," says Altman as she opens the connecting gate to a larger paddock. "She gave me the confidence to know I could do more than I thought I was capable of. She allowed me to be myself and would not get mad at me or judge me for making a mistake."

Saucy moves on into the other field; she knows it is close to feeding time, when all the Brook Hill horses come inside to receive their individualized rations. Hers is fed as a soup; several years ago, Saucy had a softball-sized tumor removed from her throat, and she now lives on a liquid diet. The four days Saucy spent at Virginia Tech's veterinary hospital to remove the tumor were among the most terrifying in Altman's recent memory.

"I know losing horses is part of life," says Altman. "Horses' bodies are more complicated. But losing her was a big fear of mine, and I had a hard time with it, because of my abandonment issues, and not wanting anyone to leave me. That's one of my biggest fears—and still is to this day.

"It was very scary, but she survived, and so did I," Altman continues. "I got to go help pick her up. It was awesome—I was so happy to see her again."

Saucy belongs to another category of horse living at Brook Hill, those surrendered to the program by caring owners due to serious injury or lameness. In Saucy's case, a torn suspensory ligament effectively ended her high-performance career. But with time, rest, and rehabilitation, even the toughest ligaments can heal, and at Brook Hill, horses are offered each ingredient in abundance. Some—like Saucy—recover enough to join the working herd on the farm and participate in programming or are adopted out. Those who don't join the sanctuary herd. When I visit, 39 horses and one donkey call Brook Hill home, but this number is fluid.

Because Brook Hill is a retirement center, most of the animals coming to them are older; here, any horse under the age of 15 is considered "young." Some horses arriving at Brook Hill were seized by law enforcement and have unknown histories. Like the participants in the youth programs, many have suffered mistreatment at the hands of others and need time, patience, and structure before they begin to trust. But when they do, Miller says they often discover plenty of pearls.

"We have a horse we just found out was doing Olympic-level dressage before he was abandoned from an injury," says Miller. "Another, a Thoroughbred abandoned in a field in North Carolina, is a biter—someone mistreated him. We were schooling him a little bit, maybe the third month he was here, and we had some jumps up, and we decided to see what he knows. He jumped every jump.... I said, 'You've obviously had some good training down the line, and we just need to tap that piece of your brain.'"

Brook Hill's approach to helping horses is quite similar to how they help youth—by focusing on their strengths, it becomes possible to build skills in areas that are not as well developed. At one point, Brook Hill took in a number of older broodmares, none of whom had ever been ridden. But broodmares tend to be handled frequently, lead well, and possess a nurturing instinct. One of the first to arrive, a Thoroughbred mare named Princess, became a guinea pig of sorts for a specialized broodmare retraining program.

"Everyone says, 'You can't teach an old horse how to ride,'" says Miller. "Princess had been a broodmare her whole life. We did a lot of desensitizing with her, and she was not fazed by anything. She didn't care that we put sacks of feed, and later, a saddle, on her back. Eventually, we got on her, and we asked her to move forward with our legs. If you kicked her hard, what would she do? Nothing.

"If you think of our therapeutic population, the physically disabled who may not have control of their bodies, well, she was the best horse ever," Miller continues. "She just walked, and followed on the lead line, and mothered all our children. That carried over to all the broodmares that came. Now, can you ride her independently? No—but we didn't need her to ride independently. For those kids that happened to kick with their legs and give the signal to canter, this horse had no clue."

Outside the window of Miller's office is one of several large pastures. A small bay mare with a tiny white star and finely chiseled nostrils is napping in the sun. This is Bree, a Welsh pony broodmare, one of the farm's newer residents and already a favorite mount of children in the Rockin' Riders therapeutic riding program. Miller regards this owner surrender fondly while she continues an earlier train of thought.

"We have found a job for broodmares," Miller says softly. "That was an eye-opener for us. I've never met one who didn't take to it—not at all. They all just seem to think it's their job, to take care of these children."

TO GET TO THE BARN ENTRANCE at Brook Hill, visitors must pass through a tree-lined walkway leading to a small wooden gate. A generous-sized covered arena is to the left; to the right stands a series of low structures including the barn, feed room, tack area, and the former 1909 schoolhouse, now converted into offices and a classroom. A smaller arena containing toys, ground rails, and a plastic basketball net is used for therapeutic riding lessons; a jump course is set within a larger arena just next to it. Horses graze contentedly in fields in nearly every direction.

For youth arriving at Brook Hill from the city of Lynchburg, the bucolic and peaceful atmosphere is a tangible departure from their everyday lives. Although at first some students are so intimidated by the horses they refuse to have anything to do with them, most are intrigued enough they slowly begin to engage. Lessons focus more on discovery than the goal of emphasizing any particular horsemanship concept, although those skills tend to come in their own time.

"I've come to look at horses as a lifelong experience," says Tracy Russler, who has been Brook Hill's assistant director for 15 years. "I take my time, and I start at a basic level—this is a brush, this is a horse, how do those two combine together. I discuss horse behavior. I am very specific with the kids—you are partnering with the horse. It's a working relationship like you'd have with anyone—your foster parent, your colleagues at work. We are trying to make a relationship where it is beneficial for both."

"At the end of each session, we talk about their horses, but it always relates back to them," says Miller. "For example, I had a biracial child who felt they didn't fit in. We go out in the field—and don't ask me why—but the grays all hang together, the bays hang together, and the palomino and appaloosa are like, 'Where do I go?' We can bring up the things going on with the horses, in response to what is happening in their lives."

During their time at Brook Hill, each student is partnered with one horse, and as much as possible, the educators try to let the student choose which horse they will work with. Anna Baucum, who is Brook Hill's resident vet tech as well as a PATH International Certified Equine Specialist in Mental Health and Learning, says they employ what they call the "three date rule" to be sure the choice is a good match.

"We find they seem to pick horses that have similar backgrounds or issues to what they do, even without knowing the history of the horse," says Baucum. "We have some kids who've been abused, and they gravitate toward a horse that has abuse in his past. One girl with a limp chose a horse with an injury who also walked with a limp. She wanted that one, she said, 'Because he is still worth something.'"

Not all participants will learn to ride, and some attrition out before the two-year mark that Brook Hill educators feel is the minimum threshold to ensure lasting change in behavior. But those who do stay will progress in their own time to more advanced groundwork, then later, mounted work, even though their lessons may look very different from what you may expect to see at a traditional riding center. Miller gives an example of her approach with a novice rider learning to trot.

"Obviously, at first they are bouncing everywhere," says Miller. "Instead of barking out orders like a drill sergeant, I ask, 'How did that go?' and they usually say, 'Not so well.' We talk about some ways we can avoid bouncing, like posting. We break it down."

Later, teachers in the United Neigh program will use the same approach in the classroom, giving students a chance to explore their circumstances when events don't go as planned. For example, if they fail a test, students are asked to assess what was missing from their preparation, and what they can do to change the situation in the future.

"We try to make it all about choice," says Miller. "Most of these kids have never had choice, and they need to learn to make good choices. This is part of the whole program."

Brook Hill's young people also need stability, and that is why they remain partnered with their chosen horse for every visit. But for students who are involved long-term, the desire to learn more advanced horsemanship skills may require them to move on to a new mount. The timing of that change is always left up to the student—and if their former mount is then deemed ready to go up for adoption, the final decision regarding the timing of that transition becomes the student's as well. Otherwise, as long as horses are partnered with a student, they will remain at Brook Hill—even if they are "adoptable" animals; even if in another setting, the time would be right for them to move on. At Brook Hill, it is the relationship between horse and human that is always paramount.

A SMALL ORANGE TABBY CAT dashes past the door of a highly organized grain room, where Altman is mixing up the horses' evening meal. The late-afternoon midsummer sun is beating down, and programming at the farm has finished for the day. The entire week has been exceedingly hot and humid, and most of the equine residents are currently napping in the shade in small groups or are camped out in front of fans in a shelter. Altman, whose journey at Brook Hill has taken her from participant to key staff member, has experienced its positive impacts from both perspectives—yet she is struggling to succinctly articulate why its work matters so much.

"Being part of Brook Hill means a lot to me, because I had it to put me on a correct path," Altman says as she sorts through the feed buckets. "To be part of the team now and watch how it helps all the others—no matter the disability, no matter the family background, or anything else…." She pauses and wipes her face. I'm not sure if she is removing sweat or a tear. "To see the horses connect with the kids and help them all in their own special and unique ways, is a big eye-opener for everybody," she goes on. "To show that we're just as capable as everybody else, and we can achieve a lot more than we think we can. That's what being part of Brook Hill means to me."

Like so many other successful programs, Brook Hill's growth has been organic, responding to evolving needs and designing solutions. Along with that growth has come more structure, including an application and screening process for youth participants, the development of extensive partnerships with local and state-level social and educational agencies, and the cultivation of a dedicated volunteer base collectively contributing over 260 hours of time each month. Some of those volunteers were once participants themselves, and alumni are always welcomed back with open arms.

It is this sense of belonging that is perhaps one of Brook Hill's greatest gifts to its participants.

"The farm provides a safe place to come, and just be who they are, with the horse," says Russler. "I see them grow in confidence; I see them grow in being more comfortable with themselves. A lot are not with their biological families, and some have had many foster families. These kids learn to be chameleon-like, and that's something we maybe can't identify with. It's about just letting them be here, be who they are, and giving them an hour or an hour and a half to just be in their own skin."

JUST OVER 350 MILES NORTH, Gleneayre Equestrian Program in Lumberton, New Jersey, is also capitalizing on the benefits veteran mounts offer to youth. Since 1998, Gleneayre has offered hands-on, experience-based learning for youth facing challenges in their lives through its flagship working student program and offerings in equine-facilitated learning and equine-facilitated psychotherapy. Horses donated to Gleneayre are often highly experienced show horses needing to step down due to age or other limitations. As they continue to age, their role within the program changes, until they are ultimately retired on the property.

I visit Gleneayre on a mild day in early August 2023. The skies are gray and threaten rain, but they do nothing to detract from the elegance of the stunning 120-acre property. Pristine white fencing delineates generous-sized grass paddocks where horses peacefully graze in small groups. Stately trees dot the fields and line their edges, their leafed limbs offering shelter from the elements and adding a bucolic aura to the property. Well-manicured shrubbery lines a lane leading to a small cluster of buildings, including the main offices, several barns, and a classic white farmhouse that is still home to Gleneayre co-founder Ellen Healey. She and her late husband Bob—who both held a strong belief in the importance of education—conceived the initial idea for Gleneayre after seeing the positive effects involvement with horses had on their own children.

"People always ask, 'What is your background?' I went to school to be a secondary education teacher, but I never taught a day in my life," Ellen tells me with a laugh. "I went into real estate, got married, adopted four children and had three more. I raised them all, and had foster children. Does that qualify me for any of this? I have no clue, but I'm doing it."

It all started in a low-key manner in the late 1990s, when the Healeys began loaning their children's former mounts to local youth to care for and ride on the farm. It wasn't long before the Healeys determined they needed an equestrian professional to mentor these young people in a more formal way. They found just the right fit in the husband-wife team of Jason and Alison Newman, who came on board in 2002. Together, they helped design the framework for what today is known as the Gleneayre Working Student Program. Twenty years later, Alison (now Johnson) remains Gleneayre's Managing Director (sadly, Jason passed away in 2013).

Most of the young women in the Working Student Program come from a family facing a challenge—illness, a deceased parent, financial difficulties, suicide. Some are also navigating developmental adversities, such as learning disabilities or mental health challenges, or have otherwise made choices negatively impacting their lives. Most, but not all, have previous experience with horses before coming to Gleneayre. Although the Working Student Program and its curriculum are not specifically geared toward girls, throughout its tenure, only two boys have ever enrolled, both named Evan. One finished, one did not.

With a program cap of 20, the annual application process can be competitive, and both the child and her parent must separately explain why being at Gleneayre would benefit her more than attending a traditional riding program. An external firm evaluates each applicant's financial situation and recommends a monthly participation fee based on a sliding scale that starts at "zero." Participants may be as young as 10 years old, and once accepted, they can stay involved with Gleneayre through their thirteenth year of school, although occasionally, a few remain active even a bit longer than that. With nearly a decade to work with each participant, Gleneayre has plenty of opportunities to make a big difference in the course of a young person's life.

"Our Working Student Program is small in terms of the number of students we are reaching," Alison explains to me one afternoon from her office off the main barn aisle. "We keep it that way, because it's beneficial. We are able to give them that personalized attention."

"It's something we struggle with sometimes, when looking for sponsors or donors," adds Ellen. "'How many children do you serve in the course of a year?' Don't ask me that—ask me how many children I have on my farm in the course of a *day*, then multiply that by 365. *That's* how many children."

Although working students come to Gleneayre ostensibly to learn about horsemanship, they are also exposed to a curriculum that teaches them how to embody 40 character traits critical for success in life. These include qualities such as respect, bravery, and self-confidence—even time and money management—all concepts easily taught alongside learning about the everyday care of horses. All Gleneayre staff are trained in this curriculum and are expected to model these qualities in their words, deeds, and interactions with others. Tacitly, working students are constantly being exposed to models of positive relationships—of people who work collaboratively and can overcome conflicts in a healthy way.

"We do not tolerate gossip or drama—it's like a cancer, it spreads," explains Alison. "Our philosophy here is we are building pedestals for these kids to go up on, not knocking them down. Everything is based on positive reinforcement. Rather than pointing out negatives, shortcomings, what you did wrong, instead we focus on what you have done right, and what you've accomplished.

"I try to treat this like a job for them," Alison continues. "We are producing young adults who will eventually be able to contribute to the world, that have the character skills needed. One of the biggest ones is perseverance, or resilience. To be able to get up, and every single Saturday, be here at 7:30 in the morning, when there are more tempting things to do. It's understanding that the *team* needs you, and that every person on the team plays a role and is important."

THERE ARE FIVE WORKING STUDENTS on duty today. Each girl is expected to work at least one weekend and two weekday shifts each week, year-round, but many come as often as they can. Several are currently in the barn aisle, untacking after a morning lesson that included a drill practice. They are laughing, and loud, and full of joy. These young women share many things in common, including a love for horses, and have gained a sense of belonging here at Gleneayre. I also soon learn that for each of them, for different reasons, coming to Gleneayre and working with its horses represents far more than just a means to ride.

Sophia Bull, 16, joined Gleneayre in April 2018, just a few weeks shy of her eleventh birthday. Prior to that, she had done a little "horse therapy," but she wasn't even taught how to handle a horse there, never mind ride one. After that program ended, she was still intrigued by the idea of learning to ride—she loved to watch videos of riders and envied the partnership they had with their horses. It was her mother, Koeberle, who—despite being scared of horses herself—suggested that Sophia apply to Gleneayre.

"It was a little intimidating at first," admits Sophia of her early months at Gleneayre. "I had this gut feeling I had started too late. Usually when people get into horses, they have a mom or someone who's very interested. They're kind of born into it, or they've grown up around horses. The girls helped me get acclimated super-fast, and allowed me to start slow, then gradually work my way up.

"I was not confident at first," Sophia continues. "I was a little timid and pretty awkward. But it happened really fast—I started to make friends, and people were really nice to me. It was a whole community that I was quickly welcomed into."

Julianna Williams, 14, started riding at another facility when she was just six years old, but she craved more opportunities with horses than they would be able to offer her. She was 11 when she learned about Gleneayre through a family member.

"I thought I could learn a bunch, and there would be many benefits for me from this," says Julianna of her decision to apply to the program. "Like, developing a work ethic, and trying to find a balance between work and outside time. The more time I spend here, the more I want to stay here. Every day that I'm here, I'm always looking forward to coming back."

Lily Miller, 16, started coming to Gleneayre in 2019; she admits that for the first several years, she was too nervous to talk to anyone at the barn. Listening to her speak so confidently now, it is almost hard to believe this young woman hasn't always known her own voice.

"I'm a very anxious person in general, and I was really hard on myself," says Lily. "I'm a perfectionist—it's going to be my downfall. I'm still hard on myself, but everyone here was very welcoming. It took me a while to open up, but these past two years, I feel like I've really blossomed."

It is a refrain I will hear again and again during my visit to Gleneayre—the absolute transformation experienced by the young women who fully commit to the Working Student Program. The culture of the program is one that promotes both growth and absolute support for wherever they are at in their journey.

"It is the structure that helps them be able to navigate," says Alison. "This is a refuge for some of the kids that are here. It is noisy or chaotic at home, and this is where it is quiet. This is where there is peace. This is where, 'I have a friend, where I'm not picked on, where I'm accepted for who I am, versus who I have to pretend to be when I'm at school.' It's somebody pushing them to the next level, believing in them, asking them to do more, achieve more, where they may never have been asked to do anything more, because the family can't provide that support or assistance at that time."

With such a wide range of ages and experience levels, the types of duties assigned to working students vary. During the week, Gleneayre employs a full-time staff responsible for mucking and other cleaning, but on weekends, the working students take over those duties. New students often start with easy chores like cleaning stall bars and polishing tack boxes. Later, they learn to fill waters, pick paddocks, or groom the "motherless horses"—animals that are part of the program but don't currently have a student assigned to them. Each task teaches the students that attention to detail matters and builds a sense of responsibility.

Kennedy Newman, 12, is Alison's daughter. She was not quite four when her father succumbed to a heart attack on the property, and for her, the farm holds a different meaning than it does for the others. As a very young child, she looked up to the working students, and at 10, she became one of them. With quiet pride, Kennedy tells me she can take care of a whole barn of horses by herself—including mucking, bedding, throwing hay, and feeding—if she has to.

"I keep working because that builds my confidence up," says Kennedy. "I feel like part of the program, not just the trainer's daughter. I get to meet more friends, get more responsibilities. I can speak up to people. As I get more strength, heavy things are lighter to me."

She pauses, and I wonder if perhaps the strength she is speaking of has nothing to do with physical ability.

Working students are partnered with at least one specific horse, whose routine care becomes mainly their responsibility. This is the horse they take lessons on most frequently, and when they feel ready, they may choose to take their horse in one or more of the horse shows held on the Gleneayre property throughout the year. Alison coordinates horse assignments, usually partnering each rider with a new mount in the late autumn, giving them the winter to learn the ins and outs of that animal before the next show season.

Na'riah Danser, 11, only joined the Working Student Program about eight months before my visit to the farm. She came with a passion for horses but no equine experience, and so far, she has only ridden one horse— 26-year-old Theo. When she describes him to me, Theo sounds like the quintessential lesson horse: he can be opinionated, sometimes refuses to trot when she asks, and is generally more compliant when the instructor is leading him. When he wants to be turned out, Theo kicks the stall door and paces in circles; given any opportunity, he is a voracious cribber. He may sound like a barn manager's nightmare, but Na'riah thinks Theo is pretty much perfect, because he knows what he wants—a quality she is learning to emulate.

"Once you get something started that you really like, you shouldn't stop," says Na'riah to me quietly. "I used to get made fun of and be called the 'horse girl' in school. But I don't care what other people think or say, because it's what I like, and I'm not going to change for them."

GLENEAYRE'S 36 HORSES range from Sugar, the ever-so-reliable beginner's pony, to Conley, the beloved jumping schoolmaster who always forgives a mistake, to newer arrival Fruit, a strapping bay Warmblood, and at 18 hands, currently the largest horse on the farm. Gleneayre's horses typically come from high-end hunter seat programs, where they were kept tuned up by professionals and competed by well-educated amateur or junior competitive riders. They are used to living in stalls and avoiding the elements. In general, these are horses accustomed to the finer things in life, and just like the working students themselves, they require a transition period and some grace as they adjust to their new lifestyle.

But gradually, these former circuit hunters and jumpers and equitation horses learn how to embrace their best selves—they begin to learn how to enjoy rolling in the mud, how to spend most of their days turned out, and eventually, how to function within a small herd. In reality, these animals often have to learn "how to be horses" again, and as they make that adjustment, they typically become more relaxed and better able to accept unfamiliar experiences in general.

"We have to teach them to be okay with 'letting down,'" says Alison with a laugh. "The longer they're here, the more that begins to happen."

It is yet another example of how the horses' experience mirrors that of the youth working with them.

To be accepted into the Gleneayre herd, horses must still be capable of jumping at least 3', which gives them greater longevity in the mounted program. As their needs change, the intensity of each horse's workload will decrease, until finally, they move across the Rancocas Creek, which bisects the property, and onto the Landing Street side of the farm. The Landing Street animals are retired from riding, but many still offer solace to participants in Gleneayre's equine-facilitated learning programs.

Alison tells me about the progression and impact of one horse,

Leo, a former Grand Prix show jumper who at one time was ridden by Olympian McClain Ward. By the time Leo arrived at Gleneayre, he had already stepped down quite a bit from his previous competition level and was initially ridden by a working student in the 3' equitation classes. Later, he popped around cross-rail courses with novice jumping riders, and still later, he became a walk-trot stalwart. After that, he moved to the Landing Street side, and despite—or perhaps, because of—his intimidating 17.3-hand stature, became one of their most valuable equine-facilitated learning teachers.

"My favorite thing is watching how these horses change in their own journey," says Alison. "With a horse like Leo—watching how many people that one horse touched along the way shows how important his role was to every single one of them. How cool is that to see! And we have nearly 40 of them."

Having a range of horses, all at different levels, allows great flexibility when it comes to matching each working student with the perfect equine teacher. Each of the girls is excited to tell me about some of the horses they have worked with, and what they have learned from the experience. From several of them, I hear about Cooper, a gray pony with a mind of his own. Cooper prefers smaller fences and wants to be first—until he *is* first. The girls say he has taught them how to "stick with it," how to be a leader, and sometimes, to understand that "progress is better than perfection." Then there is Casco, an elegant chestnut Warmblood with a thin blaze, who I'm told looks easier to ride than he is. Riding Casco taught his rider to believe that she was capable of more than she imagined. And of course, there is Eres, a newer member of the equine team at Gleneayre. Eres prefers to counterbend and to take the long spot when jumping; he is also very bouncy. But his rider shares with me that Eres makes her feel taller, braver, and like she has a friend near her, always.

One of the reasons some equestrians are unwilling to take on an older horse is because they know the laws of time are not in their favor. Typically, sooner rather than later, something will happen, health-wise, and the horse will need to work at a less intense level or even be retired completely. And of course, eventually, the caretaker of an older horse will be tasked with making some difficult decisions. Only rarely does a horse peacefully pass away on his own. Equestrians willing to care for an older horse are implicitly agreeing to be their stewards, and to do the hard—but ethical— thing when the time comes.

At a facility like Gleneayre, where the average age of equine on the property is trending well north of 20, saying goodbye is simply a fact of life. I soon learn that preparing working students for this inevitability is also part of the program's curriculum.

"We talk a lot about resilience," says Alison. "All along, we help our children understand the nature of what we are doing—that we have older horses getting a second chance at life. We give them the absolute best life they can have, and if it is their time to go, we allow them to do that with dignity, and then we carry on."

Not infrequently, whether due to divorce, death, addiction, illness, or some other reason, working students have already experienced acute loss in their lives. When students lose their project horse unexpectedly, it becomes an opportunity for the staff to model healthy ways to grieve and to cope with loss. The Gleneayre community surrounds them with love and support, often coordinating a small memorial in honor of the horse. They take time to acknowledge the student's feelings, and the connection she still feels with the animal, without allowing the loss to turn into an overly dramatic or traumatic experience.

"We teach them that we are thankful to have these horses, that we were able to learn from them and have the ride we did, and we carry that memory as we move on to help the next horse," says Alison. "We carry on, and we allow the next horse to take that space, for as long as possible."

I AM SITTING IN THE PASSENGER SEAT of a golf cart driven by Gleneayre's Executive Director, Bill Rube, heading to visit the Landing Street side of the farm. A lifelong equestrian, Bill is a jocular man with an unmitigated passion for Gleneayre's work. He is also fully open about his own previous struggles with loss, substance abuse, and engaging in other self-destructive behavior. It is largely thanks to those experiences that Bill believes wholeheartedly in the power of horses to pull people through difficult times. Ellen rides on the golf cart's back seat—her choice—and as Bill navigates the bumps on the dirt road bordering the Rancocas Creek, she is explaining how Gleneayre's unmounted equine-facilitated programming came to be.

It has been nearly two decades since the first cohort of horses donated to Gleneayre began to reach the stage of life in which complete retirement was warranted, and program staff were faced with several challenging ethical questions. The nascent Gleneayre Working Student Program had been built, at least in part, thanks to the contributions of these older horses, and although no longer suitable for riding, they were generally in good health. Everyone agreed the animals still deserved respect, care, and safety. But how best to achieve that? Who could they entrust with fulfilling these critical needs for their special elder animals?

One day, Alison—who studied psychology in college—learned about the emerging field of equine-facilitated psychotherapy, and she immediately recognized an opportunity. Here was yet another way for Gleneayre to fulfill its mission to help local youth "develop character, learn ethics and responsibility, and grow physically and emotionally," all while giving their retired horses a purpose they could embody simply by being horses.

"It opened the possibility of another world out there, that these horses were not just to be cast aside," Alison told me later. "They could be healers, later on in life."

Gleneayre's first equine-facilitated learning program reached 10 children, who visited the farm for two hours weekly for 10 weeks. It was so successful that in the ensuing years, the range of activities offered grew exponentially, and a small covered arena with an attached classroom was built on the Landing Street side to accommodate unmounted programming. With the new offerings in equine-facilitated learning (led by program staff) and equine-facilitated psychotherapy (conducted by a licensed mental health professional in collaboration with an equine specialist), Gleneayre's reach went from 20 working students a year to dozens of young people annually, while also ensuring their animals lifetime care and sanctuary.

Bill parks the cart opposite the entrance to a tidy beige-colored barn, and we climb out. The sun is starting to peek through the clouds, and several horses are grazing in nearby pastures. If the main Gleneayre property can be described as "bucolic," somehow the Landing Street side takes that peaceful atmosphere even a step further. Perhaps it is thanks to the scent of fresh-cut hay from the field next door, or the raptor lazily rising on a thermal above it, or maybe, it is simply the knowledge that the horses living here now lead a life of relative leisure. Most are veterans of the Gleneayre Working Student Program; a few of the eldest were once ridden by Ellen's now adult children.

But not all of the Landing Street horses have always enjoyed the comfort and safety they are afforded today. Ellen pauses to point out a black-and-white pinto pony, who is so busy eating she can't even bother to glance in our direction when Bill gives a low whistle.

"That's Rosie," says Ellen. "She was found tied to a chain link fence in the center of Philadelphia. No one knows who she is, or how she got there."

Rosie was saved from that situation by Last Chance Ranch, an animal rescue in Quakerstown, Pennsylvania, and eventually found her way to Gleneayre. Then there are Snowflake and Angel, two gray-faded-to-white Miniature Horses living together in a smaller dirt paddock under the trees. These Minis each experienced neglect and trauma before being rehabilitated by Artemis Farm Horse Rescue in New York. It is almost hard to imagine as I regard them now, looking as round as little butterballs. But Ellen tells me Angel was once used as bait in a dog fighting ring, and she still retains an air of wariness and caution around strangers.

Gleneayre has developed partnerships with several schools and other organizations working with youth at risk, who underwrite the funding and provide the logistical support for the young people attending EFL programming at the farm. In their sessions, participants are exposed to an unmounted curriculum called "Cowboy Poetry," which focuses on developing the 40 essential character traits working students are also striving toward, all through the lens of the Old West.

"We ham it up," says Ellen with a chuckle. "Cowboys ran their lives on the 'Cowboy Code of Ethics.' When a cowboy gave his word, that was his bond. He respected it, and he respected you, and you lived up to it."

Participants—along with their aides, facilitators, and other support staff—begin each session seated in a circle, and everyone is expected to contribute to a discussion on the character trait being presented that day. From there, the group moves into the covered arena, where they will be joined by one or two horses to complete a related activity. One day, they might be "Dancing with Horses," an activity that challenges the youth to place their hands on the side of the horse, close their eyes, and simply focus on what they feel, hear, and think, while music plays softly in the background. Another time, the group will collaborate to build an obstacle course representing elements of the Pony Express, and then individually, each participant must lead their horse through, around, and over the obstacles.

Participants are taught to respect the horses, themselves, and each other—but beyond that, there are few rules.

"So many kids today will want to quit when they encounter a problem," says Ellen. "Why couldn't a cowboy quit? Well, if they quit, they didn't eat, they didn't live. They had so many obstacles in their way, they had to think outside the box. In our program, we talk about finding alternative solutions to a problem."

Rarely do EFL participants have any experience with horses before visiting Gleneayre. Some are first-time juvenile offenders; some belong to gangs and have a rap sheet as long as the program's agenda. Some of these "kids" are 6'2" and weigh 300 pounds. Others attend alternative schools established for children requiring specialized support with various developmental, psychological, or learning conditions. Although not every participant is initially willing to engage with the activities presented, most eventually choose to take part, in their own way—because the allure of the horses themselves simply becomes too much to resist.

"The horse matters, because it draws the kids in," says Ellen. "The horse matters, because it is something different. That is on the surface: 'We're going to go see horses, and work with horses.' They're usually very excited about that. But there is a true connection that people make with horses. Horses will reflect back to you what you're sending out. The horse is an equal facilitator to us humans."

"Horses are such amazing animals," adds Bill. "They are so intuitive. Once you let your guard down, they let their guard down, and I think that's what really works for this program."

During her time as a facilitator and educator with Gleneayre's EFL programs, Ellen has seen hundreds, perhaps thousands, of young people evolve through their exposure to the Cowboy Poetry curriculum or their newer offering, Journey of the Spirit Horse, which is based on Native American culture. And although she has always believed in the positive effects of horses on youth, she wasn't sure she could attribute those changes to the horse specifically—until she met a young man we will call Max (not his real name).

Max was 14 years old when he first came to Gleneayre with his classmates, most of whom were either on the autism spectrum or navigating another diagnosis that caused them to move through the world in a unique way. When Ellen met him, Max seemed completely shut down; he didn't speak, or make eye contact, and she couldn't see that he made any effort to engage with his peers. When it was his turn to share during discussions, he would always pass, even turning down lower-stakes options such as speaking with someone one-on-one and having them share on his behalf.

One day, the theme was "problem solving," and the task was to take a halter and lead rope, go out into one of the paddocks, put it on a horse, and lead the horse back independently. To that point, no instruction had been given regarding how to put a halter on, and part of the challenge was for the student to figure that out. Max entered the paddock and made a beeline for Archie, a 17.1-hand, slab-sided former equitation horse that the staff had nicknamed "Landshark."

"We didn't really use Archie in the equine-facilitated programs, but he was turned out over there," remembers Ellen. "He was sort of a loner and always stayed down over the hill. He had a history of nipping and didn't care for people on the ground."

Ellen assumed that Archie would simply move away when Max got closer, as was his wont. Instead, what happened next is still perhaps one of the most powerful moments Ellen would witness during her career.

"Max goes over to Archie, looks at the halter, looks at Archie," says Ellen. "He puts his hand out, and then Archie puts his head in Max's hand, then puts his head in Max's chest. And Max pats Archie. They stand there for a bit, and then Max takes the halter, puts it on Archie, hooks the lead, and brings him up the hill."

The halter may have been on sideways, but Max's peers were impressed. And from that day forward, Max and Archie shared an unshakable bond. When Max's bus pulled in, Archie would be waiting at the gate.

"They were two loners who identified each other immediately," says Ellen. "Archie became a program horse, but only for Max. From that day forward, Max began to share, and other kids starting seeing him differently. It changed his position within the group.

"I don't have the passion for horses that some people do," Ellen continues. "I love my horses, and I will give them the best care that I can. But I have a passion for children, and that moment with Max—well, you can read all the jargon you want on equine-facilitated stuff, the textbook explanations of why it works. I agree with them. Can I voice them to you? I don't know that I can. But it can work."

Most of Gleneayre's equine-facilitated learning programs end with a celebration. Family is invited, and everyone enjoys a cowboy-style buffet meal featuring baked beans and cornbread. Each participant receives a small wooden plaque with their self-designed "cowboy brand" on it to commemorate the experience. Some choose to leave their plaque behind, and the edge of the covered arena is lined with these squares, creating a mosaic that tells a story of healing and hope.

We pile back on the golf cart to return to the main farm; we are all quiet for a moment. I look to the fields where Gleneayre's retired teachers graze, and I feel their contentment. In EFL, the horse becomes a confidant, a judgment-free friend, even a way to express the participant's own emotions through interpreting what the horse is doing. I wonder how many people these horses have touched, how many young people realized they had choices in their lives, or that there were ways to overcome obstacles and challenges, simply because these horses were there.

Throughout a lifetime, one horse may indeed fill many roles, and will mean different things to different people. In terms of their service to humans, the horses on Landing Street have come full circle.

BEFORE I FINISH MY DAY at Gleneayre, I have one more person to meet. Alexandrea Williams, 18, started at Gleneayre when she was 11 and is now a proud program alumna about to start her first semester at Rutgers University's New Brunswick campus. She is equal parts nervous and excited to be taking this first official step into adulthood—but thanks to her years at Gleneayre, she feels ready.

"I feel like the program has done everything it needed to do for me, as in teaching me things about horses, about riding, about myself," says Alexandrea (though they share a last name, she is not related to working student Julianna). "It was my time to go. What more was there for me to do?"

Alexandrea has just come back from her college orientation, about an hour away from her home in nearby Mt. Laurel, New Jersey. While there, she managed to make two new friends, one of whom will live in her dorm; she tells me of her plans to study marketing and join the university's intercollegiate equestrian team. Although she sounds excited, Alexandrea's body language tells me she is perhaps a bit more nervous about her impending transition than she will admit. But a moment later, her tone grows more serious and her affect changes, and I see resolve and determination in her eyes.

"I started here on August 1, and it was hot," remembers Alexandrea of her first few weeks at Gleneayre. "There is no seniority for some of the chores, so mucking the fields with a wheelbarrow and pitchfork—even if you're new, we'll take you, and you're going to do it. And they are big fields—they require at least two people.

"I had never done anything that physically demanding before," she continues. "And this is something I have struggled with personally, but when something is hard, I want to quit. Like, I'm not going to do it. But this place has taught me perseverance. When something is tough, you buckle down and get through it. Tough isn't permanent, and it will all be fine."

Alexandrea is a young woman who has learned a thing or two about tough times. Her parents divorced when she was quite young, and although her mother was supportive of trying to find affordable opportunities for her horse-loving daughter to ride, her father was not. She learned about Gleneayre through her first riding instructor, and it sounded like the perfect chance to access a world otherwise out of financial reach. Alexandrea wrote her Gleneayre admissions essay about her father's battle with stage 4 prostate cancer. He died on her thirteenth birthday. Her eyes well with tears as she remembers navigating his last months with the support of one special four-legged therapist in particular.

"Conley was really there to help me," says Alexandrea. "He was my safe space. If he was lying down in the stall, he would let me come up to him, and I could sit in his stall with him. They told us not to do that, but Conley would never freak out. He'd just look at you and go about his day."

Focusing on her horse kept Alexandrea's mind on something easier to process than the difficult emotions she faced outside the barn, while the farm atmosphere provided comfort and security. She tells me that during her teen years, nearly all her closest friends were at Gleneayre, but then she corrects herself.

"They aren't my friends—they are my family," says Alexandrea. "They are just my everything, really, and that got me through not having a lot of things. It got me through that difficult time with my dad.

"The girls here now are like my children—they call me mom," Alexandrea goes on with a laugh. "I had a graduation party with them, and the three older girls in the group came for a sleepover. When I tried talking about how much they meant to me, I could not get through it. I was crying the whole time—it's too hard, and would take too long, to describe what they mean to me."

After speaking with me, Alexandrea popped into the barn for a visit; several students attached themselves to her side immediately, and one even hopped on for a piggyback ride. It was like any joyous family homecoming, with laughter and smiles all around, their voices fading as they disappeared into the barn. As I watched them walk away, I remembered something Ellen had told me earlier—when program alums come back to visit, some with their own children in tow, they frequently cannot recall the reasons why they needed a program like Gleneayre in the first place. Instead, they remember their experience in the program as being an enjoyable time in their life, one during which they were able to be successful, develop lifelong friendships, and feel the support of a community willing to weather life's ups and downs with them. It's about helping young women like Alexandrea understand that who they are is not defined by their circumstances or the bad things that have happened to them, and that when they are able to embody qualities such as patience, resilience, and perseverance, rewards will come.

AFTER VISITING BROOK HILL and Gleneayre, I feel inspired and hopeful, not just for the positive benefits programs like these offer to older equines, but also for the young people whose lives will be irrevocably improved by engaging with these wise teachers. Further, these programs provide viable alternative models for the care of our older equines, examples of how animals may age with grace and dignity, and a guarantee of their safety, while they continue to offer their wisdom and experience to those in need. Models like these prove it is possible, with just a bit of creativity and inspiration, to make powerful connections between horses-at-risk and people-at-risk that may, in the end, save them both.

"We talk a lot about resilience...we help our children understand the nature of what we are doing—that we have older horses getting a second chance at life. We give them the absolute best life they can have, and if it is their time to go, we allow them to do that with dignity, and then we carry on."

ALISON JOHNSON
GLENEAYRE EQUESTRIAN PROGRAM
MANAGING DIRECTOR

Chapter 10

FINDING YOUR WAY BACK HOME

A YOUNG WOMAN IN JEANS and a hoodie has her arms wrapped around the neck of a fuzzy bay yearling. His black mane is twisted into tendrils and as she scratches his crest, they push aside to reveal a white freeze mark. "Tango" is an American Mustang, born in a Bureau of Land Management (BLM) holding facility to a dam gathered from Adobe Town, Wyoming; the young woman is a US Army veteran who spent 14 months serving in Afghanistan.

When the pair first met a few months earlier, in fall 2019, Tango had only recently arrived at the EquiCenter in Honeoye Falls, New York. Separated from his herd and in a new environment, this intelligent young Mustang was distrustful, hypervigilant, and anxious; even though she had no previous horse experience, "Marie" (not her real name) felt like she understood Tango immediately. Since returning from her service overseas, Marie had been reclusive and felt disconnected from friends, family, and the outside world. She suffered from hypervigilance so severe that she rarely ventured out in public without her service dog.

But working with Tango changed all that.

Marie is one of the dozens of veterans who have participated in the EquiCenter's Mission Mustang program since its inception in 2018. Initially, the program was born out of an official Memorandum of Understanding between the BLM and EquiCenter, a Professional Association of Therapeutic Horsemanship International Premier Accredited Center, with the goal of developing a replicable model and best practices for integrating wild horses and burros into therapeutic programming. The pilot version of Mission Mustang was so well-received by EquiCenter veterans that today, it has become one of the organization's core program offerings for that population (other opportunities include therapeutic horticulture, beekeeping, a cooking program, and therapeutic riding). But Mission Mustang is unique among them in that it is dedicated to connecting Mustangs and veterans specifically—two American icons—for the betterment of both.

"You're tapping into the veteran's DNA of service," explains Katherine Hatch, EquiCenter's Executive Director. "That's key to recovery. For so many of us, if you feel like you're doing something outside of yourself, it's very impactful."

There is a clear need for this type of work. As a group, veterans have a greater likelihood of experiencing post-traumatic stress disorder, or PTSD, than do civilians. But new statistics are especially chilling—up to 30 percent of veterans from our most recent named conflicts, Operations Iraqi Freedom and Enduring Freedom, suffer from PTSD, a larger percentage than veterans from any other era. PTSD can have a crippling effect on both the afflicted individual and those who live within their orbit; symptoms may include vivid flashbacks, hyperarousal and hypervigilance, depression, and avoidance of any situation that may trigger memories of the traumatic event. According to a 2023 US Department of Veteran's Affairs report, of the roughly 18 veterans who take their own lives every day, at least one quarter have a PTSD diagnosis.

Standard treatment for PTSD is a combination of one-on-one or group therapy and medication, but for many veterans, these options have proved ineffective in relieving their symptoms. In fact, due to stigma, cost, and limited availability of practitioners, fewer than 50 percent of veterans seek any treatment for their PTSD at all, and of those who do, more than a third discontinue before completion.

But it isn't just veterans who are in need of help. Mustangs, considered by many to be an iconic symbol of the American West, have increasingly been caught in the crossfire among the BLM, animal advocates, and the American public.

The BLM is legally tasked with the protection and management of Mustangs, but it also has the daunting responsibility of managing 245 million acres of federally owned land, some one tenth of the United States land base, more than any other government agency. Their mandate is to maintain this public resource for consumptive uses such as energy development, livestock grazing, and timber harvesting, while also preserving relics of the nation's natural, cultural, and historical heritage. It is a delicate line to tread, balancing the use of some natural resources with the protection of others. But perhaps nowhere is the BLM put into deeper internal and external conflict than when it comes to the management of wild horses and burros alongside the ecosystems they inhabit. Today, their Wild Horse and Burro Program is in financial distress and is hopelessly overburdened with gathered animals.

By January 2024, the BLM was caring for nearly 65,000 Mustangs and burros living in off-range corrals and pastures. By the end of the 2023 fiscal year, the cost for the care and feeding of these gathered animals hovered around $109 million a year, nearly two-thirds of the Wild Horse and Burro Program budget, and the capacity for animals in long-term holding had almost been reached. Meanwhile, over 73,500 animals still remain on public lands, and except in a select few areas where mountain lions are found, there are no natural predators to control herd growth.

With such a large percentage of the agency's dedicated funding going simply toward the care and feeding of those animals in holding, there are only minimal financial and human resources remaining to train, promote, or otherwise enhance future opportunities for Mustangs. Instead, the BLM has increasingly sought partnerships with nonprofit organizations, volunteers, and even prison rehabilitation programs to establish gentling opportunities for gathered Mustangs. Trained animals have a much higher rate of adoption by the general public than those who are unstarted.

"Programs like Mission Mustang may only assist a few animals, compared to the broader challenge we have right now," explains Jason Lutterman, Public Affairs Specialist for the BLM's National Wild Horse and Burro Program. "But it's not all about the exact number of animals that are placed into private care. It's also about demonstrating how versatile and how useful these animals are, in a variety of activities, including these types of therapeutic programs that help veterans.

"We hear there can be a stigma about wild horses—that they're too wild, or can't be trained for anything," Lutterman continues. "These programs turn that stigma on its head, and show these animals are actually extremely valuable. They can become important parts of people's lives, and a part of people's recovery."

But for veterans like Marie, the experience is about more than just gentling a wild horse—it is about feeling the connection with an animal who does not judge them for anything they have done or seen. It is about relearning how to trust, both themselves and others. It is about creating a space in which, for at least a few minutes, they can be free from the nightmares that continue to haunt them.

The free-roaming horses of the American West most of us call Mustangs aren't truly wild—like the Appalachian Brumbies, they are technically feral, the descendants of horses lost or stolen from Spanish settlers. Our word "Mustang" comes from the Spanish *mesteño*, which can be used as an adjective or noun, but typically describes a cow or horse who has escaped from his owners and is now living wild. Today's animals also include genetics from ranch stock, cavalry mounts, and other modern breeds, but some isolated populations still retain traits clearly revealing their original Iberian heritage. Their story is a mixture of legend and fact, irrevocably etching the Mustang into the iconography of a nation's evolution.

In 1971, Congress passed the Wild Free-Roaming Horses and Burros Act, which states Mustangs "are living symbols of the historic and pioneer spirit of the West, which continue to contribute to the diversity of life forms within the Nation and enrich the lives of the American people." The Act transferred Mustang management from state to federal jurisdiction and initiated the Adopt-a-Horse-and-Burro program.

But the Mustang was not always so revered. In the early 1900s, herds were decimated by "mustangers," who gathered the animals for use in the growing dog food industry, and there has long been conflict between livestock ranchers and wild horse herds competing for similar resources on federally owned grasslands.

It was in the post-war years that public sentiment toward Mustangs began to change. While many individuals were involved in what was essentially a grassroots movement, few names are as synonymous with wild horse protection as that of Velma B. Johnston, a former secretary from Nevada. Better known as "Wild Horse Annie," Johnston was horrified to witness the widespread abuse and rough treatment that Mustangs endured, and she used her considerable skills of prose and persistence to advocate for legislative protection. Over the years, she coordinated several letter writing campaigns supporting pro-Mustang legislation. Nicknamed the "Pencil Wars," thousands of citizens, including school children, flooded Congress with more correspondence than on any other single issue of the day besides the conflict in Vietnam. Her efforts contributed to the creation of first the 1959 "Wild Horse Annie Act," and later the 1971 Act that sealed federal protection.

At that time, the population of wild horses and burros on the range was estimated at 25,000, just beneath the "Appropriate Management Level" of 26,690 (which is still the target population today). But under protection, herd numbers began to double almost every four years. Wild horses live in family bands and prefer to frequent familiar areas for watering and grazing. As population increased, overgrazing contributed to loss of native plant species, and Mustangs competed with wildlife for scarce resources like water. Something clearly had to change.

In the years that followed, the BLM implemented several strategies to control herd numbers, including increasing the frequency of routine gathers and administering reversible fertility control vaccines to mares. Soon, the agency was gathering more horses annually than it could place in good homes, and in 1988, it began contracting with private landowners, mostly in Kansas, Oklahoma, and Nebraska, to create some 289,000 acres of long-term "holding pastures" to handle the overflow.

Two fertility control vaccines, one using *porcine zona pellucida* and often simply called PZP, the other a gonadotropin-releasing hormone variant called GonaCon, were widely hoped to be the magic cure. Injected or darted into a mare, they seemed effective in preventing conception for a year or more. However, wild horses have survived in their rough and barren environment due to their natural wariness and speed. Volunteers might successfully dart a mare once. It was unlikely she would be darted twice.

Add in the expansive range and rough terrain that is Mustang country, and it is no wonder the use of these vaccines has mostly been a failure, although both are still utilized by the BLM in their herd reduction plans. One individual familiar with the situation says the strategies the agency is using in an attempt to limit the prolific growth of the wild horse and burro population is "kind of like putting a finger in the hole of a dam."

"The challenge we are facing is these horse herds can grow very rapidly—between 15 and 20 percent a year," explains Lutterman. "That means they are doubling in size every four or five years—that's exponential growth for these herds. Our challenge is trying to stabilize those herds as much as we can, so they are at a healthy level for the land and the animals. We don't like to see any animals out there starving, or fighting for water or other resources."

In 2004, the so-called "Burns Amendment" was added to the original 1971 act. Named after its sponsor, Senator Conrad Burns of Montana, it directed the BLM to sell "without limitation" to any willing buyers those animals in long-term holding over the age of 10, and those which had been passed over for adoption at least three times. When a wild horse is sold instead of adopted, the title of ownership for the animal passes directly from the federal government to the buyer, giving the new owner the right to immediately re-sell the animal, if they are so inclined. In an adoption, the transfer of title does not occur for one full year, during which time the horse may not be sold or given away; additionally, the BLM may conduct compliance checks to ensure the horse's well-being. Although the agency has always (and continues) to maintain that it is against their policy to sell wild horses or burros to slaughter, either directly or through "kill buyers," animal advocates were outraged by the Burns Amendment, feeling that it opened the door to exactly that eventuality.

Currently, wild horses live in 10 states west of the Mississippi River, on some 31.6 million acres of remote, hardscrabble land dubbed Herd Management Areas (HMAs). By 2023, Nevada was home to well over half of the national total of 73,500 mustangs living on the range. And remember, the BLM still estimates that the Appropriate Management Level (AML)—meaning, the total number of horses the range can sustainably accommodate—is just under 27,000 animals. This means there are almost *three times* as many horses still living on the range as it can theoretically support; in some areas, the local population may be *five* or even *ten times* the established AML.

"That creates a lot of pressure on the resources out there," says Lutterman. "These are high desert ecosystems. There's not a lot of precipitation, not a lot of water or forage growth."

With the number of animals both on the range and in holding constantly, and exponentially, increasing, by the early 2000s, BLM employees tasked with implementing Wild Horse and Burro Program policies considered finding new opportunities for gathered mustangs to be a top priority. It was around this time that BLM Wild Horse and Burro Program employee Debbie Collins (now retired) met Jonathan Friedlander, founder and then CEO of a new therapeutic program called the EquiCenter. Collins had heard that some therapeutic programs were already using "horses with a freeze brand" in their programming, and she and Friedlander discussed the possibility of incorporating Mustangs into the EquiCenter's work. At the time, Friedlander felt the organization was too new to make that kind of commitment—after all, taking on an unhandled Mustang requires both logistical resources and knowledgeable personnel. But the conversation started a relationship, and the two stayed in touch for nearly a decade.

During those years, the EquiCenter moved to its current location at the William and Mildred Levine Ranch, a 200-acre property located just outside of Rochester, New York. The move allowed for growth in their therapeutic riding program and expansion into diverse new areas of programming to serve the local community. Veterans, in particular, looked for any opportunity to spend additional time on the property, but with a waitlist at that time of over 40 riders, there wasn't capacity to allow them to do more riding.

Mustangs taken from the range share many qualities with veterans suffering from PTSD and other invisible wounds; both Mustangs and veterans often struggle to adjust to their new life. Frequently, there is an immediate connection between veteran and Mustang, and a feeling they can relate to each other. The seed of an idea was born and evolved into the Mission Mustang pilot program.

The BLM was not able to offer any financial support to Mission Mustang, but the agency did assist in the initial horse selection process and transport. The first group of BLM Mustangs—later named Trooper, Ranger, Hero, and Sergeant Baker—arrived at the EquiCenter in May 2018, and 10 nervous yet excited veterans stood outside of a newly built steel corral to greet them. As they waited, a bald eagle flew over the property. An unusual visitor to the area, its symbolism was noticed by all present.

The veterans who signed on to be part of the pilot did so because they wanted to help save the Mustangs; little did they know that in the end, the Mustangs would save them.

WHEN MSGT. LUANN VAN PEURSEM retired after 33 years in the service, she was a highly decorated combat veteran, having earned the Air Force Medal of Honor with Valor for saving the lives of two fellow airmen during an attack in Baghdad. But when she returned home, the attacks stayed with her. She couldn't sleep, was hypervigilant, and lost trust in those around her. Nightmares and flashbacks consumed her.

"I was very close to becoming a statistic," says Luann, of Rochester, New York. "I was contemplating suicide. Thankfully, I had an intervention through EquiCenter. From the minute I set foot on it, there was just something about it. It was like magic."

Luann was one of the original veteran participants in Mission Mustang. She was there the day they arrived, ran off the trailer, and huddled together in the lean-to style shelter built specifically for them. Her connection to the scared animals was immediate and profound.

"If they had arms, they would have hugged each other for security," remembers Luann. "I am watching them, and I realized that I was seeing the same symptoms I have experienced. We all looked at each other, and just said, 'Oh my God, that's us. We get it.'"

Over the next 10 weeks, Luann and her fellow veterans gained the animals' confidence and trust, taught them to wear a halter and lead, to load onto a trailer, and have their feet handled. When a Mustang can do these things, they stand a better chance of being adopted.

"I just fell in love with the horses," says Luann, who worked mostly with Ranger. "A simple thing like learning how to approach the horse, and within time that horse comes up to you—you realize that you are so focused on this horse that the triggers and memories that haunted you are in the back seat. You can let your body relax for that time."

Pairing inexperienced handlers with untrained, feral horses may seem risky. But Mission Mustang's trainers have always worked one-on-one with each veteran, first teaching important basics such as watching the horse's front feet, the position of their nose, and being aware of body language—both theirs and the horse's. Veterans are never allowed in with the Mustangs until the trainers have determined the situation is safe.

Once a veteran is part of Mission Mustang, there is no "expiration date" for their enrollment; currently, an average of 25 men and women participate each week, working one-on-one with the EquiCenter's six Mustangs. Usually, the veterans work with the same horse in each of their sessions, which gives them a chance to establish a relationship with that animal. But with far more veterans in the program than horses, each animal is exposed to different handlers each day of the week. This is ultimately a good thing, as a horse that works with different types of people will hopefully end up being easier to place in a new home when they are ready. At the time of writing, over half a dozen Mustangs had found new homes as a result of the program, and Ranger, who Luann worked with, was "employed" as an equine instructor in the EquiCenter's unmounted therapeutic horsemanship program .

Many veterans who participate in Mission Mustang end up finding other ways to become involved at the EquiCenter. Some choose to volunteer as a means of "giving back," while others participate in or even initiate other aspects of the veterans' programming (Luann, for example, is responsible for establishing the beekeeping program).

"It becomes kind of a community for them," explains Lindsay

Alberts, EquiCenter's Director of Equine Operations. "I've had a few veterans say, 'I was going down a dark road, and this is what brought me back.' Knowing you had someone that far down that road say that horses are the thing that brought them back—hearing that from one person is enough to keep the program. But I've probably heard it from five or more. That is huge."

It is a raw, gray December morning in 2019, and two days of late-season rain have turned everything to mud. A sharp wind blows icy cold air, tentacles of northern winter reaching across the Finger Lakes. I pull my hood closer around my face and stomp my feet in a futile attempt at warmth. But DS (not her real name) is oblivious to external discomfort; she is wholly focused on the body language of a chestnut Mustang named North Star. She needs to get close enough to the yearling to slip a pink rope halter over his nose, but so far, the timing of her responses to his behavior hasn't been fast enough. Instead, the gelding canters past, sending a spray of muddy ice water over her jeans and patch-festooned vest.

"You're not making him work hard enough," says Emma Minteer, a professional equestrian who specializes in colt-starting and Mission Mustang's main trainer. "He can do this all day. You have to give him an incentive not to leave you."

Emma has been fascinated by Mustangs since a presentation on the subject back in her 4-H days. Now a married mother of three, Emma still considers herself a horse-crazy kid, and today, she looks like one—she is wearing a thick brown Carhartt jacket layered over a maroon hoodie, and the brim of a camouflage green ball cap sticks out beneath a knit winter hat. Her ranch-cut jeans are tucked into worn, square-toed cowboy boots, accented with turquoise embellishment. Emma is the embodiment of feminine toughness. She has a perpetual smile and nerves of steel.

Emma remains calm as she coaches DS through the process of connecting with North Star. Communicating with these nervous animals is all about controlling human body language and energy, helping the horse to understand that this bipedal predator actually means him no harm. Force and intimidation rarely work; applying pressure released exactly when the horse demonstrates the preferred response often does.

After the youngster canters by DS several more times, Emma tactfully helps by positioning her own body in such a way that the animal chooses to stay in a smaller space. With less distance to cover, there are just another few moments of back and forth before DS triumphantly slides the crownpiece of the halter over the gelding's poll and ties a knot just below his eye. Together, they move through a chute and into a connected round pen. There is no specific goal for the day's training session—just an opportunity for two wary beings to practice trust with each other.

Other than an 18-month window around the time of the pandemic, Emma and her husband Jack have been part of Mission Mustang since the beginning. Emma's brother served 21 years in the Air Force, and she welcomed the opportunity to give back to the veteran community. But most importantly, the Minteers have extensive experience starting Mustangs "from scratch," when the animals are still in their most instinctive, fearful state. In 2012, both husband and wife began participating in the Extreme Mustang Makeover, a program of the Mustang Heritage Foundation that gives trainers an untouched Mustang and 100 days to produce a horse capable of completing an all-around equestrian competition, in an arena, in front of a packed house (the Makeover was the inspiration for Heart of Phoenix's ATFO). Emma won the Makeover in 2016 and 2017.

There are many reasons why Emma loves working with Mustangs, but mostly, she appreciates their spirit and the fact they were previously unhandled by humans.

"With a Mustang, you don't have to go back and wonder, 'What happened to you two owners ago?'" explains Emma. "You don't have all that baggage. The horse is scared—but it's scared because that's its instinct. You start with a clean slate."

Back in the round pen, DS waves a stick topped with a small pink flag next to North Star, working to desensitize him to unfamiliar stimuli. With each flick, the flag snaps, and North Star's ears swivel rapidly, assessing the threat. Once, it accidentally brushes the hairs of his copper coat, and he anxiously steps away. But DS persists with the motion, and soon he is standing calmly while she flicks the flag up, down, up, down. He has learned enough for one day.

DS is beaming as she leads North Star back to his corral. Before joining Mission Mustang, injuries from a 2016 auto accident ended DS's nearly 35-year career as a sign language and tactile interpreter, causing the PTSD and depression she had long held at bay to resurface. She felt like her life was meaningless; she considered suicide.

"I'd been real depressed," says DS. "I was a mess, because without work, I didn't have a purpose. It was amazing coming to Mission Mustang. It was having a reason to get up in the morning…and knowing that the horses aren't going to judge you. I was finally finding a purpose, and a reason to live."

It is this process of coming back to one's self that is so transformative to veterans participating in the program.

"It's so outside of traditional therapy," explains Executive Director Katherine Hatch. "And the Mustangs are such a personal experience. For so many people, traditional therapies don't work, or they're not enough. This is just another route to wellness. When traditional therapies are not enough, this moves the needle."

Later, DS and I regroup in the EquiCenter's heated tack room, shaking off the chill. A tortoiseshell cat hops into DS's lap, and she strokes the animal's fur. The cat's hair is crackling with static but neither of them seem to mind. DS loves animals; she rode a little as a child growing up in Georgia. She joined Mission Mustang partway through its first session and worked with Sergeant Baker (she calls him Sarge) for nearly eight months. When the gray gelding left for his new home in late 2019, she felt like a proud mother.

"It was bittersweet, but seeing how far he had come, from being a wild Mustang to having a saddle on, that was like the graduation moment," says DS. "That was cool."

Sarge's training had already been well underway when DS met him; she hadn't had the opportunity to work with a horse brand new to the program. So when the EquiCenter brought in a pair of yearlings to join

Mission Mustang not long before Sarge's departure, DS was feeling ready for a new challenge.

When the Mustangs arrive, they are still completely feral, unhandled and unnamed; in holding, they are distinguished only by their color, gender, and the number on a plastic BLM identification tag they wear on a cord around their neck. At the EquiCenter, the veteran responsible for removing that tag has the honor of naming the horse.

"As soon as I heard the thing about the tag, that was my goal," says DS. She gestures to a red and white tag with the number 9259, hanging on the tack room wall above her head, then shows me a grainy photo on her phone. It is a sunny day, and DS has her arms wrapped around North Star's neck, the tag and its string just barely visible and hanging from her hand. By learning to remain calm and controlling her own fear, she had earned his trust—lessons she can take into other spheres of her life.

"In learning how to work with him, it helps me learn how to control my own fight or flight," says DS. She looks fondly at the photo for a moment. It shows the gelding's broad white blaze, which reminds DS of a compass.

"In the Navy, if you ever lose your way, you find the North Star," she says. "I think the whole point is finding your way back home, and I think this place is a good place to find that, a reason to get out and go on."

AROUND THE SAME TIME DS gave North Star his name, Army Signal Systems Support Specialist Phil Wytrwa was struggling to find his own way home. He had served in the Army for eight years, including 15 months spent in Afghanistan, where he called in medivacs and airstrikes, and set up equipment inside armored vehicles and base camps—basically, handling anything communications-related. When the PTSD symptoms started, Phil wanted—needed—them to stop. He attempted suicide twice; after the second attempt, he spent a week in the restricted wing of a dedicated hospital before returning home, not yet feeling whole.

"I was becoming part of the statistics," says Phil simply.

Not long after he was released from the hospital, Phil and his wife Alisha were watching the morning news when a segment came on about the EquiCenter's Mission Mustang program. Phil thought horses were interesting, but other than riding one once during his elementary school days, he had never really spent any time around them. Yet when the narrator began to interview Marine Cpl. Brett Avery, a member of the first group of veterans through the program, Phil began to pay closer attention.

"I want to say it was the emotion in Brett's face, and how he presented the Mustangs—it sounded very appealing," remembers Phil. "From his interaction with them, I could see there really was a benefit to these horses. My wife was quite adamant that we go check it out."

So the next day, the couple made the 30-minute drive from their home in Henrietta, New York, to the EquiCenter, where they had a brief tour and learned about the EquiCenter's offerings. Phil was immediately intrigued by the Mustangs, but just a short time later, the program took a brief hiatus when the COVID pandemic was officially declared.

But Phil stayed in touch, and by 2021, he was finally an official Mission Mustang participant, working with a horse named Sierra and a trainer named Steve Stevens (who briefly replaced the Minteers in the Mustang program). Along with teaching Phil horsemanship basics, Stevens focused heavily on developing an emotional, empathetic understanding of the horse. Phil found he could readily identify with Sierra, a fiery chestnut mare, who was both highly anxious and reactive—just like many of the veterans who worked with her.

"Sierra—well, she is the one who taught me how to be in that moment, even in a hostile situation," says Phil. "She would throw her head around, paw at the ground some, even pin her ears back. She was a very wild horse, for sure."

Sierra was later adopted by one of the EquiCenter's trainers, and in 2022, Phil began working with North Star and Emma. He started spending more and more time at the EquiCenter, volunteering and working as an equine care specialist to further his knowledge. Those who watched Phil with the horses called him a "natural." One day, he approached Emma directly.

"I spoke to her and said, 'This is something I really want to do,'" remembers Phil. "'I don't want to splice fiber optic cables anymore. I want to do *this*.'"

Phil began visiting the Minteers' Rose Hill Ranch in Naples, New York, working under their direction with some of the horses on their property, all while continuing in the Mission Mustang program. Eventually, he and Alisha purchased North Star and moved him to the Minteers' ranch, too. Today, Phil is an "assistant instructor in training" for Mission Mustang, and he teaches veterans unmounted horsemanship basics there in several sessions each week. He is also working toward attaining PATH International's Equine Specialist in Mental Health and Learning credential.

"I'm still relatively green," says Phil. "I'm not to the point where I'm helping veterans take the tags off the Mustangs yet, or any of the heavy groundwork with Mustangs and veterans. I'm essentially getting them accustomed to knowing body parts, recognizing body language—teaching them how to stay safe."

Despite his own growth since working with the wild horses, Phil admits that his belief in the program was recently put to the test when the sound of nail guns from a scheduled construction project at the EquiCenter triggered an onset of his PTSD symptoms. For a few days, Phil stayed home, avoiding both the facility and working with his beloved horses. He considers the fact he was able to overcome this setback as concrete proof of the program's efficacy.

"I wholeheartedly believe in the power that the Mustangs have to be able to create change, and to allow you to think differently and outside of the box," says Phil. "From the benefits it's given me—I know it will work, and I've seen that it works for other veterans, as well."

North Star is now five years old, and Phil and Alisha share the gelding—he mostly rides, she prefers groundwork. When I caught up with Phil early in 2024, he had never heard the story of how North Star received his name. DS had moved back to Georgia before Phil began working with North Star, but he knew who she was—he and Alisha have their horse's old BLM tag with DS's name written on the back.

"It gives me chills," he admits, when I tell him the story. "The thing is, my wife and I, we got compasses tattooed on us. It all falls into place with North Star. It really goes hand in hand."

As of early 2024, the EquiCenter was home to six Mustangs, representing members of four different "batches" of horses to arrive at the property: Ranger (one of the originals), Tango, Beacon, Faith (the newest to be named), and two other as-yet-to-be named mares who were simply called "the pinto" and "the bay."

Emma is principally responsible for selecting the Mustangs for the program, and she does her best to choose animals that, beneath their fear and inherent caution, show signs of a willing temperament. Although she remains partial to horses that originated in the Adobe Town Herd Management Area (largely because one of "the best horses she will own in her whole life" came from there), Emma admits she has worked with other horses from Adobe Town who ultimately proved more difficult, and in reality, "There are good horses all over the place." Ultimately, the truth is that the suitability of any animal she selects is really just a best, albeit well-considered, guess.

"It's like judging a book by the cover—you don't know what you're going to get until you get it home," she says.

But despite the uncertainty, there are a few variables Emma takes into consideration when she studies the available horses. First, she watches the way in which each animal interacts with the others in the pen, and how they each respond to challenges regarding the pecking order. Next, she looks at their eye: like many horsemen, Emma believes the quality of the expression found there provides insight into their temperament. Finally, she evaluates their conformation, to determine if their build will set them up for success in whatever future career she has in mind for them.

Early in 2023, Emma headed to Tennessee to select the most recent "crop" of Mustangs for the EquiCenter. She spent almost a day and a half observing the horses available; ultimately, she selected three younger mares. Younger horses, in general, have proven to be a better match for the program, although of course there can always be exceptions. North Star and Tango are a case in point—they are the same age, came from the same Herd Management Area, and both arrived at the EquiCenter at the same time as yearlings. While North Star has moved on with Phil and Alisha, Tango still remains at the EquiCenter.

"He still needs work," says Emma with a laugh. "Tango's a really nice horse, but his instinct, anytime he's not sure about something, is to bolt. He's super reactive. But a lot of veterans can relate to stuff like that. We're trying to get him to the point where he can go on and find a permanent home."

Emma has to balance the needs of her own business and family with the work she does at the EquiCenter; currently, she spends three days a week there, but knows she could easily fill more time, if she had it available. But another motivator for Emma are the 65,000 mustangs still living in BLM holding. She compares them to children in the foster system, saying they all need to be adopted. These are some of the reasons why the enthusiasm of Mission Mustang alumni like Phil is so important, because cultivating additional instructors will ultimately give the program an opportunity to expand.

"Honestly, I've seen what the power of a horse can do for a person," says Emma. "That's what it comes down to. I know a horse can bring healing to somebody who is hurting, whether that's what they're looking for or not.

"I've seen lives change, in just being able to work with a horse," she continues. "I feel weird for saying this, but God gave me a gift—why not use it? It would be just throwing it away to not offer what I can offer. I want to be able to help somebody not hurt as much."

ON THE AFTERNOON of my first visit to the EquiCenter, I watched as Marie was teaching a young Tango to lift his feet. They shared a give and take that was as beautiful as the dance the horse is named for—small pressure, a toe lift, a release.

Due to the weather, we were in the facility's cozy indoor, normally used for therapeutic horsemanship lessons. A few other horses joined Tango in the ring for schooling sessions, but not one broke the nonverbal connection between veteran and Mustang. As I watched the joyful choreography between them, I was struck, not for the first time, by the truly awe-inspiring power of horses. Not in their sheer physical capability, which far outstrips that of any *Homo sapiens*, but in their willingness to trust. A trusting horse keeps his physical power completely under control and gives himself so freely over to the requests of the human. They do not do it because they have to—they do it because they *choose* to. It is their belief in us during those moments when we do not always believe in ourselves that makes the connection so compelling.

Finally, Tango freely allowed all four legs to be held. It was an ultimate display of trust—the prey animal offering his flight to the predator. Marie gave the horse a hug.

Though it was Tango who was in training that day, it was perhaps Marie who was most transformed.

CERTAINLY, INDIVIDUAL PROGRAMS like Mission Mustang, on their own, will never make a significant impact on the total number of untrained wild horses in BLM holding. But for the individual animals in the program—and the humans they touch—future prospects improve exponentially. And perhaps, as word about the impact of this type of unique programming continues to spread, hopefully other facilities will be brave enough to take the logistical and financial leap that the EquiCenter did back in 2018.

For centuries, horses have served humans as work animals, a niche that is no longer needed in our mechanized, modern world. But what horses can still offer us is partnership and a bond. Their sensitivity mirrors our own emotions, and to connect with them requires us to examine hard truths about ourselves.

Perhaps the niche the horse fills today is that of healer.

"I saw something in that horse that I saw in myself," says Luann Van Peursem. "It has just been unbelievable, not just for myself but my fellow veterans. All of a sudden, we have a purpose again. We are part of a whole."

Afterword

THE FIRST STEP

A FEW MONTHS AFTER completing the first draft of this book, my 25-year-old Thoroughbred mare, Lee, began acting strangely. Always a bit of a "quirky" horse, her behavior became more unusual, beginning with excessive pacing along the fence line of the run in paddock she had lived in for several years, instead of quietly snoozing in her shed (her more typical way of spending the day). Within a few weeks, her odd behavior had escalated to periods of trotting, cantering, and even spinning in her paddock, combined with panicked vocalization; all of this, despite no discernible change in the environment around her. When one of these episodes started, she was nearly impossible to console. Her palpable fear was agonizing to watch.

Working closely with my veterinarian, I spent the next three months trying to determine what was driving the behavior. We installed cameras to unobtrusively watch her; we experimented with supplements and medications, moved her to different paddocks, and ran relevant diagnostic tests, none of which led us closer to resolving the problem. In between Lee's episodes, there were periods of relative normalcy, sometimes for several days in a row. But whenever I started to hope that perhaps whatever was triggering her panicked behavior had resolved, she relapsed.

With a northeastern winter rapidly approaching, I worried about her slipping on ice, sweating through blankets, breaking through a fence, or colicking. I knew the situation was becoming critical.

In the 1960s, a British author named Ruth Harrison wrote a book called *Animal Machines*. It was an excoriating inquiry into the conditions that livestock and poultry species faced under the factory farming methods that still dominate production agriculture today. Its publication led to widespread public outcry and inspired the British government to launch an investigation into the welfare of farm animals. The governmental committee that resulted ultimately drafted an 85-page report in which they identified what are commonly known today as "The Five Freedoms." These guidelines have served as a baseline benchmark for many animal welfare rules, regulations and guidelines around the world ever since.

The Five Freedoms are:

1 Freedom from Hunger and Thirst

2 Freedom from Discomfort

3 Freedom from Pain, Injury, and Disease

4 Freedom to Express Normal Behavior

5 Freedom from Fear and Distress

Creating conditions that assure The Five Freedoms represents a minimum standard for the well-being of domestic animals of all species, and concomitantly can serve as a quality-of-life assessment for animals facing adversity. Although physically Lee seemed well, emotionally and mentally, there was clearly a problem we could not resolve—she was not *free from fear and distress*. Whenever she had a panic attack, Lee suffered, and I suffered along with her. When it became increasingly clear that we could not fix the problem, I was left with no other choice but to let her go.

Lee and I had been a team for nearly two decades; I felt her loss acutely. But having just penned this narrative, her decline and ultimate passing also felt like a test of my own convictions around the importance of humanely caring for animals throughout their life cycle. As agonizing as her final months were for me, and as helpless as I felt to change the circumstances, I remained committed to taking on her agony as my own. Our understanding is that horses live only in the present. When I said goodbye, Lee was at peace, and I knew I had done the only thing possible to alleviate her further suffering.

Horses—in their majesty, strength, and grace—inspire powerful emotions. You don't have to be an equestrian to admire them, and the unique and intertwined history of our two species, horse and human, dictates a far deeper connection than what we hold with many other non-human animals. Unfortunately, direct access to horses, and equestrian educational opportunities, is becoming harder to come by in many areas across the country. The importance of activities like Hidden Pond Farm's Camp Desperado, or the Gleneayre and Brook Hill equestrian programs, cannot be overstated. Not only are they helping horses, they are giving young people the opportunity to become compassionate, empathetic, and responsible members of society. Without compassion for others, we are all lost.

The realm of equine-assisted services—including hippotherapy, recreational therapeutic riding, equine-assisted learning, equine-assisted psychotherapy, and more—is proving to be just the salve many wounded souls need. From trauma victims to the disabled to veterans, working with horses is turning feelings of adversity and "otherness" into success and capability. Certainly, the veterans at Mission Mustang will tell you about the horses who changed their lives, as will the formerly incarcerated people who participated in the Thoroughbred Retirement Foundation's Second Chances program. Though not strictly equine-assisted service programs, each serves as a model for how interacting with horses makes people's lives better. In my work as a narrative journalist, I have profiled dozens of equine-assisted service programs, and nearly to a one, they share that they are fully enrolled, with a healthy waitlist. Often, participants have no previous experience with horses when they come to one of these programs, but the general public is learning about the horse's capacity to heal humans.

When you become intimately aware of just how profound a connection with the horse can be, it becomes impossible to tolerate the idea that these animals should be subject to conditions denying them The Five Freedoms. Yet within the equine industry itself, there are still those among us who would turn a blind eye to the fact that we have more work to do in this regard. If we want to ensure that no horses end up unwanted, we must use our considerable collective knowledge, skill, and wisdom to make the best decisions possible for each individual animal at every step of that animal's journey.

What does this look like? I don't profess to have all the answers, but I would offer you this: it will require a cultural shift, across the industry, from the grassroots up. I expect it will look like everyday horse lovers, people like you and me, saying, "Enough." Each of us has the ability to make simple changes in how we think about a horse's life and well-being to effect powerful change. It starts with doing better for the individual horse (or horses) we care for, or love, or admire.

In speaking with the many sources whose stories have appeared in these pages, one consistent theme emerged: hope. Despite what might, at times, seem like insurmountable odds, the advocates, rescuers, lobbyists, executive directors, trainers, owners—*horse lovers*—you have met in *Unwanted* are all operating from a belief that *we can make a difference*. We can change things for horses at risk or in transition. But it will take each and every one of us setting aside gross differences and coming back to the one fundamental core value we share: we each love the horse.

My fervent hope is that, after reading these stories and pondering the questions raised, you, too, will believe that you can make a difference for horses. It is not my place to tell you what that first step looks like. I only ask that you be willing to take it.

Christina Keim, MEd, MFA
Cold Moon Farm, Rochester, New Hampshire

ACKNOWLEDGMENTS

WHEN I FIRST BECAME interested in the topic of unwanted horses, intuitively, I believed reopening US slaughterhouses was a losing proposition, not only because it would cost us our social license with the broader public, but because doing so would let the equine industry too easily off the hook for a problem of its own creation. At the same time, I appreciated the arguments of those who were concerned for the well-being of those equines who might fall through the cracks, and the need for broader safety net services, support for shelter and rescue organizations, and a revised mindset around caring for our animals across their life cycle. To better educate myself, I searched bookshelves and archives for a reference that could help me, an equine professional, better understand the events that led our industry to this place of conflict. What I found were articles in popular press and niche magazines and newspapers, and posts on blogs and advocacy websites, but no single source sufficiently detailing the complexity of the situation. If I, as an equine professional, couldn't readily sort truth from fiction, what hope did the average horse enthusiast have? This realization is, in part, what led me to attend the Lebanon Valley Livestock Auction in 2019 (detailed here in the introduction), and to explore the topic further in my MFA thesis, published in 2020.

The book you hold now is the continuation of that project and represents nearly five years of ceaseless exploration of the beliefs around, perceptions and misconceptions of, and possible solutions to the unwanted horse problem in the United States. Throughout this project, there were dozens of individuals who were tremendously giving of their time, knowledge, experience, and expertise to help me better understand where those of us in the industry have come from, where we are, and where we might be headed in regards to helping horses at risk. Additionally, there were many individuals who shared their insight around the craft of researching and writing about such a complex—and potentially heartbreaking—topic, who were instrumental in helping me shape this journey in a way that hopefully kept the reader turning the pages.

First, I am grateful to the support and wisdom imparted by my most definitely non-equestrian MFA thesis committee, helmed by Sue Hertz and supported by Tom Haines and Jaed Coffin. During my time in the program, Jaed frequently reminded me, "This is the story you came here to tell." I will admit I have frequently replayed this comment in my mind—first, while completing my thesis during the early days of a worldwide pandemic, and later, while navigating the challenges and setbacks inevitable in tackling any large-scale, long-term, and complex project. Sue, Tom, and Jaed each were wonderfully generous in offering their suggestions and feedback around turning this seed of an idea into a book-length manuscript, and for this, I am deeply grateful.

In addition, for helping me shape the arc and scope of this book, I would like to thank Kathryn Miles, whose own work has been so influential to mine, and the unofficial "master of research," Keith O'Brien, who taught me, "There is no such thing as writer's block," as well as reminded me to "think in terms of what is 'gettable.'"

To the Saturday Scribes, particularly the extremely talented and dearly departed Mary Duquette (who taught us all about grace and acceptance in the face of insurmountable odds), and my MFA colleagues, especially Susan Geib and Kristen Luciano (who both reviewed early drafts of this work)—thank you for your support, encouragement, and patience in listening to an awful lot of horse talk over the past five years. Being part of this community has helped me more than I can properly articulate!

Thank you so much to my dear friends (not all of whom even like horses that much) for listening to me, encouraging me, and tactfully *not* asking how things were going on the book from time to time. Heather Salisbury, Becky Lord, Melissa Burdette, Sally Batton, Sally Oxnard, and

Cindy Burke—you all have been the most wonderful cheerleaders, and so kind to lend an ear when I needed it. Jessica Joyce, you did all this and more, helping me keep my own farm going when I was on the road visiting facilities and organizations, completing interviews, and working on finishing the draft. Thank you, all.

Thank you to Dr. Amanda Rizner, DVM, of Ross Corner Animal Wellness Center in Shapleigh, Maine, for reviewing portions of an early draft and telling me with tears in your eyes, "I think I have just read your first book." And to Jen Verharen of Cadence Coaching—I appreciate you giving me the nudge I needed to send my proposal to the perfect publisher for this story and for being an incredible role model of self-acceptance, honesty, and compassion for yourself and those around you. To Donna Bixby, who willingly and, dare I say, *enthusiastically* drove nearly 15 hours each way from New Hampshire to West Virginia and back, camper in tow, to attend the Appalachian Trainer Face Off because "I thought there might be a story there." (I am still sorry we ended up driving over that one mountain, and also for the beginnings of the hurricane we drove home in—it was still a great road trip, though.)

As I started delving into the complex world of equine rescue and welfare work, horse auctions, and other realms of the industry about which I knew not enough, I reached out to many strangers who have become professional connections and even friends. Along my journey, many people went out of their way to help me, and though they may not be quoted in this work, their influence is present throughout. This list is by no means complete, but I am particularly grateful for the help and support of Laura "Phoenix" Jumpp, Colleen Segarra of Equine Rescue Resource Inc. in New York, Kelly Smith of Omega Horse Rescue in Pennsylvania, and Janine Jacques of Equine Rescue Network, for offering their time to share insights and experiences with me. This book also benefited from information and anecdotes shared by Bernice Amburgey, Cpl. Brett Avery, Cheryl Barnes, Meris Bickford, Vania Carr, Debbie Collins, Jonathan Friedlander, Ginny Grulke, "Marie," Erin O'Neill, Diana Pikulski, Katelyn Reese, Elizabeth Rine, and the late Robyn Cuffey. Thanks as well to Robyn Kent and others who, in conversation, helped me to identify my own blind spots on these subjects.

Partially as a result of my research for this book, I came to write a monthly column for *The Chronicle of the Horse* digital edition called "From Rescue to Ribbons." In this feature, I spotlight stories of horses who have been discarded, neglected, or otherwise cast aside, but thanks to the help of compassionate equestrians who refuse to give up on them, go on to shine in new homes and careers. These stories helped fuel my fire for this project and reminded me how important it is for the equestrian community to remember that "rescued" is not synonymous with "broken."

To the team at Trafalgar Square Books—Becca, Martha, and Caroline—for believing so wholeheartedly in the importance of this project, I bow in gratitude.

To my father, Thomas Keim, and his wonderful wife, Terry Lee— thank you for your endless support of my sometimes bold dreams.

And finally, to Miah, for your patience, tolerance, help, and general awesomeness—I could not have done this without you.

END NOTES

INTRODUCTION

On the Federal Definition of Livestock and its impacts on the Equine Industry:

29CFR B.V §78.120B (Code of Federal Regulations) *Raising of "Livestock"* https://www.ecfr.gov/current/title-29/subtitle-B/chapter-V/subchapter-B/part-780/subpart-B/subject-group-ECFRd236f5a25dee61f/section-780.120

Interview: Julie Broadway, President, American Horse Council

On the percentage of "working horses" in the United States:

(2024) *2023 Economic Impact Study of the US Horse Industry.* American Horse Council Foundation.

On the Amish and Mennonite communities in Lancaster and Lebanon County, Pennsylvania:

Wesner, E. (2024). *Exploring Amish culture and communities.* Amish America. https://amishamerica.com/

The Young Center (2024). *Amish Studies.* The Young Center for Anabaptist and Pietist Studies at Elizabethtown College. https://groups.etown.edu/amishstudies/

On the ending of US equine slaughter in 2007

Ahern JJ, Anderson DP, Bailey D, Baker, et al. (2006) The unintended consequences of a ban on the humane slaughter (processing) of horses in the United States. *Animal Welfare Council, Inc. Colorado Springs CO.* http://naiaonline.org/pdfs/AWC_UnintendedConsequences_5%5B1%5D.16.06.pdf

Hamilton, A. (Jan 24, 2010). Horse abandonment rises. *The Daily Sentinel/ Casper Star Tribune.* https://web.archive.org/web/20170805181103/http://trib.com/news/state-and-regional/article_97d6bcfc-2298-561e-963c-9b87c2817687.html

Larkin, M. (July 27, 2011). Closing of US horse slaughter plants still reverberates; GAO study asks Congress to fund inspections or institute permanent ban. *American Veterinary Medical Association.* https://www.avma.org/javma-news/2011-08-15/closing-us-horse-slaughter-plants-still-reverberates

Whiting TL. The United States' prohibition of horsemeat for human consumption: is this a good law? Can Vet J. 2007 Nov;48(11):1173-80. PMID: 18050800; PMCID: PMC2034431.

PART I: THE ROAD TO SALVATION?

CHAPTER 1: RESCUE ME

Quoted Interviewees: Phyllis Elliott, Jeff Greenleaf, Kathy Woodbrey

General Information regarding Hidden Pond Rescue and the Maine State Society for the Protection of Animals:

https://hiddenpondequinerescue.org/

https://www.msspa.org/

Keim, C. "A Closer Look At: The Maine State Society For the Protection of Animals." *UnTacked.* Spring 2022, pp. 90-93.

On Full Circle of Life Shelters:

(n.d.) *Full Circle of Life Horse Shelter Network.* Horses Plus Humane Society. https://horseshelternetwork.org/

On Maine's record for Animal-related law and policy:

(February 1, 2023). *States' Animal Protection Laws Ranked by Animal Legal Defense Fund: Maine is # 1, New Mexico #50.* Animal Legal Defense Fund Press Release. https://aldf.org/article/state-animal-protection-laws-ranked-2022/

(2023) *Animal Protection: U.S. State Animal Protection Laws Ranking Report.* Animal Legal Defense Fund. https://aldf.org/wp-content/uploads/2024/02/2023-U.S.-State-Animal-Protection-Laws-Ranking-Report-Animal-Legal-Defense-Fund.pdf

(n.d.) *Animal Welfare Program.* Maine Department of Agriculture, Conservation and Forestry's Division of Animal and Plant Health. https://www.maine.gov/dacf/ahw/animal_welfare/index.shtml

Background information on Lawrence J. Keddy and Marilyn L. Goodreau:

(July 16, 2023). *Obituary: Marilyn L. Goodreau.* Portland Press Herald. https://www.pressherald.com/2023/07/16/obituarymarilyn-l-goodreau-2/

Lunt, Walter. (March 19, 2019). *Before the Memory Fades: Lawrence J. Keddy, industrialist, philanthropist, entrepreneur, animal lover, genius.* The Windham Eagle. https://lifestyles.thewindhameagle.com/2019/03/before-memory-fades-lawrence-jkeddy.html?m=1

CHAPTER 2: FINDING YOUR NICHE

Quoted Interviewees: Alexandra "Ali" Chipman Baker, Tannetta "Tet" fentener vanVlissingen

General Information on Home At Last Farm Mini Horse and Donkey Rescue and Horses With Hope:

https://homeatlastfarm.org/home

Home At Last Farm Articles of Agreement of a New Hampshire Nonprofit Organization (filed and approved by State of New Hampshire Secretary of State William M. Gardner on 09/11/2019)

https://horseswithhopeme.org/

Background Information on Miniature Horses:

(n.d.) *About the Breed.* American Miniature Horse Association. https://www.amha.org/about-the-breed

(n.d.) *Streptococcus equi/ Strangles Culture and Testing.* Cornell University's College of Veterinary Medicine Animal Health Diagnostic Center. https://www.vet.cornell.edu/animal-health-diagnostic-center/testing/protocols/streptococcus-equi-strangles-culture

(2023). *Vaccinations for Adult Horses.* American Association of Equine Practitioners.

https://aaep.org/wp-content/uploads/2024/02/Adult_Horse_Vaccine_Chart_2023_SUB.pdf

Background Information on P. Fentener Van Vlissingen:

(n.d.) *African Parks Strategic Partners Listing.* African Parks. https://www.africanparks.org/strategic-partners

CHAPTER 3: THE BUSINESS OF EQUINE RESCUE

Quoted Interviewees: Penny Parker

General Information on Horse Angels:

https://horseangelsrescue.org/

CHAPTER 4: NEW HOLLAND: A LAST CHANCE FOR LOST SOULS

Quoted Interviewees: Dr. James Holt, V.M.D.

On Lily the Paintball Pony:

Knapp, Tom. (May 20, 2016). *Rhode Island man convicted on all counts for abuse of lame, paint-covered horse abandoned in New Holland.* Lancaster Online. https://lancasteronline.com/news/local/rhode-island-man-convicted-on-all-counts-for-abuse-of/article_e8fd40a8-1eac-11e6-aa85-33d7e846fdb8.html

Knapp, Tom. (June 20, 2016). *Lily, the 'paintball pony' adopted by comedian Jon Stewart, died Sunday after a fall.* Lancaster Online. https://lancasteronline.com/news/local/lily-the-paintball-pony-adopted-by-comedian-jon-stewart-died-sunday-after-a-fall/article_126401de-3717-11e6-8bca-8f350926f5a7.html

Maye, Fran. (June 20, 2016 and updated September 24, 2021). *Lily, the horse shot 130 times by paintballs, dies.* The Pottstown Mercury. https://www.pottsmerc.com/2016/06/20/lily-the-horse-shot-130-times-by-paintballs-dies/

On the Amish/Mennonite Community of Lancaster County, Pennsylvania:

(n.d.) *Amish History and Beliefs*. Discover Lancaster. https://www.discoverlancaster.com/amish/history-beliefs/#:~:text=Members%20of%20this%20conservative%20Christian,United%20States%2C%20numbering%20about%2030%2C000.

Wesner, Erik. (May 15, 2024). "The 10 Biggest Amish Communities (2024)." *Amish America*. https://amishamerica.com/10-biggest-amish-communities-2019/

(n.d.) *History*. New Holland Borough, Lancaster County, Pennsylvania. https://newhollandborough.org/history/

General Information on New Holland History and Events:

Hoopes, Karl, Thacker, Eric, and Greenhalgh, Linden. (November 2019). *Body Condition Scoring for Horses*. Utah State University. https://digitalcommons.usu.edu/cgi/viewcontent.cgi?article=3075&context=extension_curall

Worden, Amy. (April 2017). *New Holland Auction Bans Photography, Hampering Rescues*. East Coast Equestrian. https://www.eastcoastequestrian.net/news2017/april/New-Holland-Auction-Bans-Photography.php#/

(n.d.) *Animal Health and Diagnostic Commission*. Pennsylvania Department of Agriculture. https://www.agriculture.pa.gov/Animals/AHDCommission/Pages/default.aspx

On American Association of Equine Practitioners/ American Veterinary Medical Association Guidelines for Humane Euthanasia

Leary, Steven, et al. (2020). *AVMA Guidelines for the Euthanasia of Animals*. American Veterinary Medical Association. https://aaep.org/wp-content/uploads/2024/02/AVMA_2020_Euthanasia_Guidelines.pdf

(March 8, 2021). *Euthanasia Guidelines Position Statement*. American Association of Equine Practitioners. https://aaep.org/resource/euthanasia-guidelines/

(April 13, 2019). *AAEP Rescue and Retirement Guidelines*. American Association of Equine Practitioners. https://aaep.org/resource/aaep-rescue-and-retirement-guidelines/

PART II: A TANGLED WEB

CHAPTER 5: LIVING IN THE GRAY ZONE

Quoted Interviewees: Julie Broadway

On the definition of livestock:

(n.d.). *Livestock*. In Merriam-Webster.com dictionary. https://www.merriam-webster.com/dictionary/livestock

(n.d.) *Livestock*. Oxford English Dictionary. https://www.oed.com/search/dictionary/?scope=Entries&q=livestock

On Equine and Livestock Law:

Rollins, Brigit and Rumley, Elizabeth. *Equine Activity Statutes*. The National Agricultural Law Center. https://nationalaglawcenter.org/state-compilations/equineactivity/

(n.d.) *Companion Animals*. Animal Legal Defense Fund. https://aldf.org/focus-area/companion-animals/

(n.d.) *Farmed Animals*. Animal Legal Defense Fund. https://aldf.org/focus-area/farmed-animals/

Smith, Craig M. (2009) "Detailed Discussion of Horse Related Legal Issues". Michigan State University College of Law Animal Legal and Historical Center. https://www.animallaw.info/

(February 2024). 2022 Census of Agriculture US Summary and State Data Volume 1 Geographic Data Series Part 51. US Department of Agriculture's National Agricultural Statistics Service. https://www.nass.usda.gov/AgCensus/

(March 19, 2024). *National Veterinary Accreditation Program: Category I and II Animals*. US Department of Agriculture's Animal and Plant Health Inspection Service. https://www.aphis.usda.gov/nvap/category1-2#:~:text=Food%20and%20fiber%20animal%20species,animal)%2C%20zoo%20animals%20that%20can

On Food Taboos and Why Americans Don't Typically Eat Horsemeat:

In this section, I have drawn heavily from the work of Susanna Forrest, in particular the excellent chapter titled "Meat" in her book, *The Age of the Horse: an Equine Journey Through Human History* (New York: Grove Press, 2016).

Forrest, Susanna. (June 8, 2017). "The Troubled History of Horse Meat in America." *The Atlantic*. https://www.theatlantic.com/technology/archive/2017/06/horse-meat/529665/

Forster, Tim. (December 15, 2017). *Why Don't Americans Eat Horse?* The Eater. https://www.eater.com/2017/12/15/16741848/horse-meat-restaurants-america-diners-canada

Meyer-Rochow VB. (June 2009). *Food taboos: their origins and purposes.* J Ethnobiol Ethnomed. 2009 Jun 29;5:18. doi: 10.1186/1746-4269-5-18. PMID: 19563636; PMCID: PMC2711054.

On the status and sentiment of equine slaughter in the United States:

(2024). *Horse Slaughter Legal States 2024.* World Population Review. https://worldpopulationreview.com/state-rankings/horse-slaughter-legal-states

(February 9, 2022). *New Poll Confirms That Overwhelming Majority of Americans Oppose Horse Slaughter.* American Society for the Prevention of Cruelty to Animals. https://www.aspca.org/news/new-poll-confirms-overwhelming-majority-americans-oppose-horse-slaughter

CHAPTER 6: MOVING TOWARD A COMMON GOAL

Quoted Interviewees: Tessa Archibald, Kelsey Buckley, Ashley Harkins, Christie Schulte Kappert

General Background Information:

American Society for the Protection of Cruelty to Animals Right Horse Program https://www.aspcarighthorse.org/

Equine Welfare Data Collective: https://unitedhorsecoalition.org/ewdc/

Homes for Horses Coalition https://homesforhorses.org/

United Horse Coalition: https://unitedhorsecoalition.org/

Additional Data and Information:

Weiss E, Dolan ED, Mohan-Gibbons H, Gramann S, Slater MR. Estimating the Availability of Potential Homes for Unwanted Horses in the United States. Animals. 2017; 7(7):53. https://doi.org/10.3390/ani7070053

(n.d). *ASPCA Equine Transition and Adoption Center.* American Society for the Prevention of Cruelty to Animals. https://www.aspca.org/aspca-equine-transition-and-adoption-center/equine-transition-and-adoption-center-pilot#:~:text=Launched%20in%20late%20 2021%2C%20the,at%2Drisk%20horses%20

finding%20homes.

(n.d.) *ASPCA Vet Direct Safety Net Program Researches Increased Welfare, Retention, of Owned Horses.* American Society for the Prevention of Cruelty to Animals. ASPCA Pro. https://www.aspcapro.org/topics-equine-welfare-keeping-horses-safe/aspca-vet-direct-safety-net-program-researches-increased

(n.d.) *Vet Direct Safety Net: What Owners Need to Know.* American Association of Equine Practitioners. https://aaep.org/guidelines-resources/horse-owner-resources/vet-direct-safety-net/#:~:text=The%20Vet%20 Direct%20Program%20is,Wound%20 management

(n.d.) *Encouraging Research Regarding Homes for Horses.* ASCPA Pro. https://www.aspcapro.org/resource/encouraging-research-regarding-homes-horses

(February 2024). *Equine Welfare Data Collective Sixth Report: Analysis of Data Reported for: January 1, 2022-December 31, 2022.* Equine Welfare Data Collective/United Horse Coalition.

(March 4, 2024) *American Horse Council's "Datapalooza"* (webinar). Hosted by the American Horse Council.

(April 3, 2024) *Discover the Future of Equine Welfare with Tessa Archibald.* (webinar). Hosted by Horses and Humans Research Foundation.

On Horse Slaughter/SAFE Act:

(n.d.) *Horse Slaughter Statistics.* American Welfare Institute. https://awionline.org/content/horse-slaughter-statistics

Martinez, Dennis. (January 18, 2024). *SAFE Act and Horse Slaughter Update.* American Horse Council. https://horsecouncil.org/press-releases/safe-act-and-horse-slaughter-update/

(June 23, 2023). H.R.3475 - 118th Congress (2023-2024): SAFE Act of 2023. https://www.congress.gov/bill/118th-congress/house-bill/3475

(June 23, 2022). H.R.3355 - 117th Congress (2021-2022): SAFE Act of 2021. https://www.congress.gov/bill/117th-congress/house-bill/3355/text

(Spring 2013). *Bill to Ban Horse Slaughter Introduced.* American Welfare Institute. https://awionline.org/awi-quarterly/2013-spring/bill-ban-horse-slaughter-introduced

Larkin, Malinda. (July 27, 2011). *Closing of US horse slaughter plants still reverberates.* American Veterinary Medical Association. https://www.avma.org/javma-news/2011-08-15/closing-us-horse-slaughter-plants-still-reverberates

On the Great Recession of 2008:

(March 1, 2008). How Recession Proof is the Horse Industry? American Farrier's Journal. https://www.americanfarriers.com/articles/6269-how-recession-proof-is-the-horse-industry?

Lewis, James M. (August 1, 2009). *Recession to blame for unwanted horse problem.* DVM 360. https://www.dvm360.com/view/recession-blame-unwanted-horse-problem

Medina, Carlos E. (December 30, 2009). *Recession Hits State's Horse Industry Hard.* The Ledger. https://www.theledger.com/story/news/2009/12/30/recession-hits-states-horse-industry-hard/26238497007/#:~:text=%22The%20downturn%20has%20caused%20there,as%20much%20as%20a%20third.

Hiers, Fred. (December 3, 2010). *Horses once highly valued now starving amid economic downturn.* The Gainesville Sun. https://www.gainesville.com/story/news/local/2010/12/03/horses-once-highly-valued-now-starving-amid-economic-downturn/64296138007/

Mance, Steven M. and Goodman, Christopher J. (April 2011) *Employment loss and the 2007-2009 recession: an overview.* US Bureau of Labor Statistics Monthly Labor Review. https://www.bls.gov/opub/mlr/2011/04/art1full.pdf

Duggan, Wayne. (June 21, 2023). *A Short History of the Great Recession.* Forbes Advisor. https://www.forbes.com/advisor/investing/great-recession/#:~:text=The%20Great%20Recession%20of%202008,down%2057%25%20from%20its%20highs.

https://www.horseadoption.com/

Thoroughbred Aftercare Alliance https://www.thoroughbredaftercare.org/

Thoroughbred Retirement Foundation https://www.trfinc.org/

Amato, Natalli. (July 17, 2023). *Thoroughbred Retirement Foundation and the Art of Caring.* Saratoga Living. https://saratogaliving.com/thoroughbred-retirement-foundation-and-the-art-of-caring/

Blood Horse Staff. (December 30, 2009). *TRF Founder Koehler to Get Special Eclipse.* https://www.bloodhorse.com/horse-racing/articles/144718/trf-founder-koehler-to-get-special-eclipse

Drape, Joe. (March 17, 2011). *Ex-Racehorses Starve as Charity Fails in Mission to Care for Them.* The New York Times. https://www.nytimes.com/2011/03/18/sports/18horses.html

Flatter, Ron. (n.d.) *Secretariat Remains No.1 Name in Racing.* ESPN.com. https://www.espn.com/sportscentury/features/00016464.html

Glauber, Bill. (May 2, 1993). *'It Was Like He Was Flying;' In Five Weeks in 1973, Secretariat Went From a Potentially Great Horse to a Racing Legend.* The Los Angeles Times. https://www.latimes.com/archives/la-xpm-1993-05-02-sp-30060-story.html

Hegarty, Matt. (November 19, 2013). *Thoroughbred Retirement Foundation, New York attorney general settle lawsuit.* Daily Racing Forum. https://www.drf.com/news/thoroughbred-retirement-foundation-new-york-attorney-general-settle-lawsuit

Klayman, Ben. (May 7, 2016). *A Year After American Pharaoh, US Horse Racing Faces Uneasy Future.* Reueters. https://www.reuters.com/article/idUSKCN0XY08R/

Pagones, Rachel. (December 1, 2022). *Great Tracks We Have Lost: Hollywood Park and the Dawning of the Breeder's Cup Era.* Thoroughbred Racing Commentary. https://www.thoroughbredracing.com/articles/5636/great-racetracks-we-have-lost-hollywood-park-and-dawning-breeders-cup-era/

Riess, Steven. (March 26, 2014). "The Cyclical History of Horse Racing: The USA's Oldest and (Sometimes) Most Popular Spectator Sport." *The International Journal of the History of Sport.* Volume 31: 1-2, 29-54.

PART III: TRANSFORMATION

CHAPTER 7: AFTER THE FINISH LINE: THE RISE OF THOROUGHBRED AFTERCARE

Quoted Interviewees: Jenna Encheff, Katie Gardner, Dot Morgan, Chelsea O'Reilly, Pat Robinson, Stacie Clark Rogers, Samantha "Sam" Smith, Julianne "Jules" Stowell

General Background Information:

New Vocations Racehorse Adoption Program

(June 21, 1987). "America UnTracked". *The Boston Globe.*

(June 10, 2002). "That 70's racing show unequalled." *The Chicago Tribune.* https://www.chicagotribune.com/2002/06/10/that-70s-racing-show-unequaled/

On the Life, Death, and Impact of Ferdinand:

Associated Press. (July 23, 2003). *Ex-Ferdinand Owner Says Derby Winner has Died.* ESPN.com. https://www.espn.com/horse/news/2003/0721/1583900.html

Bayer, Barbara. (December 16, 2003). "The Search for Ferdinand." *BloodHorse.* https://www.bloodhorse.com/horse-racing/articles/178402/the-search-for-ferdinand

Ehalt, Bob. (April 27, 2016). "Legends: Whittingham's Derby Winner Ferdinand." *BloodHorse.* https://www.bloodhorse.com/horse-racing/articles/211136/legends-whittinghams-derby-winner-ferdinand

Finley, Bill. (July 23, 2003). "HORSE RACING: 1986 Kentucky Derby Winner Was Slaughtered, Magazine Reports." *The New York Times.* https://www.nytimes.com/2003/07/23/sports/horse-racing-1986-derby-winner-was-slaughtered-magazine-reports.html

Hall, Tom. (February 3, 2021). "Ferdinand Made Impact During His Life and After; Ferdinand's fate led to the rise of Thoroughbred Aftercare." *The BloodHorse Daily.* https://www.bloodhorse.com/horse-racing/articles/246023/ferdinand-made-impact-during-his-life-and-after

Nack, William. (August 5, 2003) *No, Not Again.* ESPN.com. https://www.espn.com/horse/columns/misc/1589423.html

Paulick, Ray. (July 25. 2003). "Death of a Derby Winner: Slaughterhouse Likely Fate for Ferdinand." *BloodHorse.* https://www.bloodhorse.com/horse-racing/articles/180859/death-of-a-derby-winner-slaughterhouse-likely-fate-for-ferdinand

(June 2, 2005). "New York Horsemen and NYRA Initiate Ferdinand Fee to End Horse Slaughter." *BloodHorse.* https://www.bloodhorse.com/horse-racing/articles/170210/new-york-horsemen-and-nyra-initiate-ferdinand-fee-to-end-horse-slaughter

On the Life and Legacy of Exceller:

https://www.excellerfund.org/

On The Jockey Club's Annual Registration Numbers and Other Statistics:

Singer, Dan and Lamb, Michael. (2011). *Driving Sustainable Growth for Thoroughbred Racing and Breeding: Findings and Recommendations.* The Jockey Club. https://www.jockeyclub.com/default.asp?section=RT&year=2011&area=6

Highet, Ian D. and Gagliano, James L. (2018). *McKinsey Report 2018: A Situation Analysis for Horse Racing.* The Jockey Club. https://www.jockeyclub.com/default.asp?section=RT&year=2018&area=4

(2024). *Annual North American Registered Foal Crop.* The Jockey Club. https://www.jockeyclub.com/default.asp?section=FB&area=2

On Thoroughbred Aftercare, Broadly:

Clark Rogers, Stacie. (August 2, 2023). *Revisiting the Conversation on How to Solve Thoroughbred Aftercare.* Thoroughbred Aftercare Alliance. https://www.thoroughbredaftercare.org/revisiting-the-conversation-on-how-to-solve-thoroughbred-aftercare/

Voss, Natalie. (December 2, 2019). *A Decade In, How are we Doing with Thoroughbred Aftercare?* The Paulick Report. https://paulickreport.com/horse-care-category/a-decade-in-how-are-we-doing-with-thoroughbred-aftercare

Voss, Natalie. (December 3, 2019). *Emptying the Ocean with a Teaspoon: the Challenges of Aftercare.* The Paulick Report. https://paulickreport.com/horse-care-category/emptying-the-ocean-with-a-teaspoon-the-challenges-of-aftercare

Voss, Natalie. (December 4, 2019). *Aftercare Should Not Be an Afterthought: Solutions for the Future.* The Paulick Report. https://paulickreport.com/horse-care-category/aftercare-should-not-be-an-afterthought-solutions-for-the-future

CHAPTER 8: SAVING THE HORSES OF APPALACHIA: A MODEL FOR SUCCESS

Quoted Interviewees: Tinia Creamer, Jordyn Dominguez, Brenda Hanson, Samara Manich, Colby O'Connor, Eric Pottrafke

Background on Heart of Phoenix and the ATFO:

https://www.wvhorserescue.org/

https://www.appalachiantrainerfaceoff.com/

Keim, C. "A Closer Look At: Heart of Phoenix." *UnTacked.* Summer 2021, pp. 70-75.

On Tinia Creamer:

(November 19, 2019). *The Extraordinary Recipients of the 2019 ASPCA Humane Awards.* American Society for the Prevention of Cruelty to Animals. https://www.aspca.org/news/extraordinary-recipients-2019-aspca-humane-awards

(January 14, 2007). *7 Dead in W. Va. Apartment Fire.* CBS News/Associated Press. https://www.cbsnews.com/news/7-dead-in-w-va-apartment-fire/

Guay, Jessica. (January 14, 2017). *10 years later, sister remembers siblings killed in Emmons Apartment fire.* WCHS/WVAH Fox 8 & 11. https://wchstv.com/news/local/10-years-later-sister-remembers-siblings-killed-in-emmons-apartment-fire

Regarding Appalachian Region: Culture, Economics, Coal Mining, and more

(n.d.) *About the Appalachian Region.* Appalachian Regional Commission. https://www.arc.gov/about-the-appalachian-region/

(2011). *Economic Overview of Appalachia-2011.* Appalachian Regional Commission. https://www.arc.gov/wp-content/uploads/2020/06/EconomicOverviewSept2011.pdf

(February 2019). *Strengthening Economic Resilience in Appalachia: a Guidebook for Practitioners.* Appalachian Regional Commission. https://www.arc.gov/wp-content/uploads/2019/02/StrengtheningEconomicResilienceGuidebook-Feb2019-1.pdf

(April 7, 2022). *The Horse That Built Kentucky.* PBS. https://www.pbs.org/video/the-horse-that-built-kentucky-3qcw3s/

Hatem, Andy. (January 6, 2020). *The Great Recession Occurred Twelve Years Ago. In Appalachia, it Never Really Ended.* Federation of Appalachian Housing Enterprises, Inc. https://fahe.org/the-great-recession-occurred-twelve-years-ago-in-appalachia-it-never-really-ended/

Ziliak, James. (September 16, 2010). *The Appalachian Regional Development Act and Economic Change.* Center for Poverty Research, University of Kentucky Department of Economics. https://www.irp.wisc.edu/newsevents/workshops/2011/participants/papers/12-Ziliak.pdf

(n.d.) *Reclaiming Abandoned Minelands: Title IV of the Surface Mining Control and Reclamation Act.* US Department of the Interior, Office of Surface Mining Reclamation and Enforcement. https://www.osmre.gov/programs/reclaiming-abandoned-mine-lands

On Free-Roaming Horses in Appalachia:

Kobin, Billy. (December 18, 2019). Who shot and killed 15 horses? The reward has grown to more than $15k for answers. Louisville Courier Journal. https://www.courier-journal.com/story/news/crime/2019/12/18/horses-shot-killed-along-strip-job-floyd-pike-county-kentucky/2684594001/

Menderski, Maggie. (March 3, 2020). *East Kentucky is Still Littered with Dead Horses. How One Farm is Recovering from a Massacre.* Louisville Courier Journal. https://www.courier-journal.com/story/money/louisville-city-living/2020/01/30/kentucky-horse-shooting-survivors-rehabilitate-human-society-farm/4468324002/

Coyne, Caity. (April 23, 2018). *Wild horses present challenges in WV coalfields.* Charleston Gazette-Mail. https://wvpress.org/uncategorized/wild-horses-present-challenges-in-southern-wv-coalfields/

Kessler, Lisa. (December 5, 2012). *All the Pretty Horses.* Blue Ridge Outdoors. https://www.blueridgeoutdoors.com/go-outside/all-the-pretty-horses/

(n.d.) *History of Free-Roaming Horses.* Appalachian Horse Project. https://appalachianhorseproject.org/history-of-free-roaming-horses

(n.d.). *Free-Roaming Horses in Eastern Kentucky.* Kentucky Humane Society. https://www.kyhumane.org/equine/free-roaming-horses/

CHAPTER 9: THE PROFESSOR IS IN: LIFE LESSONS THROUGH HORSEMANSHIP

Quoted Interviewees: Jordan Altman, Anna Baucum, Sophia Bull, Na'riah Danser, Ellen Healey, Alison Newman Johnson, Jo Anne Miller, Lily Miller, Kennedy Newman, Bill Rube, Tracy Russler, Alexandrea Williams, Julianna Williams

Background Information on Brook Hill Retirement Center for Horses and Gleneayre Equestrian Program:

https://brookhillfarm.org/

https://gleneayreequestrianprogram.org/

Keim, C. "A Closer Look At: Gleneayre

Equestrian Program." *UnTacked.* January/February 2020. pp 82-86.

CHAPTER 10: FINDING YOUR WAY BACK HOME

Quoted Interviewees: Lindsay Alberts, Katherine Hatch, Jason Lutterman, Emma Minteer, LuAnn Van Peursem, Dragonslayer (in text as D.S.), Phil Wytrwa

In composing this chapter, I have additionally pulled from previous work I have written on the EquiCenter and Mission Mustang:

Keim, C. "A Closer Look at: Mission Mustang." *UnTacked.* November/December 2019. pp 94-98.

Keim, C. "Partnering Mustangs With Veterans." *Strides.* Spring 2020. pp 17-22.

Background Information on EquiCenter:

https://www.equicenterny.org/

On Veterans and PTSD:

Keim, C. "A Closer Look at: The Man O'War Project," *UnTacked.* July/August 2019. pp.88-91.

(n.d.) *The Man O'War Project (Overview).* The Man O'War Project. https://mowproject.org/about/

(n.d.) *How Common is PTSD in Veterans?* U.S. Department of Veterans Affairs. https://www.ptsd.va.gov/understand/common/common_veterans.asp

(n.d.) *PTSD Basics.* U.S. Department of Veterans Affairs. https://www.ptsd.va.gov/understand/what/ptsd_basics.asp

(n.d.) *Overview of VA Research on Posttraumatic Stress Disorder (PTSD).* U.S. Department of Veterans Affairs. https://www.research.va.gov/topics/ptsd.cfm

(n.d.) *Mental Health and Suicide Prevention.* U.S. Department of Veterans Affairs. https://www.mentalhealth.va.gov/suicide_prevention/data.asp

(n.d.) *Veterans and PTSD: Understanding Causes, Signs, Symptoms, and Treatment.* Wounded Warrior Project.

https://www.woundedwarriorproject.org/programs/mental-wellness/veteran-ptsd-treatment-support-resources#:~:text=PTSD%20is%20a%20very%20common,a%20person%20thinks%20and%20feels.

November 2023. *2023 National Veteran Suicide Prevention Annual Report.* U.S. Department of Veterans Affairs Office of Mental Health and Suicide Prevention.

https://www.mentalhealth.va.gov/docs/datasheets/2023/2023-National-Veteran-Suicide-Prevention-Annual-Report-FINAL-508.pdf

O'Brien, Soledad. (Interviewer) (March 29, 2017). *The Stigma That Stops Veterans from Getting Help with PTSD.* PBS Newshour. https://www.pbs.org/newshour/show/stigma-stops-veterans-getting-help-ptsd

Fisher, P.W., Lazarov, A., Lowell, A., et al. Equine-assisted therapy for posttraumatic stress disorder among military veterans: an open trial. *Journal of Clinical Psychiatry.* 2021; 82(5):21m14005.

Reisman M. PTSD Treatment for Veterans: What's Working, What's New, and What's Next. P T. 2016 Oct;41(10):623-634.

Committee on the Assessment of Ongoing Efforts in the Treatment of Posttraumatic Stress Disorder; Board on the Health of Select Populations; Institute of Medicine. Treatment for Posttraumatic Stress Disorder in Military and Veteran Populations: Final Assessment. Washington (DC): National Academies Press (US); 2014 Jun 17. 2, Diagnosis, Course, and Prevalence of PTSD. https://www.ncbi.nlm.nih.gov/books/NBK224874/

On Mustangs and the BLM:

For one of the most comprehensive and well-researched works on the complex history of the American Mustang, I highly recommend David Phillips' *Wild Horse Country: the History, Myth, and Future of the Mustang.* (W.W. Norton and Company, 2017).

(n.d.) *Wild Horse and Burro Program.* US Department of the Interior Bureau of Land Management. https://www.blm.gov/whb

(March 1, 2024). *Program Data.* US Department of the Interior Bureau of Land Management. https://www.blm.gov/programs/wild-horse-and-burro/about-the-program/program-data

(n.d.) *What We Manage Nationally.* US Department of the Interior Bureau of Land Management.

https://www.blm.gov/about/what-we-manage/national

(March 1, 2023). *Herd Area and Herd Management*

Area Statistics. US Department of the Interior Bureau of Land Management. https://www.blm.gov/sites/default/files/docs/2023-04/2023_HMA-HA_PopStats_4-3-2023_Final.pdf

Staff Report. *With 22,000 Animals in its Care, BLM puts $4.7M Toward Wild Horse and Burro Training, Adoption Programs.* Craig Press. (April 4, 2023). https://www.craigdailypress.com/news/with-22000-animals-in-its-care-blm-puts-4-7m-toward-wild-horse-and-burro-training-adoption-programs/

The Use of GonaCon in Wildlife Management. Report on Human Health and Ecological Risk Assessment for the Use of Wildlife Damage Management Methods by USDA APHIS Wildlife Services. (July 2022). https://www.aphis.usda.gov/wildlife_damage/nepa/risk_assessment/11-gonacon.pdf

Text of the Wild Free-Roaming Horse and Burros Act of 1971 (Public Law 92-195), as amended. (Compiled, organized, and reproduced by the Bureau of Land Management as of January 2006). https://www.blm.gov/sites/default/files/programs_wildhorse_history_doc1.pdf

(n.d.) *History of Mustangs*. Mustang Heritage Foundation. https://mustangheritagefoundation.org/learn/#history

Report to the Chairman, Committee on Natural Resources, House of Representatives. *Bureau of Land Management: Effective Long-Term Options Needed to Manage Unadoptable Wild Horses.* (November 10, 2008). https://www.gao.gov/assets/a282669.html

(n.d.) *The Story Behind the Burns Amendment.* American Wild Horse Conservation.

https://americanwildhorse.org/story-behind-burns-amendment#:~:text=The%202004%20Burns%20Amendment%20to,picked%20up%20by%20kill%20buyers.

Leigh, Laura, and Brown, Mary. *Burns Amendment.* Wild Horse Education: Effective Advocates for Public Lands, Public Horses. (March 31, 2013). https://wildhorseeducation.org/burns-amendment/

GLOSSARY OF REFERENCED MEDICAL TERMS

African Horse Sickness: A life-threatening hemorrhagic disease of equids characterized by respiratory and circulatory impairment.

Ataxia: A neurological condition causing lack of coordination, balance, and control over movements.

Equine Herpes Virus (EHV): Common DNA viruses in horse populations worldwide. The two most significant are EHV-1 (causes respiratory disease, abortion, and neurologic disease) and EHV-4 (primarily causes respiratory disease).

Equine Infectious Anemia (EIA): A noncontagious infectious viral disease of equids, causing fever, depression, muscle weakness, thrombocytopenia, anemia, jaundice, increased heart and respiration rates, hemorrhages on mucous membranes, epistaxis, collapse, and death. Infection identified by a *Coggins Test*.

Equine Protozoal Myelitis (EPM): A central nervous system infection of equids with signs that are highly variable, with the most common being asymmetric ataxia and weakness of limbs and regional neurogenic muscle atrophy.

Laminitis: The inflammation and subsequent separation of the laminae of the hoof caused by carbohydrate overload, excess weight bearing, and endotoxemia.

Paraphimosis: The inability to retract the penis into the prepuce.

Strangles: A highly infectious and very common disease of equids characterized by upper respiratory tract lymph node abscessation secondary to infection with *Streptococcus equi equi.*

Vesicular Stomatitis: A viral disease of primarily horses and cattle, resulting in characteristic vesicular lesions on the muzzle, lips, tongue, ears, sheath, udder, ventral abdomen, and/or coronary bands.

RESOURCES

American Horse Council (AHC)
https://horsecouncil.org

American Association of Equine Practitioners (AAEP)
https://aaep.org

American Society for the Prevention of Cruelty to Animals (ASPCA)
www.aspca.org

American Wild Horse Horse Conservation
www.americanwildhorse.org

Animal Welfare Institute
https://awionline.org

Appalachian Trainer Face Off (ATFO)
https://www.appalachiantrainerfaceoff.com

ASPCA Equine Transition and Adoption Center
www.aspca.org/aspca-equine-transition-and-adoption-center

ASPCA Right Horse
www.aspcarighthorse.org

Animal Legal Defense Fund (ALDF)
https://aldf.org

Artemis Farm Rescue
www.facebook.com/ArtemisFarmRescue/

Brook Hill Retirement Center for Horses
https://brookhillfarm.org

EquiCenter Mission Mustang
www.equicenterny.org

Equine Welfare Data Collective (EWDC)
https://unitedhorsecoalition.org/ewdc/

Extreme Mustang Makeover
www.mustangheritagefoundation.org/extreme

Gleneayre Equestrian Program
https://gleneayreequestrianprogram.org

Global Federation of Animal Sanctuaries (GFAS)
https://sanctuaryfederation.org

Heart of Phoenix
www.wvhorserescue.org

Hidden Pond Farm Equine Rescue
https://hiddenpondequinerescue.org

Home at Last Farm (HALF) Mini Horse and Donkey Rescue
https://homeatlastfarm.org

Homes for Horses Coalition
https://homesforhorses.org

Horse Angels Rescue
https://horseangelsrescue.org

Horses With Hope
https://horseswithhopeme.org

Humane World for Animals
www.humaneworld.org/en

International Forum for the Aftercare of Racehorses (IFAR)
www.internationalracehorseaftercare.com

Maine State Society for the Protection of Animals (MSSPA)
www.msspa.org

Massachusetts Society for the Prevention of Cruelty to Animals (MSPCA)
www.mspca.org

Mustang Heritage Foundation
www.mustangheritagefoundation.org

New Vocations Racehorse Adoption
www.horseadoption.com

PATH International
https://pathintl.org

Retired Racehorse Project
https://www.therrp.org

Standardbred Transition Alliance
https://www.standardbredtransition.org

Standardbred Retirement Foundation
https://www.adoptahorse.org

Thoroughbred Aftercare Alliance
https://www.thoroughbredaftercare.org

Thoroughbred Retirement Foundation
https://trfinc.org

United Horse Coalition
https://unitedhorsecoalition.org